*Passing on the Faith*

# *Passing on the Faith*

## Transforming Traditions for the Next Generation of Jews, Christians, and Muslims

EDITED BY JAMES L. HEFT, S.M.

FORDHAM UNIVERSITY PRESS
NEW YORK 2006

The Abrahamic Dialogues Series, No. 6

ISSN 1548-4130

Library of Congress Cataloging-in-Publication Data

Passing on the faith : transforming traditions for the next generation of Jews, Christians, and Muslims / edited by James L. Heft.—1st ed.
    p.   cm.—(The Abrahamic dialogues series no. 5)
    Includes bibliographical references and index.
    ISBN-13: 978-0-8232-2647-4 (cloth : alk. paper)
    ISBN-10: 0-8232-2647-6 (cloth : alk. paper)
    ISBN-13: 978-0-8232-2648-1 (pbk. : alk. paper)
    ISBN-10: 0-8232-2648-4 (pbk. : alk. paper)
    1. Monotheism.   2. Judaism.   3. Christianity.   4. Islam.   I. Heft, James.
    BL221.P37 2006
    207′.5—dc22

                                                        2006035677

Printed in the United States of America
08  07  06   5  4  3  2  1
First edition

# Contents

# *Preface*

James L. Heft, S.M.

The chapters of this book were originally given in somewhat different form as papers at an international conference held at the University of Southern California in October 2004. The conference, "Faith, Fear and Indifference: Constructing the Religious Identity of the Next Generation," drew speakers from Europe and North America, and focused primarily on how three religious traditions—Judaism, Christianity, and Islam—pass on their religious traditions to their youth in the context of the contemporary culture of the United States. The conference itself would not have been possible without the generous support of the Lilly Endowment; the University of Southern California's College of Letters, Arts and Sciences, and its Center for the Study of Religion and Civic Culture; the Omar Ibn Al Khattab Foundation; the Institute for Advanced Catholic Studies; Peter and Merle Mullin; Ruth Ziegler; Mark and Peachy Levy; The Angell Foundation; the Wilsey Foundation; and Thomas and Katie Eggemeier, Jr. Without the wise counsel and constant support of Rabbi Reuven Firestone of Hebrew Union College; Professor Don Miller, the director of the Center for the Study of Religion and Civic Culture; Dafer Dakhil, the executive director of the Omar Ibn Al Khattab Foundation; Rabbi Susan Laemmle, Dean of Religious Life at the University of Southern California; and Brie Loskota, the conference director, this conference could not have happened.

Preparation for the publication of this volume is largely the result of the superb editing skills of Carol Farrell, my excellent assistant. Dr.

Donald Wigal prepared the subject and author index, which provides easy access to the contents of the volume. I am also grateful to the wonderful support of the University of Southern California for a whole series of initiatives that allow for the careful study of religions and interreligious dialogue. This kind of study is just one of the key research agendas of the Institute for Advanced Catholic Studies, which played a key role in organizing the conference and seeing this book through to publication.

*Passing on the Faith*

# Introduction: Youth and the Continuity of Religious Traditions

*James L. Heft, S.M.*

Jaroslav Pelikan, the well-known Yale historian of Christian doctrine, worried whether his grandchildren would have a religious tradition to reject. So pervasive did he consider the acidic effects of modern Western culture on religion that he feared that communities of faith would, over the coming generation or two, simply dissolve. Historians are rarely given to apocalyptic prediction; rather, they typically warn us about repeating the history from which we have never learned. But Pelikan has not been the only person who has worried about religion's future in the West. Religious leaders and sociologists and theologians have been asking similar questions: Is the latest generation of young people simply absent from traditional congregations? Isn't it naïve to think they will return to the congregations they were raised in once they marry and have their own children? Will the future be populated instead by people who think of themselves as "spiritual but not religious"? Will the virtual world of iPods and electronic information and entertainment replace face-to-face communities? To attract young people back to their religious traditions, is it necessary to perform extreme makeovers on those traditions, adapting them to the visual, audio, and entertainment patterns of many young people in the West?

Rabbi Reuven Firestone of Hebrew Union College in Los Angeles, Rabbi Susan Laemmle, the Dean of Religious Life at the University of

Southern California, Dafer Dakhil, the executive director of the Omar Ibn Al Khattab Foundation in Los Angeles, Professor Don Miller of USC's Center for the Study of Civic Religion, and Fr. James L. Heft, S.M., president of the Institute for Advanced Catholic Studies at the University of Southern California, began discussing these issues in spring 2003. While no one in this group disputed the data that showed that quite a few young people in the United States disassociate themselves from the religious traditions in which they were raised, they all knew that in the three religious traditions they personally represented—Judaism, Christianity, and Islam—a number of congregations have successfully resisted the declining trend. That is to say, a number of religious congregations have found ways of remaining connected with their youth. As a group, they decided to organize an international conference held in October 2004 at the University of Southern California. It was entitled "Faith, Fear and Indifference: Constructing the Religious Identity of the Next Generation."

Don Miller and Jim Heft described the seriousness of the current situation in a proposal submitted to the Lilly Endowment:

> Christianity in the West is on the threshold of a seismic shift over the next quarter century. In spite of the fact that a considerable number of teens and young adults are interested in spirituality, including mystical revelation and supernatural events, they are relatively indifferent to institutional religion, except for a minority who are energized by various expressions of fundamentalist religion. This is worrisome, because unrooted spirituality quickly lapses into narcissism. The pursuit of meaning and the exercise of life commitments are enriched when they are informed by tradition, religious practices that have evolved through the centuries, and an informed understanding of the role of religious faith in shaping our collective destiny.

But it is also obvious that Christianity is not alone in this crisis. The Jewish community in the United States has suffered considerable loss of its youth, many of whom see little reason to be observant or to perpetuate the religious traditions of their ancestors. The gulf that exists between many young Jews and their parents is at least as wide as the gulf between many mainline Protestants and Catholics and their offspring. The one exception to this trend is among observant Muslims, the majority of whom are immigrants in this country. Perhaps because of the suspicion cast upon all of them, especially since 9/11, they assert their religiosity in a much more striking fashion than do mainline Protestants, Catholics, and Jews. Muslim communities in the United States simply do not identify with the "spiritual but not religious" description.

The conference planning team decided that they wanted to explore that minority of congregations—Jewish, Protestant, Catholic, and Muslim—that has successfully engaged their youth. They wanted to tell a different story than the one dominating the current discussion; they wanted, if you will, to submit a "minority report." In the United States, these three religious traditions encounter the same liberal, democratic, and consumerist culture; any differences in how they respond to that culture could be most instructive. The team also wanted to give an overview of the situation of religious practice, both in the North Atlantic countries and especially in the United States. Finally, they wanted to make sure that the results of several important recent national studies on youth and religious practice in the United States were presented at the conference. A generous grant from the Lilly Endowment[1] allowed original research into congregations that have successfully engaged their youth. In an era of polarization and lagging social capital, especially what Robert Putnam identifies as "bridging social capital," the planning team understood that the crisis facing them, and all people concerned about the religious identity of the next generation, was the transmission of religious memory, practice, and tradition to that generation, especially by nonreductive and nonpandering expressions of faith traditions and moral commitments.[2]

## A Brief Retrospective on the Youth Crisis

Before previewing the major themes and insights in this volume, it might be helpful to situate historically some of the earlier studies of the challenges posed by youth, especially for the transmission of religious traditions. Raise the question of how far back goes the crisis with young people, and invariably someone will quote Plato, who said, "What is happening to our young people? They disrespect their elders, they disobey their parents. They ignore the laws. They riot in the streets inflamed with wild notions. Their morals are decaying. What is to become of them?"[3] Plato also worried about the invention of writing; he feared that the written word would reduce students to mindless passivity, much as educational critics today deplore the effects of television.

Other authors telling the story of religion in the United States often begin with the observation of Alexis de Tocqueville, who, shortly after he visited the United States in the early 1830s, remarked that a free democracy cannot exist for long without morality, and that morality depends on religious beliefs. But in the following decade, Ralph Waldo Emerson expressed a lasting and deep trend in religion in America when in 1841 he called upon his fellow Americans to distance themselves from the conformity and dullness of New England Congregationalism, and instead urged them to "do your thing," to "insist on yourself" and "never imitate," to be the kind of person who "puts off from himself all external support, and stands alone."[4] While no one then used the now common phrase "spiritual but not religious," Emerson had already expressed the cultural context for a more personal and individual approach to religion.[5]

In our own century, the late Jesuit Walter Ong, who spent his life studying the impact of various technologies on how we think and learn, explained that both the time of Plato and our own time mark great turning points in human consciousness. According to Ong, people read less today and learn more through pictures and sounds—because of electronic media, television, movies, and computers. Ong explained that Plato objected to written texts because they are unresponsive; they do not understand us, nor do they talk back the way people do. Modern media do not return us to Plato's ideal of a community of conversation, the oral culture. They do create, however, "secondary orality"—the orality you find in dorms where stereos blast CDs and iPods deliver directly to ears a nearly endless selection of favorite songs.[6]

As provocative and insightful as a study of the impact of different technologies on consciousness and learning styles of youth might be, authors in our own time have focused more on the formation of distinct cultures among age groups, especially teenagers. Most important in this regard are the writings of the late University of Chicago sociologist James Coleman, whose 1961 study, *The Adolescent Society: The Social Life of the Teenager and Its Impact on Society,*[7] documented how the high school, an educational institution that grew rapidly around the turn of the twentieth century, created an adolescent society in which peers often exercised more authority than adults when it came to teenagers' social practices and behavior. Coleman believed that athletes and other teenagers with good looks and popular personalities created the models that influenced peer behavior, perhaps much like today when movie and music-video stars populate the normative imagination of many young people. Coleman also developed the idea of "social capital," that is, the power of social relationships that can work positively or negatively and, when built up in and through solid families, can greatly enhance the effectiveness of education. Finally, his study provided a basis for the charge of anti-intellectualism in a youth culture submerged in audio and visual stimulation. However, Ong argued that significant learning can and does take place through "secondary orality," a form of learning that has little to do with the reading of texts. How best to "read" the transmission of a religious tradition to youth requires careful analysis of several trends, which, isolated from each other, could lead a person to conclude that today's youth are profoundly "illiterate" and therefore anti-intellectual, or orally informed, and therefore intellectual in a different way.

## MORE RECENT STUDIES

In the past decade or so, generational studies that focus on the younger generation, named variously "Gen X" or "Gen Y" or "The Millennials," have been booming. I will mention those studies I know best.[8] All these studies point to a major shift in understanding of the practice of, for example, the Catholic faith among American Catholics at the time of the Second Vatican Council (1962–65). In quite general terms, the baby boomers who raised their families after 1965 remained committed to many of the core teachings of the Catholic religion (the celebration of the Mass, the reality of Jesus as both human and divine being, the Trinity, and dedication to helping the poor), but began with much greater regularity to show greater independence on a number of moral issues, starting with the decision of a majority of them not to accept the 1968 teaching against the use of artificial birth control. And given a culture even more individualist than the one their boomer parents grew up in, today's young adults have, for the most part, become even more autonomous in the way they decide what they want to continue of the practices and beliefs that their parents have handed on to them. They do not feel as obligated as their parents to participate regularly in Sunday worship, and their departure from official church teachings on a number of doctrinal and moral issues is even greater than that of their parents.[9]

In more recent years, however, a small but quite visible group of what have come to be called "evangelical Catholics" has appeared on many Catholic campuses.[10] They have been described as "evangelical" because of their emphasis on personal conversion and witness, typical of evangelical Protestants. These young Catholics, the children of the post–Vatican II boomers, might be representatives of the third-generation phenomenon of immigrants. The first generation, the parents of the boomers, embodied a "thick" culture, both socially and religiously, replete with many distinctive religious practices and devotions, which they maintained—including parochial schools, Catholic Youth Organizations, May crownings of Mary the Mother of Jesus—even as they moved to the suburbs. The second generation, the boomers, raised in the suburbs, left much of that "thick" religious culture behind them, including many of the devotions and organizations that secured the Catholic subculture of their parents. They assimilated into the mainstream culture, which was affluent and suburban. Their children, now immersed in a pluralistic culture with few religious identity-markers, have a different attitude than their parents toward the religious life of their grandparents. In fact, they actually seek to establish boundaries and identity-markers in order to practice in a more particularistic and devout way than their boomer parents at least some of the religious practices and devotions of their grandparents. The number of evangelical Catholics is not great, but their presence and vitality deserve careful attention.

Such movements toward more explicit identification with traditional religious practices have been reported as well among some Jewish and mainline Protestant youth. Sometimes they can be described as various forms of fundamentalism: the absolutizing of certain beliefs and practices in such a way as to feel that anyone who does not also affirm these same beliefs and perform these same practices is condemned by God. However, the movement toward more particular forms of devotion and communal observances among youth today often includes, as shown by the original study examined here (chapter 5) done on congregations that connect with their youth, expression of tolerance for other religions and openness to new ideas.

## THE CONTRIBUTIONS OF THIS BOOK

This book seeks to show how in fact three religious traditions can pass on to their next generation of believers a robust and vital understanding and practice of their faiths. More specifically, most of the essays in this volume focus on success stories, in which spiritual searching and religious tradition join hands and enhance each other.

TWO OVERVIEWS

But to situate these success stories, the planning team asked two people to paint the larger landscape of youth and religious practices. In the first chapter, which describes trends in religious practice and religious indifference throughout the world, Melchor Sánchez de Toca, of the Vatican's Pontifical Council for Culture, reports that since 1985 atheism seems no longer to be growing in Europe, though the impact of secularization remains widespread. The world context, however, has changed dramatically with the fall of the Soviet Union, increasing globalization, new communication technologies, and the spread of various forms of terrorism. While the peoples of Asia, Africa, and Latin America remain deeply religious, the intellectual elite of these parts of the world are often secular. In Muslim countries, religious youth join in traditional practices (e.g., the fast of Ramadan), but also seem more prone to adopt Western practices, such as the celebration of New Year and the use of alcohol. About 10 percent of Muslims that immigrate to Europe leave the Muslim religion. It is in the West, however, that the "deconfessionalization" (the "spiritual but not religious") movement is growing, along with an increasing indifference to and agnosticism about religion.[11]

Chapter 2 also paints the large landscape, but focuses on the United States. Sociologist Nancy Ammerman begins her chapter by posing questions that many religious parents and grandparents are asking:

Will our children have a faith to guide them? Will they be able to leave behind the chains and fears and dysfunctionalities of some religious traditions without losing their sacred and moral grounding? Will they forgive the bad religious behavior of some and find common cause with others who are more admirable religious exemplars? Will our own doubts breed religious indifference in the next generation? Will this generation of independent individualists be willing and able to make real commitments to religious ideas and ways of life that may make demands on them?

Ammerman identifies two cultural trends that she believes pose the greatest challenges to passing on religious faith in the United States:

diversity and skepticism. The former is strengthened by religious pluralism and the culture's long support for individualism; the latter has grown with the rise of the scientific method that makes religious claims suspect, since such claims cannot be empirically verified. Instead of advocating a liberal path of accommodation to the culture, or a conservative one of separation from the culture, Ammerman recommends a sort of "postmodern" strategy of cultural bilingualism by which religious people, through extensive religious formation in local communities, become "elective parochials." She believes that such strong faith communities will actually contribute to the common good of the country, skilled as they will be in building not only diverse communities of faith, but communities of tolerance as well. It is within such communities that the faith will be more effectively passed on to the next generation.

## THREE NATIONAL STUDIES

Two important but rather different recent national studies shed light on the issues involved in passing the faith on to the next generation. One, led by Christian Smith while at the University of North Carolina, focuses on the religious understanding and practices of teenagers in the United States. The other, led by Sandy Astin of the Higher Education Research Institute of the University of Southern California, focuses on college students and their sense of spirituality. Succinct summaries of their findings may be found in chapters 3 and 4 of this book. As good as these studies are, they also have their limitations. The Astin study emphasizes, as we shall see, "spirituality" without much attention to its religious roots; Smith's study is more nuanced, but the project design does not include the linkage between survey data and interviews on the one hand, and congregational practices on the other. Later, with the support of the Lilly Endowment, the planning team was able to conduct original research, the third national study in this section of the book, on how specific synagogues, congregations, and mosques successfully connect spirituality and religious practices.

Before looking at the third original study, with its focus on the ambiguous relationship between spirituality and religion, a brief comparison of the Astin and Smith studies will show some striking differences and similarities. First, the two studies are different in that Smith focused on teenagers and Astin on college students. Somewhat surprisingly, Smith found that the deepest desire of the vast majority of teenagers is for a deeper relationship with their parents. Along with that finding, the Smith study explains that the "spiritual but not religious" trend seems to have missed teenagers completely: they do not describe themselves as spiritual, just religious—but religious in a particular way. Nevertheless, when it comes to articulating their faith, they lapse into a language of tolerant "inarticulacy,"[12] to borrow a term from the philosopher Charles Taylor. To describe these teenagers' idea of God, Smith coins the phrase "Moralistic Therapeutic Deism." For teenagers, God is distant but on call when needed, a nondemanding, "cosmic therapist or counselor, a ready and competent helper who responds in times of trouble but who does not particularly ask for devotion or obedience." Like a number of contemporary sociologists of religion, including Peter Berger most recently, Smith does not accept the classic theory of secularization, namely, that with modernity religion will wither until it dies. However, he does think that Thomas Luckman was on to something quite insightful when as early as 1967 Luckman said that while religion was pushed to the margins of society in Europe, in the United States religion became more "modern" through a process of internal secularization—that is, through a process that led religious traditions in the United States to internalize the secular ideas of the American Dream: happiness, freedom, and choice. Smith's conclusion is hardly encouraging for religious leaders and educators: the historic faith traditions are not being handed on in any substantial form.

Turning to Sandy Astin's study, conducted only four years later, one wonders whether we are talking about the same population. Part of the reason for the difference between the two studies is not only that Astin's is focused on college students rather than teenagers, but also that it quite intentionally seeks to understand the "spirituality" of college students, not their religious practices (though it does ask about frequency of attendance at religious services). The distinction made by Jennifer Lindholm, one of Astin's co-researchers and the author of the chapter, between *spirituality* and *religion* is instructive. She defines spirituality, derived in part from the Greek word *enthousiasmos*, as meaning "the God within."[13] Consequently, she writes that spirituality points to our subjective awareness, our "interiors," what we experience "privately"; it has to do qualitatively with our affective experiences. By contrast, religion points to the "objective domain of material objects that one can point to and measure," and has to do with "reasoning or logic" and with "our beliefs about why we are here." She concludes that "spirituality may well exist apart from religion altogether."

One of the significant findings of the Astin study is that today's secular colleges and universities pay little attention to the inner development of their students. Rather, they emphasize "individual achievement, competitiveness, materialism, and objective knowing." More than half the students reported that their professors "never provide opportunities to discuss the meaning and purpose of life."[14] The Astin study finds that, compared to nearly forty years ago, many more students are preoccupied today with being financially secure than in developing a meaningful philosophy of life. Moreover, the percentage of students who claim "no religious preference" has tripled (from 6.6 percent in 1966 to 17.6 percent in 2002). The study also reports that religiously involved students report less stress, alcohol consumption, and casual sex. Women are more spiritual than men, and more involved in serving others. Finally, students in the humanities and fine arts are three times more likely to report high levels of spirituality than students in the physical sciences, business, and computer science—a finding that may also reflect gender imbalance in these majors.

How is it that Smith's teenagers have little contact with the "spiritual but not religious" trend that seems all-pervasive among college students? One college student quoted in the Astin study may provide the answer:

> I think [the distinction between spiritual and religious] is something unique to actually being at college. I never heard anyone distinguish between spirituality and religion when I was back home at my high school and junior high. They were always the same thing. Then I got to college, where you are allowed to be more freethinking or whatever. . . . That's when I started to see that there could be a difference between the two.

Even if college students are allowed to be more freethinking, they seem to think very much like Smith's teenagers do about God, whom they regard as a person who wants to see us happy and fulfilled. Smith's study argues that the single most profound religious influence on teenagers is not their peer group, as Coleman argued some forty years ago, but their parents. But Smith also points out that teenagers' religion is pretty much that of their parents. It may well be that at the end of the day the deepest influence on parents, teenagers, and college students is a democratic, affluent culture of consumption and choice.

It was because of the limitations of the otherwise very valuable Smith and Astin studies that the planning team for the conference commissioned its own research on religious congregations that more or less successfully connect religious practices and spirituality. A report on that study rounds out the national studies in this section of the volume. A team of researchers—including a Jew, a Christian, a Muslim, and someone without a religious affiliation—visited synagogues, Protestant and Catholic churches, and mosques on both coasts and in the Midwest to see how these congregations functioned. The researchers made sure that the three congregations in each of the four groups were sufficiently different from each other so that any common characteristics would be even more valuable. Hence, they visited liberal, Conservative and Orthodox synagogues, and liberal and conservative Protestant churches. It was more difficult to find diverse polities among Catholic parishes, but the mosques visited show some significant differences.

What in essence did the researchers find out about these successful congregations? What they found is not surprising. One is reminded of Dr. Johnson's witticism: people need to be reminded more often than instructed. They found that in all these congregations youth wanted their presence and participation to be valued. They wanted to be met where they are (with all their questions and doubts and, sometimes, their lack of religious literacy), and to learn and be emotionally affected. At the same time, they expressed attitudes of tolerance toward their peers who were not involved in religious practices and toward peoples of other religious traditions. They also valued their freedom to choose whether and how much to be involved in their congregations, and their freedom to adopt many or only some of the religious practices of their traditions. In a very clear way, therefore, even those young people who are involved in historic religious traditions seem to do it on their own terms. The researchers also found that nearly all the congregations either hired staff or had religious leaders, be they rabbis, ministers, priests, or imams, who were able to connect well with youth. Most of the congregations developed liturgies for youth, and sponsored clubs and organizations led by young congregants. Though involved in traditional communal religious practices, many of these young people used the language of spirituality that has become more and more dominant in the wider culture of the United States.

*Jewish Insights*

The planners of the conference also wanted to invite from the three religious traditions individuals who have thought a lot about passing on the faith to the next generation, and perhaps have also led congregations that have connected well with youth. In the case of the Jewish tradition, Rabbi J. Rolando Matalon admirably fulfilled both these expectations. He has led the Congregation Bnai Jeshurun (BJ) in New York City for the past decade. As the spiritual grandson of Rabbi Joshua Abraham Heschel (Matalon's mentor, Rabbi Marshall Meyer, was a student of Heschel), he has built up a large and lively congregation with a substantial contingent of young participants. The congregation's vision of itself rests upon four principles: 1) the centrality of the experience of the divine; 2) the expectation of an engaged participatory membership; 3) a combination of existing and new Jewish practices; and 4) a rabbi-led congregational structure. For this synagogue, the practice of prayer is at the very center; the rabbi leads by visibly praying in a way that transforms the congregation and frees it to pray with him. The practice of study introduces the congregants to texts and teaches them how to act, and, in a form characteristic of the Jewish tradition, study is practiced as an act of devotion. The synagogue also has a strong tradition of social justice and inclusion, welcoming members single and divorced, gay and straight, young and old. And finally, BJ is a rabbi-led congregation, headed by a rabbi who works with but not for a board. Matalon's conviction is that many Jewish congregations in the United States are stifled by boards that dictate policy to rabbis.

Philip Schwadel's essay draws upon Christian Smith's national database, but focuses on a small sample of Jewish teenagers. Throughout his report, the reality that Judaism is as much a culture as a religion— and for the Jewish teenagers surveyed, understood more as a culture—is everywhere present. Despite the overall lack of interest in Judaism as a religion, these young Jews value highly their identity as Jews, are more inclined to think about and get involved in civic and political activities, and approach their religious lives in an individualistic way that allows for choosing what one likes from one's own religious tradition. Were these young Jewish teenagers to join a congregation like Matalon's BJ, their cultural Judaism would likely sink deeper roots in Judaism as a religion.

*Christian Insights*

For over thirty years, the monks of Taizé in Burgundy, France, have received weekly visits from as many as five thousand young people aged seventeen to thirty. They come from everywhere for an experience of prayer and community. These Catholic, Protestant, and Orthodox monks, dedicated originally to ecumenism but now more to their work with young adults, do not design special services for young people; rather, they simply invite them to join in their prayers, to participate in scripture study and sharing groups, to sing chants with them, and to enter periods of protracted silence. So why invite a monk from this community in France to address the issue of passing on the faith to youth living primarily in the United States? We invited a monk because, as was expected, many of the insights gained by the brothers of Taizé in working with youth can be applied in the United States. They have asked themselves why so many young people who return to Taizé for a second visit describe their return as "coming home":

> Coming from a generation raised on all the creature comforts to the $n$th degree, from young people who take for granted their own room, their own bath, their own electronics warehouse, their own car, these words [about the feeling of coming home again] have something stupefying about them. In Taizé they sleep in tents or cabins; the food is nourishing but far from gourmet, or even Burger King; they are expected to attend religious services three times a day; there is no television, movies, or popular music . . . and yet they feel at home!

Brother John's descriptions of the profound silences five thousand young people enter together, the forty-five-minute daily bible instruction, the liturgical gestures and symbols, and the emotional impact of religious practices deliberately performed in a low-key manner—taken together, these help the brothers realize their deepest aspiration for the thousands of young people who visit them weekly: that these young people might live lives rooted in the trust that God accepts them as they are, a discovery that opens the door to radical changes in themselves and the way they relate to others.

The second Christian speaker, Peter Phan, a Vietnamese priest and the only theologian in this volume, directs the doctoral program on interreligious dialogue at Georgetown University. While taking into consideration the findings of the national studies conducted by Astin and Smith, he speaks mainly as a theologian concerned about passing on the faith to the next generation in the midst of a modern culture marked by religious pluralism. He largely accepts the cultural analyses of Astin and Smith, and understands the "spiritual but not religious" movement as a direct threat to historic Christianity, mainly because Christianity makes truth claims. Rather than pinpoint religious illiteracy as the key problem, at least among Catholics, Phan believes that the real problem is that many of the Church's teachings are simply not persuasive. For religious educators and leaders to make them persuasive, they would do well to use an "indirect approach," one that emphasizes the "deep structures" of Catholicism (and Orthodoxy and Anglicanism); those deep structures include a "feel" and an "instinct" when dealing with central Christian claims. These "deep structures" include sacramentality, mediation, communion and the analogical imagination. In Phan's words, these structures are characterized by

> the inclusiveness of both-and rather than either-or thinking, a positive appreciation of creaturely realities as mediation and sacrament of their divine creator, a high regard for the community as the locus of God's self-communication, and a basically optimistic attitude of hope for the redemption of everything.

Finally, Phan offers advice to young people who wish to explore other religions. If they are wise, they will begin such explorations not from uncertainty, but from a deep rootedness in their own religious tradition—a rootedness grounded in careful study and genuine prayer. What ultimately is to be sought is neither syncretism nor synthesis, but a sort of "symbiosis," that is, a way of becoming a better Christian or Jew or Muslim by working and praying with people of other religions. Such a demanding approach to learning about another's religion is, according to Phan, a lifelong process, just as is the formation of one's own religious identity.

*Muslim Insights*

Like the Christians and Jews described in the papers in this volume, Muslims face the same affluent and pluralistic culture, but with one major difference: most Muslims now in this country are immigrants. And unlike European immigrants, they not only practice a non-Christian religion, they are also typically darker skinned. Moreover, many who come from countries with rather homogenous cultures are plunged into very heterogeneous Muslim communities in the United States. And finally, the tragedy of 9/11 has made Muslims in the West, and especially in the United States, feel unwanted and under surveillance. The anthropologists and historians who have founded their theories of immigration upon the experience of European immigrants coming to the United States need to find different explanations, at least in part, for how second-generation Muslims are dealing with the challenges of figuring out whether, as scholar Ghada Osman asks (quoting John Esposito), to "remain Muslims in America or become American Muslims."

In an effort to create an illuminating comparison, Osman looks for parallels between Muslims of the pre-*hijira* Mecca and Muslims in the United States today. In both times and places, the Muslim community constituted a minority, subject to the codes and laws of the majority. Once Muhammad died, Muslims did not have founding figures or others who exercised continuing guidance with authority. The earliest converts to Islam were youth, slaves, and women. Today, 74 percent of the American Muslim community is under the age of fifty. Somewhere between 17 and 30 percent of American Muslims are converts, and 41 percent are female. Taking these parallels into consideration, Osman concludes that American Muslims have an uneasy relationship with mainstream culture in the United States. Many second-generation Muslim youth disassociate from their parents' ethnic background, but, especially since 9/11, focus on their religious identity as Muslims. Even with regard to the severe restrictions of the Patriot Act, American Muslims differ in their reaction, with some seeing the act's measures as unfortunate but necessary, while others are shocked and possess little hope. On the whole, however, most Muslims in the United States are working within mainstream culture, but remain rooted primarily in their identity as Muslims.

The stories told by Amira Quraishi about several Muslim organizations for Muslim youth, two of which she herself has participated in, provide an encouraging portrait of both adaptation to mainstream American culture and fidelity to Muslim tradition. Like Osman, she focuses primarily on second-generation Muslims. In essence, she describes these organizations as providing "safe space" for questioning young-adult Muslims, places where they can probe their tradition without censure, and where they are encouraged to contribute to the larger culture in a variety of ways. These organizations draw upon the internal diversity of Islam, which inevitably raises questions about whose version is correct. They also provide a more informal setting for discussion than the typical mosque. They structure role-playing situations and provide opportunities for debate about many real issues faced by youth— issues such as dress, film and media, gender roles, participation in American holidays, and media coverage of Muslims in America.

Instead of reporting on organizations that operate largely independent of mosques, sociologist Ihsan Bagby studies the large, highly concentrated Muslim community (thirty-three mosques) in Detroit. Nevertheless, his principal focus, like that of Quraishi, is second-generation Muslim youth. He focuses on three questions: 1) that generation's sense of belonging to their mosque; 2) their identity; and 3) their way of understanding Islam. After explaining why traditional immigration theory (progressive and irreversible assimilation into the mainstream culture) doesn't seem to apply to Muslims, he shows how the majority of second-generation Muslims value their religious identity first, and then their identity as Americans. After sustaining their own identity as Muslims, the education and formation of their youth is the second-highest priority of the leadership of the mosques. More than two-thirds of young Muslims feel a strong sense of belonging to their mosque. They find there a place to make friends, learn, and play. That sense of belonging, higher among women than men, drops a bit for those who are away at college, but peaks for Muslims in their forties who are raising families. But despite this sense of belonging, a significant number of second-generation Muslims feel a certain disconnect with those mosque leaders who are more conservative and ethnic in their understanding of what is essential to being a Muslim. The Qur'an teaches that if parents teach something different than what the Qur'an teaches, young people should obey the Qur'an—a teaching that allows a number of second-generation Muslims to shed their parents' sense of ethnicity, and in the process become even more religiously Muslim—a change that nonetheless allows them to enjoy pizza, midnight basketball, and a greater role for both young women and men in choosing their marriage partners. Nonetheless, half of young Muslims still preferred their ethnic identity to their American identity.

Finally, Bagby describes how Muslim youth interpret Islam, that is, whether they insist on literal interpretations and strict applications, or instead "contextualize" and make more flexible their understanding of various Qur'anic teachings, or conclude there is no need to practice at all in modern culture. Less than 10 percent of Muslim youth opted for the strictest interpretation of Islam, and most looked for some flexibility. Interestingly, the most conservative among the youth are those aged thirteen to twenty. In this sense, the second generation could be said to be more religiously conservative than their parents. The youth value "authenticity" above everything else. But these young Muslims are young! With the hope that the Iraq war will become history and that tensions between the West and Islam will be mitigated, it will be most interesting to see what the third generation of Muslims will be like.

## Two Summary Essays

Jack Miles, religious scholar, winner of a MacArthur Fellowship and senior advisor to the president at the J. Paul Getty Trust in Los Angeles, and Diane Winston, the Knight Chair for Media and Religion at the Annenberg School for Communications at the University of Southern California, participated in the entire conference and then, at the end, look back on it and offer their reflections and evaluations. Miles puts his finger on what he believes is now the situation facing all religions in the West: not an ongoing win/lose battle between secularism and religion, but an all-pervasive market economy that pits unchecked commodification against religious commitment: "The encounter of religion with secularism has been overtaken by the encounter of both with American consumerism."[15] Ironically, American consumerist culture creates an especially fruitful context for interreligious dialogue, for religions now need to create something of a common idiom to address a common challenge. Smith's Moralistic Therapeutic Deism resembles closely the consumerist rule that the customer is always right. An essential part of American consumerism is ever greater individualization of entertainment media, with the top spot going to pornography. Does

Miles see any hope? Yes. It can be found, he notes, "in examples like that of Taizé, BJ, and Muslim Youth Camp, particularly when the campers rise at dawn to hear the Qur'an chanted in the cold of first light." Perhaps, suggests Miles, religious leaders should follow the advice of one advertising researcher who found that a great lure for many people, especially youth, is authenticity. Perhaps, instead of yielding to commodification, religions need to stick to mystery.

Diane Winston challenged all the participants of the conference to answer two questions that had not been asked at the conference: Why is religion important? And why is it worth saving? In the eyes of the growing number of people whom religion has alienated, religion appears as a seedbed of violence and hypocrisy, hatred and religiously based terrorism. To be sure, this perception is fueled in part by a media that focuses on scandals, violence, and conflict. Winston provides an excellent and concise summary of the major presentations and affirms their principal conclusions: religions, to be alive and attractive to youth, need to be authentic, accessible, and animating. She emphasizes especially the importance of learning religious language, of becoming articulate in the expression of not only the beliefs of one's religious tradition, but also experiences and insights gained through the practice of one's religion. Especially noteworthy in this regard, Winston writes, is the original research done on successful congregations—where a particular religious tradition and language have engaged youth's desire for participation, ownership, responsibility, and accountability.

As valuable as the sociological studies on religion and youth are, more study needs to be done on the theological dimensions of the challenge of passing on the faith to the next generation. Moreover, the impact of culture on immigrants as different as those who came to this country mainly from Europe during the nineteenth and twentieth centuries needs to be more carefully delineated from the impact of that same culture on Asian immigrants with non-Christian religious commitments, and especially on Muslim immigrants. Not enough study has been done on the power of ritual and symbol—now that we live in a culture that makes such extensive use of visual and musical media—on religious socialization. Could it be that those religious traditions that have depended so heavily on the text and the preached word are now at a distinct disadvantage? If the culture of conspicuous consumption is as ubiquitous and powerful as Jack Miles has suggested, could it not be the case that those who fashion their own approach to God apart from any historic religious tradition—that is, the "spiritual but not religious" people referred to by several authors in this volume—are in fact doubly vulnerable to being co-opted and, almost inevitably, themselves commodified by that pervasive cultural force that markets security, entertainment, comfort and the illusion that they, the customers, are always right? And finally, in an age of sophisticated marketing techniques, is there an even more important place for religious traditions that are able to escape savvy manipulation oriented toward customer satisfaction? Indeed, many important issues need further investigation.

This volume, however, shows that at least three religious traditions—Judaism, Christianity, and Islam—desire to pass on their beliefs and practices to their next generation. None of the chapters in this volume recommends full assimilation into a market-dominated, consumerist culture. Some congregations emphasized that accommodations should be made to the larger culture, but differed on how extensive those accommodations should be. Few spoke about God, the heart of any religious tradition. All religious traditions in the United States obviously face extraordinary challenges, given its pluralistic and consumerist culture. The extent to which they meet that challenge, best met, it would seem, by rooting a vibrant spirituality in a religious tradition, will determine whether Jaroslav Pelikan's grandchildren will have a religious tradition to reject.

# Section One
## National and International Overviews

# Looking for God: Religious Indifference in Perspective

*Melchor Sánchez de Toca*

As we neared the public presentation of the Pontifical Council for Culture's 2004 research into unbelief, religious indifference, and new forms of alternative religion, I somewhat absentmindedly recited to my secretary a rather detached theoretical analysis of unbelief. Unable to restrain herself, she burst out with her very own story: "My children have lost the faith." They are good boys, born to a Christian family, whose mother works in the Vatican and is active in the parish. But they no longer go to Mass on Sundays. Indeed, not only do they no longer practice, but quite simply they no longer believe. After a little questioning on my part, she informed me that they became this way peacefully and quietly, seemingly without any turmoil. At that moment, I did not realize that the problems we are dealing with—youth, unbelief, and religious indifference—are not abstract problems, nor are they distant from us. Just like in the Soderbergh's film *Traffic*, in which the president's right-hand man in the fight against drugs discovers his own daughter's addiction, for us the problem starts in the home. Unbelief is not out there, belonging to other groups, other people, other countries—the marginalized, those who live with too much luxury or in desperate conditions. Even in the stronghold of the traditional Catholic family, in a traditional Catholic country, where the mother works in the Vatican

and the children attend Catholic schools and Catholic universities—
there too the problems of unbelief and indifference exist.

Clearly, these are not new experiences. Saint Monica is a perfect
example of a woman of deep faith who suffered tremendously because
her son was at first not Christian, then became a member of a sect, and
then a first-rate skeptic. Thankfully, the son, Augustine, turned out all
right in the end! Indeed the situation of children abandoning the faith
from within the home is quite familiar. Often it's a form of rebellion
against parents and authority. A positive outcome—by which I mean a
return to the faith—is often forthcoming. But this old problem of abandoning the Church has taken on a new dimension. Today it has a *cultural dimension*. It is no longer just personal. There has been a
breakdown in the process of transmitting the faith from one generation
to the next. This cultural swing is perhaps most evident in European
countries, to the point that not long ago, it achieved the dubious merit
of becoming the cover story of *Time* magazine under the title, "Father,
Where Art Thou?" [1]

The title of this paper, "Looking for God," refers to the person's
ontological religious nature lived as quest for the fulfilling contempla-
tion of God's glory, but the subtitle, "Religious Indifference in Perspective," seeks to underline the need to examine carefully the visible
phenomenon of religious indifference and its partner—the new religiosity. This thesis is based on an inquiry carried out by the Pontifical
Council for Culture on atheism, unbelief, and religious indifference in
the whole world. The fruits of that inquiry, discussed during an international conference in Rome in March 2004, have now been published in
the form of a reflection entitled *Where Is Your God?* [2] In this paper, after
briefly presenting the survey and commenting on some of the more relevant and meaningful elements for the youth in the United States, I will
touch on some of the pastoral means available to respond to the
phenomenon.

## WHY AND HOW A SURVEY ON ATHEISM

Let us turn back the clock to the 1960s and the aftermath of the Second
Vatican Council. Paul VI created three bodies to promote dialogue with
three types of non-Catholics: other Christians—the *Secretariat for
Christian Unity*; believers from other religions—the *Secretariat
for Non-Christians*; and well-disposed nonbelievers—the *Secretariat*

*for Non-Believers*. The task of this latter office was twofold: on the one hand, to establish dialogue with unbelievers; and on the other, to study the phenomenon of contemporary atheism to identify its causes and the reasons for the spread of unbelief. They soon found that it was easier to study atheism than to find nonbelievers with whom to engage in dialogue! That problem has become more acute since the fall of the Berlin Wall and the collapse of the officially atheist regimes, who were among the principal protagonists. For these reasons the Secretariat turned its attention away from dialogue with atheists to address atheism itself, and hence the study of culture marked by unbelief and religious indifference. In 1985, a first study of the actual state of atheism was published in several languages.[3]

As we all know, over the following twenty years, the world changed radically. It suffices to mention the fall of the Soviet Union, the rapid take-off of globalization, the new communication technologies, and the new face of terrorism. From the cold war we have passed to a new global scenario. Whether or not Samuel Huntington's thesis in *The Clash of Civilizations* is correct, a radical change has already occurred at a transcultural level. All this prompted the renamed Pontifical Council for Culture, which is where I work, to update the map of unbelief created in 1985. To do this we asked ourselves some questions: Who are the unbelievers today? How many are they? Where are they? Has there been a change in unbelief? How can we spread our faith to unbelievers today?

We prepared a questionnaire divided in three parts: basic information, the new face of unbelief, and the new forms of religiosity. More than one thousand questionnaires were sent to experts across the world, particularly the members and consultants of the Pontifical Council for Culture, academics in Pontifical and Catholic universities and faculties of theology, local researchers attached to each Episcopal conference, a selection of Catholic cultural centers, and several people chosen for their competence on these issues. The questionnaire was also contained in our quarterly review *Cultures and Faith* and was offered for study to various groups.

Over three hundred replies were received enclosing or referring to an enormous quantity of material, coming from a vast range of perspectives. Together with these replies a whole host of documentation was gathered: statistical information garnered using different research methods by different authorities and agencies, interpretations of the same from different perspectives, names of atheistic groups, satanic sects, and new religious movements. We also found various publications, Web sites, reviews, journals, and centers dedicated to the pastoral study of unbelief.

## PRELIMINARY REMARKS

Before going into any depth on the findings of the survey, I would like to make some preliminary remarks. First, I intend to present the Catholic Church's understanding of the question at hand as it is seen from Rome, but based on the reports from around the world. I say this because while many of the assertions I make can also be held by people from other religions, other denominations, and Catholics from other parts of the world, sometimes the vocabulary, concepts, and backgrounds used are not shared by everyone. For example some researchers used the category "unbeliever" for those who have left the Catholic Church to enter new religious movements or Pentecostal-type communities, whereas others would rank them as "alternative believers." Also bear in mind that most of the material received came from Catholics and hence offer Catholic perspectives.

Second, the end product is not a sociological report. It was done seriously and with honesty—at least I hope so—but not by sociologists of religion. Hence rather than offering up-to-date statistics on the state of religion in the world in the style of the *European Values Study* or the *World Values Study*, it merely presents an outline or overview of the Catholic faith, atheism, and religious indifference in the world. It is intended to be a pastoral study, prepared for pastors and those responsible for Christian communities. It takes into consideration statistics and recent sociological surveys, but it goes beyond them, as its purpose is not only to know how the world is getting on, but to help transmit the faith to the people in that world.

## A PANORAMIC VISION OF THE WORLD OF UNBELIEF

The survey gave us a panorama of unbelief in the world, structured according to geographic areas: Africa (excluding North Africa); America, divided into two blocs, North America and Latin America; Asia; Europe, divided into Mediterranean, western, Scandinavian, central, and ex-Communist areas; Oceania; and, finally, Islamic areas. Offering a general impression, the survey highlighted both those aspects of unbelief that are common and those aspects that are particular to certain geographical or social areas.

The picture is obviously incomplete. Firstly, because the data we have are limited to what was supplied by those who answered our questionnaire and the limited research we could carry out. Moreover, the data are not uniform: some are official censuses, others the fruit of serious academic study, and still others are based on hearsay evidence or contain simple opinions or impressions by correspondents. Indeed, the way our correspondents categorized and collected statistics varies enormously. For obviously asking "Do you believe in God?" is not the same as asking "Do you attend church?" At the same time, I should mention that in some countries when a census asks which religion do you belong to, believers might, for very good reasons, leave the answer box empty and hence be categorised as atheists.

Putting all these statistics together and evaluating them with an interpretative eye, we painted a picture that is complex, changing, and in continuous evolution. Here are some of the more pertinent conclusions:[4]

1. *Globally, unbelief is not increasing.* It is a phenomenon seen primarily in the Western world. The cultural model it inspires spreads through globalization, exerts an influence on the different cultures of the world, and erodes their popular religiosity. Unbelief is not an Asian, African, or Latin American problem. Nor does it affect the Islamic world.

One gets the impression that in Asia the problem is not a lack of religion, but rather a surplus of it. African peoples are fundamentally religious. Modern forms of unbelief affect those of European origin, and the urban elite of these countries. The religious problem in Africa is one of syncretism rather than of absence, and the persistence of tribalism. As our correspondent in Cameroon noted: "Normal practice is that of Christians by day, animists by night. But unbelief is not a big issue in Africa."

In Latin America the people are deeply religious and the majority are Catholic. But in almost all countries ambivalence can be found. While the intellectual elite of the country is strongly marked by secularism, the popular Christian culture struggles to get a mention in the public life of the country. The extraordinary growth of sects and new Pentecostal-type communities is a common phenomenon. In some countries, such as Brazil and Guatemala, these groups have passed from 0 to 25 percent of the population in the last twenty-five to thirty years. Even if this is not so much a question of unbelief as a search for a form of more emotional and affective religiosity, for many, the continual transition from one community to another eventually leads to their exiting institutional religions, to which they rarely return.

In the Islamic world any generalization is simplistic. It is difficult to talk of unbelief in countries that have a Muslim majority, as many Muslims, even if they are not strictly observant, are and believe themselves to be Muslim. In some countries, especially in the Maghreb, some changes were noted by our correspondents. There is a reaffirmation of cultic elements and of religious practice among the youth, for example fasting at Ramadan. Yet at the same time, they adopt Western practices such as celebrating New Year with presents and even consuming alcohol. But the sense of frustration that builds in the face of globalization pushes people to a form of fundamentalism and a radical rejection of modernity.

A word should also be said about the evolution of Islam, particularly about Muslim immigrants to Europe. In some countries about ten percent of immigrants from Muslim countries abandon Islam when they feel freed from their social and family environment. However, the majority of these ex-Muslims do not adopt another religious identity: they become unbelievers.

2. *Militant atheism recedes and no longer has a determining influence on public life*, except in those regimes where an atheistic political system is still in power. Nevertheless, a certain cultural hostility is being spread against religions, especially Christianity and Catholicism in particular, notably through the means of social communication, and is promoted by groups active in different organizations.

3. *Atheism and unbelief*, phenomena that once seemed to have something rather masculine and urban about them and that were found particularly among those with an above-average level of culture, *have changed their profile*. Today the phenomena seem to be connected more to lifestyle, and the distinction between men and women is no longer significant. Unbelief increases among women who work outside the home, and even reaches more or less the same level of that among men.

4. *Religious indifference or practical atheism* is growing rapidly. Agnosticism remains at about the same level. A large part of secularized societies lives with no reference to religious authority or values.

For *homo indifferens*, "perhaps God does not exist, it doesn't matter, and anyway I don't miss him." Affluence and secular culture provoke in consciences an eclipse of need and desire for all that is not immediate. They reduce aspiration toward the transcendent to a simple subjective need for spirituality, and happiness to material well-being and the gratification of sexual impulses.

5. *A dwindling number of regular churchgoers can be seen in those societies marked by secularization.* This fact does not, however, mean that unbelief is on the increase. Rather, it points to a degraded form of believing: *believing without belonging.* It is a phenomenon of the "deconfessionalization" of *homo religiosus*, who, refusing to belong to any binding confession, jumps in and out of an endless confusion of heterogeneous movements. A number of those who declare that they belong to no religion or religious confession nevertheless declare themselves to be religious. Many Catholics who are part of the *silent exodus* join sects and new religious movements,[5] especially in Latin America and sub-Saharan Africa.

6. In the West, where science and modern technology have neither suppressed religious meaning nor satisfied it, a *new quest that is more spiritual than religious* is developing; however, it is not a return to traditional religious practices. It is the search for new ways of living and expressing the need for religiosity inherent in the heart of man. Often, this spiritual awakening develops in an autonomous fashion and without any links to the contents of faith and morals handed on by religious tradition.

7. Finally, at the dawn of the new millennium, a *disaffection* is occurring both in terms of militant atheism and in terms of traditional faith. It is a disaffection in secularized Western cultures that are prey to the refusal or simple abandonment of traditional beliefs, and affects both religious practice and adherence to the doctrinal and moral contents of the faith. But the person whom we call *homo indifferens* never ceases to be a *homo religiosus*; he or she is just seeking a new and ever-changing religiosity. The analysis of this phenomenon reveals a kaleidoscopic situation where anything and its opposite can occur: on the one hand, those who believe without belonging, and on the other, those who belong without believing in the entire content of the faith and who, above all, do not feel obliged to respect the ethical teachings of the faith. In truth, only God knows what is at the bottom of our hearts, where His Grace works secretly.

A BRIEF ANALYSIS

The typology of the unbeliever likewise varies. There are the spiritually dead, those seeking a sense of marvel, the desire for desire. There are the indifferent with their need for provocation, and the badly orientated who face up to the big questions but stop at incomplete solutions. There are those with faith but who reject any notion of the Church. Then there are the misdirected believers who need that gentle correction and advice. And finally there is the nonbeliever in each one of us, which is an invitation to each one of us to daily conversion. The terminology for these categories is also rich if multi-interpreted: atheist, nonbeliever, agnostic, indifferent, unattached, misbelieving, unchurched, nonpracticing believer, and even practicing nonbeliever.

The causes of unbelief and religious indifference pointed out in the responses are many. The Second Vatican Council's Pastoral Constitution on the Church in the World, *Gaudium et Spes*, listed some of them (nn. 19–21). These are still valid and include a) scientism, b) absolute anthropocentricism, c) the problem of evil, and d) the historical limits of Christians and of the Church in the world. Alongside these there are some new ones: the breakdown in the process of handing on of the faith, the globalization of the modern lifestyle, the influence of the mass media, and new religious movements such as New Age religions.

As I mentioned before, the changes in belief and unbelief are most evident in countries of ancient Christian tradition and in countries marked by significant pluralism, such as the United States. Some proof of this phenomenon can be found in a major Italian daily national newspaper, which recently printed an article on the religiosity of today's citizens of Rome.[6] Rome is home to the Pope, to the Roman Catholic Church with her history and tradition. For centuries it has been called, and rightly so, the Holy City, and is the destination of millions of pilgrims every year. These faithful Christians visit the tombs of the apostles Peter and Paul, and of the early Christian martyrs. But how does the journalist view today's Romans?

Citing a study by the Fondazione Roma Europea, which telephoned 504 people, the journalist describes Romans as "tolerant, religious, but rarely practicing." In very broad outline: 77 percent of those interviewed say they are Catholics; 74 percent say they feel God is near them; only 23 percent frequently attend Mass on Sundays. What is more significant is that 20 percent never attend, and this figure shoots up to 55 percent in the 18–35 age group. More than half of the Romans surveyed maintain that the religions are all more or less the same. And 49 percent of declared Catholics hold this opinion. But at the same time 65 percent believe the world would be a worse place if there were no religion in the world.

Luca Diotallevi, a sociologist at the University of Rome, gives an interesting interpretation of these statistics: "The traditional rationalist atheist is in crisis. The number of regular practitioners is neither rising nor falling. What is rising is the number of people who are open to the religious dimension, but who are not practicing." What is happening is a process of secularization in which there is a personalization of the faith, but not "in the sense of a new rationalism, but in the sense of selective consumerism, which sees Catholicism as part of a great religious supermarket." Religion is perceived as being made up of many symbols, emotions, and individual freedoms, but with few rules and little discipline. The sociologist concludes that after the Jubilee year of 2000, which the Holy Father set aside as a time for commemorating two millennia since Christ's birth and for renewing the faith, there has been no growth of the "superfaithful." "There is a brighter glow of general pleasure taken in religion, but no notable increase in rigorous belonging. There is a growing feeling of goodwill towards religion."[7]

This is the portrait of religiosity in Rome, and the rest of Europe is seeking to cope with a similar shift. In my own country, Spain, disaffection with and abandonment of the Catholic faith is notable. Perhaps this is due to the Spanish character, and the historical relations between the Church hierarchy and the people. According to an old saying, Spaniards are always behind their priests: either in procession with a candle in hand or in the shadows with a cutthroat knife! Today it is sometimes difficult to see the same level of passion about religion.

## THE NEW RELIGIOSITY

The study of the Pontifical Council for Culture and the article cited above are both consistent with the main research carried out by sociologists in the field that points to a tendency to elaborate a very personal, often narcissistic style of relationship between the individual and God and/or religion.

Hence, closely connected to unbelief and religious indifference is the theme of the so-called "new religiosity." Our study noted that this is something that is emerging clearly as a common factor across the world. It is a spirituality more than a religion. It can be defined with reference to four categories: absence of a personal God, a religion of the self, relativism in terms of truth, and rejection of the historical forms of religious traditions to pass on the truth to the individual, including the rejection of institutions such as the Church.

An examination of new religiosity might seem paradoxical in a talk that addresses unbelief and religious indifference. But these phenomena are closely connected. If on the one hand the new spiritual search is a manifestation of the thirst for the infinite and transcendent, which is innate in each and every person, it represents on the other hand a form of immanent religion, which focuses the needs of the subject, and is thus related to the forms of indifference today. This mentality also affects believers; careful attention, therefore, also needs to be paid to this aspect of religious indifference. For these reasons, the Pontifical Council for Culture also undertook a study of the New Age phenomenon to address these questions of indifference, new religiosity, and ecclesiology.[8]

RESPONDING TO THE DESIRE FOR GOD PRESENT IN PEOPLE TODAY

Many questions surround the issues we are dealing with. The first, and most obvious, is: "Are these new forms of religiosity and indifference a necessary consequence of the progress of humanity?" Or another way of putting it: "Has this state of affairs come about of necessity or are there, at least in part, some individuals or groups who are either purposefully or unconsciously promoting this indifference and state of unbelief?" If unbelief is a necessary consequence of progress, then our lot is cast, and we may as well prepare for our extinction; if certain interpretations of falling religious adherence and practice are to be believed, then within ten or twenty or so years (depending again on one's perspective) traditional religions will totally disappear and be but a subject for the history books. But this is not likely to be the case. Even in the old Soviet Union, the official line was that only the old women went to church and that when they died there would be no believers left. But they must have lived very long lives, for even during the seventy years that the Soviet regime blighted the world, those old women somehow never stopped going to church! And today the same churches are still frequented by a new generation of women with grand experience. Not even the harshest religious oppression ever known managed to uproot the faith or suppress the heart's desire for God.

The times in which we are living today are not easy, but they are our times and we are called to live them. Saint Augustine, who lived through the fall of the Roman Empire, called upon his congregation to live in their own time. He said: "Do not complain, my brothers. It is true that there are many who complain about the present times, and they say that our forefathers knew better times. But even if they had lived during our forefathers' times, they would have complained all the same. In truth, you judge other times as good because they were not your own."[9] Such fatalism is still alive today. As one colleague of mine is prone to say, "Wherever two or three are gathered in your name, Lord, they complain how badly it's all going." This is something we often remembered when reading the responses to the questionnaire. Indeed, while an enormous amount of words are spent decrying the current situation, such verbosity is absent when it comes to presenting hard-and-fast proposals to counter this situation.

Our task, though, is not to denounce but to announce. With the Second Vatican Council, the Catholic Church committed itself to reading the "signs of the times." That is to say it seeks, in the changes and evolutions the world is passing through, signs of the action of God in the hearts of people, and values that can become anchor points for a renewed proclamation of the Gospel. Such a sign of the times is the spiritual search that is prevalent today. Despite all its contradictions, this new religiosity can become fertile ground for the task of handing on faith.

Clearly a new language is needed for this task. Religiosity is taking on new forms that until now were unthinkable. What is called for is a new language that takes into account both intelligence and emotion. This was particularly commented on by our Anglo-Saxon correspondents to the survey; more so than people of any other culture, they seem to have suppressed emotions and, as a consequence, feel the need to refresh and bring to the fore the emotional nature of the faith. The culture of the significant relationship, the primacy of the person and personal relationships are essential in the opera of evangelization. New Age philosophies and the sects attract many by playing on their emotions. To respond to this challenge, and following the invitation of John XXIII to "use the medicine of mercy rather than that of severity," we can reach out to all those who in sincerity are seeking the Truth, starting with those who are passing through the difficult moments of life, which leaves them prey to the sects. *Personal relationships* within the church, above all in the larger parishes, are also important. If the large gatherings of youth are useful as starting points to recover or discover the faith, that faith can then be nurtured, shaped, and matured in small local communities where each person feels that he or she belongs and has a role to play and is no longer just another meaningless member of the anonymous masses. The joy of belonging, as a Catholic, to the family of God is the visible sign of the message of salvation. The Church, family of families, appears as the real "place" of meeting between God and men.

But that which Christians call evangelization is not only a question of language and methods, although these are always necessary. It is not enough to find a new method to fill the churches. We are not salespeople capable of saying anything to entice the customer, but we have the task of looking after a treasure that we have received and that we have to hand on—a treasure that holds in the balance the true liberty of humanity. The renewal of language must walk side by side with a renewal of ardor and fervor in the way that believers live their own faith, their relationship with God, the mystical and spiritual dimension of faith, and the coherence between religion and life. As Pope Paul VI wrote in his Apostolic Exhortation *Evangelii Nuntiandi* (December 8, 1975, no. 41): "Modern man listens more willingly to witnesses than to teachers, and if he does listen to teachers, it is because they are witnesses."

I would like, finally, to touch on an experience that has deeply marked the relation between the institutional church and youth, and which illustrates how new ways, languages, and relationships can be found to hand on the faith to the next generations: the World Youth Days.

Started in 1984 as an opportunity to let youth from all over the world meet the Pope, they have become what some have called the Catholic Woodstock—a regular date between the successor of Peter and the youth. There are many reasons to be skeptical about the real value of such big events and gatherings. "Big event syndrome" is the latest title I have heard being applied to occasions where the smallness of our hearts are left untouched by the momentum of the occasion. But experience shows that at World Youth Days the opposite is true. In the midst of a crowd, surrounded by friendship and anonymity, faces foreign and

familiar, the moments of prayer and silence help these seekers to rediscover the joy of believing. They are liberating forces for the potential
that is in each one of us. Attracted by the witness of the countless fellow
youth present, these are privileged times to discover the Gospel or to
let it enter more deeply into our lives.

When our study was first made public, the Archbishop of Madrid,
Antonio Rouco, was due to talk about this issue at the meeting of the
Pontifical Council for Culture. It was March 11, the day of the terrorist
attack on Madrid. In his prepared speech, he had paid attention to one
of the most surprising elements of these events: their ecclesial character. As opposed to many contemporary trends, he said, the faith experience resulting from these tragic days leads *toward* the Church, not away
from it: "The youth have started to feel the need to belong to the people
of God, to the Church. This is in strict opposition with the temptation
to believe without belonging, to live one's faith at the margins of the
Church."[10] Many youngsters have discovered a call to serve God in
these days, becoming priests or entering religious orders, or forming a
Christian family. These youth, then, some years later, come back as
group leaders, or animators, or bring their own families along thereby
creating a multiplication effect. Concluding the World Youth Day of
Rome 2000, the mayor of Rome, Francesco Rutelli, said that Rome had
suffered the largest but least damaging invasion in its history. In one
week, with one million youths visiting from all over the world, in the
merciless heat of mid-August, the only incidents registered were faint-
ing spells due to the heat.

Similar experiences may be found elsewhere. One could mention
meetings held at Taizé, France, and the Meeting for the Friendship of
Peoples, at Rimini, Italy; the various pilgrimages to Santiago de Com-
postella, Lourdes, Czestochowa, and Loreto that embrace thousands of
youngsters and introduce them to the life of the Church. Other confes-
sions and denominations recite similar experiences.

It would be ingenuous to imagine that there are easy recipes to
guide the young unbeliever into faith, to persuade the alternative believer of the importance of participating in the religious tradition, or
to entice the indifferent into action. But I have listed a few promising
examples—youth events, relations that foster the dignity of youth, the
recognition of their language to stimulate meaningful dialogue, the cap-
turing and harvesting of the natural search for God that is innate in each
person, and Christians simply being witnesses to the truth of a God who

emptied himself, took on human form, and died on the cross for our sake. The witness of charity reflects this pastoral outreach, the most convincing argument to "prove" the existence of God; it is the "better way" of which Saint Paul wrote (1 Cor. 13). In Christian art and in the lives of the saints shine the flame of beauty and of God's love that becomes incarnate in ever new ways in people's lives. In the end, it is beauty that will save the world;[11] a morally upright life attracts each and every individual person to embrace the good and to see God.

JOURNEYS OF FAITH: MEETING THE CHALLENGES
IN TWENTY-FIRST-CENTURY AMERICA

*Nancy Ammerman*

The questions raised by this conference are both professional and personal for me. As a sociologist, the social changes of the last forty years have provided ample fodder for research, and I'll attempt to tell you some of the things I think we've discovered in the process. But as a parent of a daughter born in 1980, I also stand before you with many of the same concerns that I suspect brought some of you here. Will our children have a faith to guide them? Will they be able to leave behind the chains and fears and dysfunctionalities of some religious traditions but without losing their sacred and moral grounding? Will they forgive the bad religious behavior of some and find common cause with others who are more admirable religious exemplars? Will our own doubts breed religious indifference in the next generation? Will this generation of independent individualists be willing and able to make real commitments to religious ideas and ways of life that may make demands on them?

I worry, for instance, that my daughter doesn't seem to have the habit of giving a regular portion of her meager and intermittent income to any church. But I rejoice that she chooses to *go* to church! I worry that her biblical knowledge may be a bit thin, but then she surprises me with the stories and characters and ideas she does know. She started her life in Southern Baptist churches of a progressive sort (yes, there used to be such things), but as that tradition was overtaken by fundamentalist forces, our beloved local church in Atlanta was eventually pushed out of the denomination entirely. We are now all members of an American Baptist church in Boston. Sometimes even when you don't set out to change traditions, your tradition itself changes! You can perhaps see why a continuing faith commitment hasn't exactly been a given for this young woman.

One morning last summer, we were doing our usual jockeying over the newspaper sections at breakfast before she headed to the campaign office of a certain presidential candidate for whom she is working. She noted that the Southern Baptists were calling on their members to vote for candidates that represented "biblical values." I expected her to scoff, reading the conservative agenda between the lines. Her response, however, was: "I intend to—just not the ones they have in mind!" In the midst of a culture in which she has many choices about how to spend her time, in which the tradition into which she was born has been transformed, in which the intersections between faith and everyday values are contentious at best—in the midst of all that, she has staked her claim to an identity shaped by biblical values. And her mother can only say "Amen!"

Those are formidable challenges—for all of us. Putting on my sociologist's hat, I want to explore two broad areas of challenge for faith in our culture, suggesting some of the ways in which faith traditions are—and aren't—stepping up to the plate.

The first area of challenge is the reality of diversity. If it ever was the case that a parent could raise a child under a single overarching sacred canopy, that is clearly not the case today. The United States remains a predominantly Christian country, but young adults today encounter compatriots from many corners of that Christian tradition, many of whom have only vague attachments to whatever tradition they may claim. About one in four young adults identifies as Catholic, but less than half of them attend church even once a month.[1] Another one in four identifies as some sort of conservative Protestant, with an additional one in ten a member of the various African American Protestant denominations. More of these Protestants attend regularly than Catholics do, but even here a substantial number of people who were raised in a tradition have little ongoing connection to it today. One in six young adults identifies as one of the mainline Protestant denominations, and again, less than half of them attend church regularly. One in five young adults has no religious preference at all, but a quarter of them actually do show up at religious services occasionally.

All the non-Christian traditions together account for only 3 percent of young adults. But their psychological presence is far greater than those numbers indicate. For one thing, they are not evenly distributed around the country, so there are pockets in the United States where Jews, Muslims, Hindus, Buddhists, and others are present and visible in far greater proportions than in other places. What's more, only about 37 percent of the young-adult population actively participates in a Christian tradition, and among them the range of beliefs and practices extends from traditionalist Catholics saying the Latin mass to hip evangelicals with praise bands to Afrocentric black Methodists and civic-minded Congregationalists meeting on New England town greens. Between the 40 percent who are minimally involved or nonparticipating Christians and the 20 percent who have no religious preference, a majority of the young-adult population is at best nominally attached to any given tradition, and the rest are spread among a very wide diversity of groups.

But more than the sheer numbers, diversity is a *cultural reality*.[2] No one makes any assumptions about the religious identity of the people they meet on the street—unless those people provide some visible signal. And even if they do, American culture has taught us well. We know that no one has the right to impose his or her religion on someone else and that each of us is supposed to choose for ourselves from the vast array of religious and secular options available to us. Even people who have grown up in much more taken-for-granted sorts of places quickly learn that in the United States, religion is far from a given. They learn that people here believe in different gods or no god at all; they worship on Saturday and Sunday and five times a day. Some fast during Lent, others on Yom Kippur, and still others between sunrise and sunset during Ramadan. Some ordain women to lead their religious communities, and others command them to be silent. The range of practice and belief is enormous, and it is not in distant lands, but all around us.

Such pluralism has, according to many observers, undermined the plausibility of any single religious tradition.[3] Because no religious tradition can define a taken-for-granted world, all religious traditions suffer. Because we are surrounded by people of faith whose god is not our god, we must confront the reality of our own god's contingency. In this modern, pluralist situation, proselytization seems impossible, impolite, even dangerous. We aren't even sure we should impose our religious beliefs on our own children!

One of the results of this American pluralism is a tendency toward individualism in matters religious. The same forces of mobility and education and commerce that have brought diverse people together have also dislodged people from traditional communities in the process. And in the dislodging from ascribed loyalties, the modern individual has been created.[4] We are not first identified by our family and town and ancestral occupation. Rather, we are identified by occupations and places and even names that we have chosen for ourselves. Faith, in this individualist mode, is an internalized meaning system that may combine elements from a variety of traditions, but is accountable to none of them.[5]

Recent studies of baby boomers—the parents of today's youth—have demonstrated the degree to which these ideals of individualism and choice abound. Wade Clark Roof has documented the spiritual lives of the generation that came of age in the midst of a "question authority" era, for whom little about religion has been taken for granted.[6] We have sought out our own paths—borrowing from eclectic religious sources, sometimes inside organized religion and sometimes not. Dean Hoge and his associates looked at a sample of boomers who began the 1960s inside organized religion as Presbyterian confirmands. Interviewing them thirty years later, however, these researchers discovered that only about a quarter were still members of Presbyterian churches. Many had left religious involvement for at least a time, and many others were in other religious traditions or outside the faith entirely.[7] When 78 percent of Americans say that a person can be a good Christian or Jew without attending church or synagogue,[8] they are often speaking from the experience of trying to chart just such an independent course. If these people are parents, we have to wonder what, if anything, they have taught their children. Diversity—and the individualism it seems to have spawned—has increasingly taken individuals outside traditional religious communities and into a vast religious (and secular) marketplace of ideas.[9]

American religious diversity is, however, by no means new.[10] One could argue that the diversity of eighteenth-century American religion is one of the primary reasons the Constitutional framers did not seek to create an established church in the first place. There was already as much diversity on these shores as in the whole of the European continent and far more than in any one European society.[11] Sidney Mead argued that religious tolerance quickly became a pragmatic necessity here, that religiously diverse groups of immigrants "learned in a relatively short time to live together in peace under the genial aegis of the Dutch and English combination of patriotic-religious fervor, toleration, cynicism, simple desire for profits, efficacious muddling through, and 'salutary neglect' that made up the colonial policy of these nations."[12] From the beginning, this country has been an experiment in religious pluralism.

Before the nineteenth century was over, the experiment expanded further. Constitutional freedom not only protected the initial broad array of faiths, but also enabled this country to give birth to dozens of new religious traditions and to become the immigrant home to dozens more. Nathan Hatch describes the first third of the nineteenth century in ways that evoke our own time. Having set loose the possibility of religious liberty, what followed was "a period of religious ferment, chaos, and originality unmatched in American history. Few traditional claims to religious authority could weather such a relentless beating. There were competing claims of old denominations and a host of new ones. Wandering prophets appeared dramatically, and supremely heterodox religious movements gained followings. People veered from one church to another. Religious competitors wrangled unceasingly."[13] Today's diversity stands in a long line of religious inventiveness and experimentation. And although dozens of groups would argue that they and they alone have the true way to live, all that inventiveness has taken place with relatively little overt or violent religious conflict.[14]

The implication for religious groups themselves was that they had to learn to be one among many and act, in effect, like radical Protestants. The Reformation had introduced Europeans to some modest notion of religious pluralism as the monopoly of the Roman Catholic church was broken. There were new dissenting sects, but most of the new Protestant movements in Europe responded by setting up their own exclusive domains—Lutherans in Germany and Scandanavia, Anglicans in England, Reformed (Calvinist) Protestants in Switzerland and the Netherlands. Only the "radical" reformers (Mennonites, Baptists, and Brethren, for instance) argued for complete separation from state power. Only these separatists ventured complete reliance on voluntary membership, on spiritual rather than earthly persuasion. And in the United States, those radical impulses won the day. Other traditions have often complained that they have been "Protestantized" as they have accommodated to American culture. Whatever else that has meant, they are right in the sense that they have been pushed to adopt a basic commitment to live peacefully alongside religious others.[15] While the resulting diversity surely poses challenges to communities of faith, we can also celebrate the relatively peaceful and civil results of these long-standing U.S. commitments.

If diversity is the first basic challenge faced by traditions that wish to survive into a new generation, the second is the equally inescapable reality of skepticism. In earlier times, people often turned to their religions to explain the unexplainable in life: Where do babies come from? Why does the moon pass through phases? What makes the crops grow and the rains come? What happens to us when we die? In the earliest days, priests and shamans offered solutions and cures, rituals and explanations for things people had no other way of understanding. But beginning at least as far back as the Enlightenment, experts located in and trained by universities began to displace priests as dispensers of approved knowledge about life's mysteries. If we want to know why we are sick, we go to a doctor. If we want to know about the moon, we ask an astronomer or even an astronaut. If we want to know about crops, we consult an agricultural scientist—or perhaps an economist. If we want to understand the mysteries of the human mind, we go to the biology and psychology departments. Wherever we go for answers, we expect them to come through systematic, *rational* methods. This epistemological move is described by Max Weber as a shift from traditional and charismatic bases of authority to authority based on "rational-legal" forms of legitimacy.[16] There are rules to be followed, ways of defending one's evidence, and recognized credentials that allow one to claim expertise. In this modern way of thinking, it is not sufficient to say "the Torah commands it" or "the priest advises it." Rather, the scripture itself is to be subjected to historical, critical, archeological, and anthropological investigation. And the priest must gain advanced training in psychology and management before his or her advice will be taken seriously.

Like diversity, skepticism is not new. [17] The struggle between science and religion has been going on for at least two centuries, and by the beginning of the twentieth century, two dominant modes of response had developed. One mode of response was the liberal path of adaptation. To survive in this skeptical world, theologians sought to make religion believable to rational, scientifically attuned minds—and offered a set of moral precepts more than any claims of miracle or transcendence. The liberal project, at least for the last century, has sought uniquely modern forms for religious faith and practice, updating old doctrine and ritual and eschewing any claims to timeless truth.

The result for many youth today is that their religious upbringing has emphasized tolerance as much as competence in their own tradition, questioning as much as faith. It was as important to their churches that they know about and accept their Buddhist and Jewish neighbors as that they know their own tradition's history and teachings. Within Christianity, ecumenism emphasized common ground and discouraged particularity. The result for many young adults is a growing indifference to those particularities—we're really all the same, aren't we?

Standing opposite this liberal project has been an equally adamant conservative one. Theorists and practitioners alike have claimed that for religion to survive the modern challenge, it would have to form relatively isolated, "sectarian" communities with strict rules, firm beliefs, and a strong collective identity. Dean Kelley advised Protestant churches a generation ago that growth depended on "strictness."[18] People wanted to have a clear sense of identity, he claimed, and that identity would come from unwavering beliefs, clear guidelines for behavior, and no doubts about the presence of God in the world. His practical advice echoed the theoretical words articulated by Peter Berger. In the face of a pluralistic world, religion could construct small sheltering—and fearful—social worlds. Various religious countercultures and sectarian groups would give up the illusory goal of dominating society and instead undertake the formidable social engineering task required for the "erection and maintenance of barriers strong enough to keep out the forces that undermine certainty—a difficult feat in the context of modern urban life, mobility, and mass communication."[19] Both belief and practice, so these theories go, can be produced and sustained in spite of modern challenges; but they require intentional work at creating religious enclaves in which those ideas and practices make sense.[20]

The challenges of the modern world, then, have appeared to present two radically different alternatives to those who would continue to be religious: a creative synthesis that merges faith with modern sensibilities and maintains the gains represented by American tolerance and civility—risking indifference—or a strategic retreat into intentionally anti-modern communities—risking the dangers of mutual fear. You can either teach your children to be good, tolerant, civil liberals, or you can teach them to be aggressively active in maintaining the boundaries between their faith and a hostile world.

I want to suggest, however, that neither the skepticism nor the diversity is perhaps quite what we have taken it to be—and our options may not be so "either/or" as the modernists and fundamentalists claimed they were.

I am proposing that our way forward may lie in a kind of "postmodern" strategy that says "yes, but" to the modern challenges we face.[21] To invoke a postmodern paradigm is to suggest that the realities of the modern situation are still with us, but their limits are recognized. Skepticism and diversity are not likely to go away, but we are beginning to recognize that modern assumptions about our necessary choices may not be the whole story. There are all sorts of cracks and crevices in that presumably modern front in which new forms of life are emerging, and old, unnoticed ones have been thriving all along.

This is not the place for an extended philosophical reflection on the limits of rationality, but I do want to suggest the commonsense observation that human beings have begun to engage in some fairly serious questioning about just how far science can and should take us and whether there are other ways we can learn about the world.[22] In the horrors of atomic war and genocidal holocaust—all so rationally planned—we have seen what science *can* do. It may only deepen our basic dilemmas. We are also recognizing that, alongside our reasoned inquiry, we have always depended on other ways of knowing. We have always trusted tradition more than we ever admitted. Vast areas of our lives are still governed by rules that come to us through habit and advice that have never been tested in any scientist's laboratory. We also know that sometimes our knowledge and insight come from sources we have a hard time explaining. Sometimes we call it a "gut feeling" or "intuition" or "a vision" or "wisdom," but we still know it is true. These days, when there seems to be a spirituality of everything from nature to business plans, the lines between "rational" and "not rational" have blurred considerably. Science is not about to disappear, but its domain has shrunk.

Nor has the modern response to diversity resulted in the universalist melting pot that was predicted. While many forms of particularity have eroded, other signs of difference persist. Not only are immigrants learning to live transnational lives,[23] but even some members of liberal denominations are celebrating their distinctiveness and teaching newcomers their heritage.[24] While fundamentalist, high-boundary solutions seem to be maintaining their appeal, I remain convinced that they will never be the primary way modern people choose to live together.

A much more promising response to diversity seems to be emerging among people who are culturally bilingual—who speak a native, parochial language and a language shared with people they do not know.[25] We live in a world where people can both be rooted in particularistic ethnic and religious communities *and* be more aware of the larger world and the choices that have brought them to their current practices. They are, to use Stephen Warner's extremely helpful term, "elective parochials."[26]

That term is useful because it recognizes two key realities. First, today's religious commitments are by definition "elective." The realities of choice are probably with us to stay. Nearly all religious communities recognize that the community of birth is not, of necessity, the community of lifelong affiliation. It is no accident that religious people increasingly use the metaphor of journey to describe their faith. At the very least, geographic mobility is likely to precipitate the search for a new congregation, and in most instances even the person who remains religiously loyal will have more than one congregation from which to choose. Many commentators have come to refer to this reality as "religious shopping," but it need not be a cost-benefit process. To choose is to make a commitment, however minimal, and to be on a journey implies conscious effort. These are not passive processes, but active engagements with tradition.

And tradition is the other reality evoked by that "elective parochial" phrase. To be a parochial is to have a community, to go beyond one's presumed autonomy as an individual. The presumption of autonomy is neither so unquestioned today nor so welcomed as it once was. We are neither as free and disconnected as the modernist paradigm would have had it nor as utterly embedded in ascribed communities as our traditionalist forebears. In the nexus of choice and community, new understandings of person and commitment are emerging.[27]

What I am suggesting is that *communities* of faith remain vitally important in supporting those who seek to live a life of faith, but the relationship between person and community is not one that can be taken for granted.[28] The American religious experiment has always meant that people have to invest voluntary resources in preserving and extending their own traditions. The Constitution guaranteed the right to gather into religious communities, but it did not guarantee that any given group would succeed in their efforts. Only the group's own voluntary energies could do that.

Faith communities that seek to build robust relationships that can sustain their youth and adults face exactly the challenges of diversity and skepticism and choice that I have been describing. Congregations cannot structure their work around assumptions that members will share common social identities or lifelong religious histories. Even if they do, they cannot count on a stable and integrated set of institutions and relationships to supply a store of conversation topics and common lore. Relationships outside the congregation—families, neighborhoods, and those formed in common places of work or leisure or shopping— cannot be counted on to supplement and reinforce the community- building efforts of the congregation. The people who find their way into local congregations bring increasingly diverse life experiences out of which a community must be intentionally constructed.

The challenge of gathering a community of common religious prac- tice is especially apparent to those who find themselves in the religious and cultural minority here. Immigrants for whom religion was a taken- for-granted part of the culture "back home" soon realize that they are going to have to organize if they want to maintain those traditions here.[29] Across the country, we see thousands of new local gatherings— masjids, temples, and study groups—all taking on the tasks and forms of American congregational life, voluntarily forming the communities that they hope will teach their children the language, music, stories, and rituals of their traditions. Beyond these local gatherings, regional and national associations have formed to provide youth camps and ritual supplies, and religious guides in English that are often posted on the Web. These religious newcomers know that they have to be intentional and that they need the help of a community. They know that American culture will not help them teach their children to practice the faith.[30]

While there are many ways to respond to the challenge of sustaining faith in the midst of diversity, investment in the worship and religious education carried on in local congregations seems to me one of the most effective strategies. What I have discovered in recent research, however, is that some congregations invest much more heavily than others in the work of worship and spiritual life. Christian congregations in the sacra- mental traditions—both Catholic and Protestant—typically offer multiple opportunities for worship each week and organize groups of members to tend to the ritual tasks surrounding those events. Collective resources are expended on special clothing and ritual objects, as well as on prayer books and hymnals. Leaders are trained in the arts of liturgical performance, and new members are offered mentorship in the skills of worship. Similarly, although the traditions themselves are vastly different, members and leaders in Buddhist, Hindu, Muslim, and other newer American traditions often spend much of their organizational energy in assembling the material necessities for proper worship and gathering to honor their Holy One. No matter what else they do, they begin with time and space for prayers and offerings.

The centrality of gathering for worship is also seen in America's African American churches. Services last longer than in most other traditions; multiple choirs are likely to contribute time and talent; ushers, pastor's-aid groups, and others support and guide the church's experience. Many churches invite worshipers back for services on Sunday, Wednesday, or Friday evenings that are filled with the prayers, testimonies, and songs contributed by all the participants. These churches are also likely to expect both children and adults to attend Sunday-school classes, with a cadre of adult teachers who spend significant time training and preparing and youth leaders who are apprenticed in the work.

For conservative white Protestants, worship and spiritual nurture receive significant attention as well, oriented in their case toward individual conversion and education in the faith. Having an additional church service beyond the Sunday morning event is typical for conservatives. Sunday nights and Wednesday nights often find these church buildings full of activity that blends fellowship and learning. While nearly all congregations, in all traditions, have at least some minimal offering of religious education for children and adults, conservative Protestant churches are likely to schedule classes for adults that meet at the same time the children are in Sunday school (when the most adults are also there). They are also likely to have weekday educational programs for children and at least some have classes for new adult members. Some members even send their children to conservative Christian day schools. A good deal of energy is devoted to learning about scripture and about how one is supposed to live, as is also the case in sectarian communities such as Jehovah's Witnesses, Christian Scientists, and Latter-day Saints.

Religious education is also important in Catholic and Jewish congregations. Youth get special attention through CCD classes in Catholic parishes and weekday Hebrew schools in Jewish synagogues, not to mention Catholic elementary and high schools and the Solomon Schechter schools. New adult members get intensive RCIA classes in Catholic parishes and comprehensive introductions to Judaism in synagogue classes for aspiring converts. What neither Catholic nor Jewish groups do as well, however, is tend to the adults who have grown up in the faith. For those who have passed through confirmation or bar/bat mitzvah, the opportunities for continued spiritual learning and growth diminish, unless one is a convert.

The religious groups that spend the least organizational energy on worship and religious education are the mainline Protestant churches. Other than the sacramental traditions of the Episcopal and Lutheran churches, these groups rarely have a worship service at any other time than Sunday morning or have any group of members that spends time planning and supporting their worship activities. Most do have some form of adult religious education, but it is less likely to be scheduled in prime time, alongside children's Sunday school, and is more likely to be a small group that meets during the week. Mainline Protestants rarely have any religious education for children during the week and almost none of them sponsor or support religious schools. While all the other traditions have some particular organizational effort that supports the spiritual nurture of their members, white mainline Protestants seem to be putting all their eggs in the basket of Sunday morning worship and children's Sunday school.

Whether this minimalist organizational structure can support robust spiritual lives is questionable. Other traditions, each in their own ways, recognize their outsider-ness in American culture, and they have built organizational structures accordingly. Mainline Protestants have never made such assumptions. For much of American history, mainline Protestants taught all the children in the public schools, ran the government, and owned the businesses. It was Protestant symbols that hung on the walls, and Protestant holidays that were honored. Protestant churches did not have to bear the full weight of religious enculturation because their stories, symbols, and practices were available in a variety of everyday contexts. Even if the stories and symbols are still there, they are now harder to find. If mainline Protestants wish to perpetuate distinct spiritual traditions, they cannot depend on institutions in the larger culture to help them. Individual congregations will need to relearn the organizational habits of voluntarism if this stream of American religious tradition is to maintain its vitality. They need not become an oppositional counterculture with high boundaries, but they will have to tend more intentionally to building their own religious traditions.

Building those traditions means, most fundamentally, experiencing and telling stories of faith. This is what congregations do as they gather for worship. In hymns, scripture, sermon, sacrament, prayer, chant, bowing, kneeling, lighting candles and incense, wearing vestments, displaying art—the words and signs and symbols tell the story of the gods and the creation and the direction of history. As people listen and move and see and smell, they are asked to encounter a reality beyond themselves. The practices carried on by organized local communities of faith are the carriers of the transcendence many modern seekers find absent elsewhere.

Strong communities of faith, of whatever sort, need to encourage their members to talk with each other in terms that acknowledge and celebrate the particular spiritual presence they come together to celebrate. Such particularistic spiritual talk may come more naturally to a conservative or sectarian group but is not impossible for liberals. Shared experiences in service projects or spiritual retreats may provide the stories members can tell each other and their children, but they need the social space in which to do it and the encouragement to risk new forms of conversation.

A pastor in a northeastern city recently challenged members of her liberal UCC church to share their testimonies each Sunday during Lent. The only rule, she said, was that God had to be part of the story. The result was a powerful experience for both speakers and listeners. The testifiers explicitly recognized God's presence in stories they might previously have told otherwise. The listeners were challenged to think of their own lives differently. And the congregation had a Lenten experience that is now the stuff of congregational lore. Creating and telling stories of faith is at the heart of how congregations provide a heritage their children can take with them. Precisely because they will indeed take that heritage to many other places as adults, the stories told and experienced are essential.

Stories, then, provide us both with the common elements that allow us to make connections with each other and the unique identities that keep us anchored in the midst of our diversity. They can be told over and over, linking us to our past, while evolving with each new telling. Unlike doctrinal propositions, they do not have to go head-to-head with scientific and philosophical skepticism. They are at once empirical accounts of what has happened and mythical accounts of what it means. Active, intentional storytelling is the basis on which all communities have always been built, and that is no less true today when communities are so fluid and fragile.

American society depends on the willingness of local communities to nurture relationships and traditions—to tell their stories—no less than it depends on the traditions to operate as tolerant parts of a plural whole. Both the voluntary investment and the stance of tolerance are essential to the relatively healthy diversity that has characterized American society. Making commitments to a local religious gathering and learning to be religious in the very particular way of that group's tradition, far from being antidemocratic, may provide exactly the sorts of experiences, skills, and commitments that enhance the abilities of women and men, native and immigrant, small-town resident and big-city cosmopolitan to engage their fellow citizens, working together to build up our store of social capital. As Warner argues, "Subcultural religious reproduction does not require antagonism towards one's neighbor. . . . In the United States, religious difference is the most legitimate cultural difference."[31] Local religious communities that sustain and express those differences are essential to making the system work. Demerath agrees that American congregations are a clue to understanding our relative lack of religious violence. "In settings where a communal or congregational grouping is lacking, the faithful may be especially vulnerable to aberrant movements that offer an equivalent to the congregational experience while pursuing more secular and political agendas."[32] The work of local faith communities may have far-reaching political consequences, but only if that work is actively tended by the voluntary participants who gather there.

Will our children have faith? They just might, if we provide them with opportunities to experience the very particular traditions of our communities and give them spaces in which to tell their stories. Will that faith lead them into fearful and defensive enclaves? It need not. In spite of the modern challenges of diversity and skepticism, we have ample evidence that a healthy religious commitment does not always lead to antagonism toward neighbors or the world. Is any of this easy? By no means. Communities that seek to isolate their youth often lose them, and communities that provide no roots can even more surely bid them farewell. The challenges of diversity and skepticism are real, but the opportunities for intentional community building are just as real for those who are willing to take up the challenge.

# Section Two

## Three Recent National Studies

# Is Moralistic Therapeutic Deism the New Religion of American Youth? Implications for the Challenge of Religious Socialization and Reproduction

*Christian Smith*

All human communities face the general challenge of social reproduction—that is, socializing subsequent generations to carry on community identities and practices. Meeting this challenge successfully requires effective practices of socialization, identity formation, role modeling, intergenerational transference of authority, and so on. Many other factors, however, typically play into the success or breakdown of social reproduction, including competing institutional demands and changing social environmental conditions that make passing on a collective way of life over time more or less difficult. Religious communities are only one among many types of human communities that face this general challenge of reproducing themselves in future generations. But many sociologists have long believed that religious communities in modern societies face particular challenges in passing on religious faith and practice to their youth. Modernity's differentiation of institutional spheres, rationalization of social life, materialism and naturalism embedded in capitalism and science, liberal disestablishment of religion in politics, and other disenchanting and secularizing modern social forces are often said by at least some sociologists to corrode religious sensibilities and undermine religious authority—making the religious socialization of the next generation all the more difficult.

In recent years, however, rival sociologists have argued that modernity does little that inevitably undermines religious beliefs and organizations. Indeed, some claim that the religious pluralism and competition of modernity can actually vitalize religion by increasing the mobilization of religious organizations and strengthening religious identities rooted in distinctive religious subcultures. Simple statistics about belief in God and church attendance suggest that religion is hardly in decline in the United States, one of the most modern countries in the world. And within our own lifetimes, many significant religious movements have asserted themselves on the national and geopolitical stages of history. How could secularization theory really be true when we consider the significance of America's Christian Right, Poland's Solidarity movement, liberation theology in Latin America, the role of religious organizations in the fall of apartheid in South Africa and communism in Eastern Europe, ongoing militant Islamic insurgencies, the booming of Christianity in Africa and Asia, and other examples of religious vitality? For these reasons, I have in my career numbered myself among sociologists who are skeptical of the traditional "secularization theory" predicting religious decline in modern societies. By extension, I would also number myself among those who believe that the reproduction of faith communities over generations is not especially problematic in modern societies, as long as it is done seriously and well.

For the last four years, however, through the National Study of Youth and Religion (NSYR), I have been intensely researching the religious and spiritual lives of teenagers in the United States. This research has given me ample occasion for rethinking my views on these matters. The research has included a nationally representative telephone survey of 3,370 U.S. teenagers and personal, in-depth interviews conducted with 267 teenagers living in 45 states around the United States. Throughout this study, I have recurrently found myself wrestling with—sometimes almost haunted by—a short passage from Thomas Luckmann's secularization-theory book, *The Invisible Religion,* published in English in 1967.[1] "Traditional church religion," Luckmann writes, "was pushed to the periphery of 'modern' life in Europe, while [in contrast] it became more 'modern' in America by undergoing a process of *internal secularization.* . . . Whereas religious ideas originally played an important part in the shaping of the American Dream, today the secular ideas of the American Dream pervade church religion." Luckmann thus argues that religion thrives organizationally in the United States, but precisely as a result and at the cost of becoming *internally* secularized. Millions of religious Americans thus still tell survey researchers that they believe in God and attend religious services but, Luckmann suggests, at the same time the internal character of their religious beliefs and practices in the United States have been dramatically transformed by faith-corrosive forces. Viewed sociologically from the outside, all may look well. But understood with more nuance internally, especially in relation to the historical norms of religious traditions themselves, Luckmann suggests, much that is important has been lost.

To be clear, I am not here declaring my conversion to the secularization-theory camp. I remain skeptical of secularization theory as a whole. But I have also come to think that there is some truth in Luckmann's observation about *internal* secularization in U.S. religion that has implications for religious social reproduction and so is well worth considering. Taking Luckmann seriously is not methodologically easy, however, because it requires that we move beyond citing generic survey statistics to the more challenging task of analyzing changes in the actual substantive content of religious faith traditions, both in official religious pronouncements and as internalized and expressed by ordinary people. This ultimately involves making theological judgments about definitions and boundaries of religious orthodoxy and orthopraxy—something many sociologists are not comfortable doing. But considering the possibilities of internal secularization means the exercising of such theological knowledge and judgments is unavoidable. Critical in this process is evaluating contemporary religious actors, not by our personal opinions or wishes about religion, but against the normative stated beliefs of religious traditions themselves and against ordinary believers from previous eras' actual norms and practices with regard to them.

In the following pages, I will explore some NSYR findings about the religious and spiritual lives of U.S. teenagers that have implications for the challenge of religiously socializing youth and that I think also shed light on the question of internal secularization. My guiding question is this: What are the prospects of success for established religious communities in contemporary U.S. culture seeking to induct their youth into the beliefs, commitments, and practices of their historical faith traditions in ways that will both form the lives of their youth as individuals and carry on with significant continuity those collective faith traditions into the future? I begin by exploring some of the social and cultural difficulties and challenges that faith communities face in this task. I then describe what I see as one of the major results of faith communities' general failure to successfully meet those difficulties and challenges: a pervasive, functional, religious belief system among teenagers that I call Moralistic Therapeutic Deism. Finally, I close by suggesting some ways that, from a sociologist's point of view, faith communities might respond to this popular "alternative" *de facto* religious faith and better form and educate their young people.

## DIFFICULTIES AND CHALLENGES

Contemporary religious communities in the United States that are interested in nurturing their children and youth in the richness and particularities of their substantive faith and moral traditions are up against a number of significant social and cultural forces that make that task quite difficult. I explore many of these challenging forces in my book on U.S. teenage religion, *Soul Searching: The Religious and Spiritual Lives of American Teenagers.*[2] There I argue, for instance, that certain larger social and institutional contexts—namely, a culture of therapeutic individualism, mass-consumer capitalism, the digital communications revolution, residual positivism and empiricism in popular culture, the structural disconnect of teenagers from the world of adults, the personal problems of adults, and other relevant cultural and institutional contradictions—likely influence the religious and spiritual lives of many contemporary youths in a variety of ways. It is not, I think, that youths are normally consciously aware of these macro social influences. Nevertheless, these larger contexts are objective, structural, institutional, and cultural realities that often powerfully form youths' lives. They can have the effect of making religious faith less centrally relevant to many teenagers' lives and more difficult to believe in the terms passed on by the religious traditions themselves. I will not elaborate on these social forces here, but will rather focus on examining other cultural structures that, in my view, can make quite difficult the religious socialization of youth today and thus the social reproduction of religious faith across generations.

The first cultural structure that I wish to highlight here that I believe complicates the nurturing of youth in faith concerns widespread cultural stereotypes about teenagers and their relationships to adults and to religion. Since the 1960s at least, adolescence has become virtually synonymous in our culture with rebellion and surliness. Of course, adolescents can be surly and rebellious, but that does not describe the entire story. Parents and other adults, it seems to us, too often take teenagers' ornery or resistant communications at face value, failing to recognize beneath the complaints and rolling eyes the profound need of adolescents to connect emotionally and relationally with adults, especially with their parents. In our personal interviews with teenagers of all kinds around the country, we asked teens what they would change about their family situations if they could change anything they wanted. The most common answer that teenagers gave—amazing as it may seem—was that *they wish they could be closer to their parents.* We suspect few parents realize this. But that is what very many teens told us in all sincerity. When we asked why they are not closer or can't become closer to their parents, they most often said that they just do not know how to do it. This is heartbreaking itself and, I think, indicative of a larger reality. Namely, too many adults appear to presume that normal adolescent moves toward greater personal independence mean that they as adults should give teens their space by leaving them alone, allowing teens to set their own boundaries and standards, and letting teens solve their own problems and deal themselves with the negative consequences of their poor choices.[3] The way this general mentality often seems to be expressed in religious communities specifically is by either simply ignoring teenagers as uninterested and unteachable—perhaps assuming that they are about to stop practicing faith anyway but will eventually return to faith when they have their own children—or shooing them off to designated "youth" spaces and activities separated from the adult world of the religious community. In fact, about the last thing today's teenagers need is to be isolated, ignored, left alone, and made autonomous. Contemporary teenagers rather desperately need—in addition to an appropriate amount of personal "space"—connection, support, guidance, instruction, and boundaries—even as they continually renegotiate their transition away from dependence and toward interdependence with adults. What makes this complicated is that teenagers do not always know or realize this, nor are they always appreciative when they do get what they actually need and often deeply want. So all too often, it seems, adults allow teenagers to dictate the terms of relating. The way this typically gets worked out in the context of religious communities I think undermines the effective religious education and socialization of youth.

Another significant cultural structure that makes the religious social-ization of youth problematic has to do with confusions about identity and discourse arising from life in a pluralistic society. Many if not most Americans know that fair and hospitable public discourse in our plural-istic society requires recognition and tolerance of, civility toward, and ideally respect for other people who are religiously or culturally differ-ent. U.S. teenagers, we learned in our research, are especially aware of these rules of etiquette in their public talk, if not private beliefs. What most religious Americans do not appear to know, however, is how any kind of serious, committed, expressive talk about religious faith is pos-sible, given these general rules of etiquette. We thus found that most U.S. teenagers appear unable to distinguish among three distinct forms of religious speech:

a) serious, articulate, confident personal and congregational dis-course of faith,
   versus
b) respectful, civil discourse in the pluralistic public sphere,
   versus
c) obnoxious, offensive faith talk that merely offends other people.

Most teenagers in the United States are very concerned to observe the second of these forms of speech and to avoid the third. But most have largely lost a sense for how to engage in the first of these ways of talk-ing. As a result of a frequent lack of distinction observed among these three forms, it appears that the first often simply gets lost. Few religious teens—and we suspect few religious adults—seem able to understand that committed and articulate personal and congregational faith does not have to be sacrificed for the sake of public civility and respect for others who are different. Pluralism, few appear to recognize, does not have to produce thinness and silence. But for pluralism not to produce thinness and silence, it would seem that religious believers need to learn to distinguish among the three forms of speech cited above. I believe that there is plenty of room for U.S. faith traditions to claim and empha-size confidently their own particularities and distinctiveness without risking intolerance or disrespect for others. Youth should be able to learn and embrace the particularities of their own faith traditions and understand why they matter, without having to be fearful that this will inevitably cause conflict and uncomfortable situations. But we found little evidence that U.S. teenagers—or those who are religiously educating them, apparently—know how to go about doing this. As a result, it appears, given the dominance of the culture's emphasis on diversity and tolerance, it is the serious, confident, articulate expressions of faith that are losing out. This matters, because it is hard to be educated into a religious tradition about which its adherents have difficulty even talking seriously and with confidence.

A third cultural structure that NSYR findings suggest significantly influences the prospects for successfully socializing youth into serious, substantive communities of faith relates to common assumptions about the very value and justification of being a person of religious faith in the first place. Very many Americans, including teenagers, appear to hold a primarily instrumentalist view of religious faith. For many parents in the United States, religion is good and valuable because it produces good outcomes for their kids. Many religious clergy, congregations, and denominations capitalize on this in order to appeal to families with children and adolescents. It is an empirical fact that religiously involved youth generally *do* fare better in life than youth not religiously involved, which should be encouraging for religious believers. But making this into faith's key reason for existence easily deteriorates into an instrumentalist, "public-health justification" model of faith as legitimate simply because it produces healthy, good, "prosocial" citizens— instead of, say, genuinely committed believers. It easily slips into a "religion-is-good-because-it-will-help-keep-my-kids-from-drinking-and-improve -their-grades-in-school" mindset. This mentality clearly undercuts larger and deeper questions of truth, tradition, discipleship, and peoplehood that inevitably matter to most American religious communities. Promoting an instrumentalist legitimation of religious faith may be effective in attracting adherents in the short and medium run. But it certainly comes at a long-term religious cost: faith and practice become redefined as instrumental therapeutic mechanisms to achieve personal goals that are probably not themselves formed by the religious traditions. In fact, most U.S. youth, we learned in our interviews with them, do tend to assume an instrumental view of religion. As I wrote in *Soul Searching*:

> Most teens instinctively assume that religion exists to help individuals be and do what they want, and not as an external tradition

or authority or divinity that makes compelling claims and demands on their lives, especially to change or grow in ways they may not immediately want to. For most U.S. teenagers, religion is something to personally believe in, which makes one feel good and resolves one's problems. For most, it is not an entire way of life or a disciplined practice that makes hard demands of or changes people. Stated differently, for many U.S. teenagers, God is treated as something like a cosmic therapist or counselor, a ready and competent helper who responds in times of trouble but who does not particularly ask for devotion or obedience.[4]

Such an instrumentalist view of religion has been deeply and widely embraced by the majority—though not all—of American adolescents. We discussed in depth with teens what religion was all about, whether religion has any value, why anyone would want to practice a religious faith, what religion does and does not do in their own lives. What we heard from most teens is essentially that religion makes them feel good, that it helps them make good choices, that it helps resolves problems and troubles, that it serves their felt needs. What most teens appear to believe is that religion is about God responding to the authoritative desires and feelings of people, not the reverse. In simple terms, for many, religion is a tool for people to use to get what they want—as determined not by their religion but by their individual feelings and desires.

As a consequence, the cultural terrain on which communities of faith have to engage youth in their work of religious education and socialization makes that task that much more difficult. Essentially it sets up a consumerist mentality about religious faith that wants primarily to know "what can it do for me?" not "what does it require of me?" Given such instrumentalist assumptions about religious faith, youth ministers are ever obliged to be entertaining, religious youth activities always need to be great fun, Sunday-school teachers must be interesting and "relevant" in ways that do not always comport well with the actual interests and priorities of religious traditions, etc. In short, religious educators inevitably hit a big, hard wall of contradiction around the fact that serious induction into a religious tradition requires the inductee to be formed and reformed in new and perhaps demanding ways according to the teaching of the faith, whereas an instrumentalist mentality about faith presumes that religion exists to serve the existing felt wants and needs of the religious consumer. It is difficult to have it both ways. So it proves quite difficult to religiously educate the next generation in this context.

## MORALISTIC THERAPEUTIC DEISM

For the reasons explained above and numerous other reasons besides, the task of religiously socializing youth and so socially reproducing with some integrity and continuity religious communities and traditions in contemporary culture is very challenging. My observation—having monitored hundreds of hours of teen telephone surveys and conducted or analyzed the transcripts of hundreds of personal interviews with teenagers—is that most, though not all, religious educators of adolescents in the United States are basically failing. To be sure, most U.S. teenagers do hold a benignly positive view of religion. Relatively few are hostile to or alienated from religion. Most are quite happy to believe in whatever is the religious faith of their parents. We also found that many teens profess that religious faith is important in their lives, that they value it a great deal. And many say that they expect to maintain their religious faith in the years ahead. At the same time, we also discovered that the vast majority of U.S. teenagers are incredibly inarticulate about their faith. They know very little of the substantive belief content of their religious traditions. They can only explain specifically how and why religion is important and influential in their lives with the greatest of difficulty, if at all. And relatively few engage regularly in elementary, personal religious practices, like reading the Bible. Furthermore, it is evident that, for most teens, school, friends, work, television, and other forms of fun play much more significant roles in their lives than do religious faith and practice. A definite minority of teen exceptions to this rule does exist, but this is the general rule nonetheless. In short, while plenty of U.S. teenagers embrace religious identities and affiliations, attend religious services, and have benignly positive things to say about religious faith, it is clear that most teens have actually not been well engaged, educated, and socialized into their religious faith traditions. Whatever U.S. religious communities are or are not doing to engage their teenagers, it does not appear to be working extremely well.

In fact, as I put together what I heard hundreds of all different kinds of teenagers from around the United States tell us about their religious beliefs, it struck me that some very common themes were emerging among teens from various religious traditions. In working over these themes, I have come to this conclusion: it may not be far off to think that the true religious faith of the majority of U.S. teenagers is not in fact Christianity or Judaism or Islam. Rather, I have come to suspect that the actual, functional religious faith of most teenagers is something I call Moralistic Therapeutic Deism. The core beliefs of this *de facto* religious faith—which I describe and explore in much greater depth in my book, *Soul Searching*—consist of five basic ideas:

1) A God exists who created and orders the world and watches over human life on earth.
2) God wants people to be good, nice, and fair to each other, as taught in the Bible and by most world religions.
3) The central goal of life is to be happy and to feel good about oneself.
4) God does not need to be particularly involved in one's life except when he is needed to resolve a problem.
5) Good people go to heaven when they die.

This Moralistic Therapeutic Deism is, first, about a moralistic approach to life. It believes that essential to living a happy life is being a good, "moral" person—which means to teens not much more than being kind, nice, pleasant, courteous, responsible, at work on improving oneself, taking care of one's health, and doing one's best to be successful. Second, Moralistic Therapeutic Deism is about providing therapeutic benefits to its believers. It is finally about feeling happy, good, safe, at peace. It is about achieving subjective well-being, being able to resolve problems, and getting along nicely with other people. Finally, Moralistic Therapeutic Deism is about belief in a specific kind of God, one who exists, created the universe, and defines our overall moral order, but who is not particularly personally involved in one's life dealings—especially dealings in which one would prefer not to have God involved. Most of the time the God of Moralistic Therapeutic Deism keeps a safe distance. He is frequently described by teens as "watching over everything from above" and "the creator of all and is up there now." For many, God does sometimes get involved in one's life, but normally only when one calls on him, mostly when one has some trouble or problem or bad feeling which one wants God the Cosmic Therapist or Divine Butler to fix. Otherwise, God can keep his distance. As one fourteen-year-old white Catholic boy I quote in my book said, "If you ask God for something I believe he gives it to you. Yeah, he hasn't let me down yet. God is a spirit that grants you anything you want, but not anything bad."

Note it is not that U.S. teenagers identify themselves as Moralistic Therapeutic Deists—that is my label, not theirs. But this nevertheless is essentially the view that emerges when U.S. teenagers talk about their religious faith and beliefs. Moralistic Therapeutic Deism is not a formal, organized religion. Rather, it is a functional, *de facto* religion.

Before proceeding, one conceptual clarification is in order: in what sense is it accurate to label this religious faith of teens "Deism"? This belief system's divinity is not the same God of the eighteenth-century Deists, insofar as this God can be called upon to intervene in life situations to solve problems or make one feel better. This God is not the divine clockmaker who created and wound up a mechanical universe and now stands entirely back from human affairs. So, this God is not technically deistic in this strong historical sense, but rather seems to be an evolved variant of this older image. The label Deism does work here insofar as God in this faith is thought of as *normally* distant from everyday life, existing "up there" and so not interfering with daily existence except when called upon. Moreover, like the God of the eighteenth-century Deists, this God's primary job is to serve as Creator and Provider of Order by establishing law and morality. This is not primarily a saving God of grace and forgiveness, or a Trinitarian God whose Son lived as Jesus of Nazareth and whose Spirit lives daily in human hearts. Finally, the Deism in this faith must be understood as conditioned by the "Moralistic" and "Therapeutic" qualifiers. This is not the God of Matthew Tindal and Thomas Paine, but rather their God who has since gotten a serious "makeover" by Leo Buscaglia, Oprah Winfrey, and *Self* magazine. Times change. So must God, it seems.

What we are dealing with here, then, seems to be a hybrid, "least-common-denominator" religious faith. It is an understanding of life and the divine that represents what sensitive and tolerant Americans would naturally gravitate toward who are looking for a belief system that facilitates personal fulfillment and smooth interpersonal relations. There is very little, if anything, that is religiously particularistic here, that might cause offense or express incivility. The only kind of people who are going to hell in this faith, for instance, are Hitler and Stalin. There is very little that stands within any specific historical faith tradition. In this way, Moralistic Therapeutic Deism provides explanation with few obligations, morality with few demands, divine assistance on call devoid of a divine calling, and assurance of eternity in heaven with the bar set very low. No wonder most teenagers speak in such positive terms about religion and faith.

Furthermore, Moralistic Therapeutic Deism appears to be a belief system that is strongly oriented toward functionality—which resonates well with the instrumentalist tendencies discussed in the previous section. This faith system is good because it is useful. It has instrumental value. It accomplishes important things for its adherents. It solves problems. It helps people be nice to each other. It provides inner peace and happiness. Indeed, in *Soul Searching* I suggest that this functional American religious faith serves a larger social purpose of lubricating public-sphere social relationships among people who are different from each other. It is, I suggest, socially functional in fostering a thin solidarity in a way that is roughly parallel to American civil religion as described by Robert Bellah; but it operates at a "lower" level than our national civil religion, more "close to the ground" of interpersonal relations in public settings and institutions, like school, work, community organizations, and neighborhoods.

From this rather Durkheimian perspective, we might observe that Moralistic Therapeutic Deism is a perfectly suited religious faith for the particular society we live in, which is characterized by its mass-consumer capitalist economy, liberal polity, individualistic culture, and socially, religiously, racially, and morally pluralistic population. It fits, for example, the kind of constituted human self needed by mass-consumer capitalism—namely, autonomously choosing individuals oriented by the advertising industry toward the perpetual consumption of commodities in order to continually satisfy subjectively felt wants and needs directed toward the goal of feeling personally good and happy. It also fits the contemporary liberal polity's emphasis on self-constituted individual interests, the priority of procedural and individual rights over collective visions of the good, and the central social need for friendly tolerance of difference. In these and other ways, Moralistic Therapeutic Deism provides minimal meaning and moral direction at the micro level that aggregates toward well-lubricated social relations in the public sphere. It seems, in short, to be a highly socially functional religious faith.

From this viewpoint, many Americans might hail the apparent pervasiveness of Moralistic Therapeutic Deism as a blessing and boon for

U.S. society. God and God's heaven are put to use to encourage social order, personal meaning and happiness, and interpersonal niceness and tolerance. The old Deist dream is at least partially realized. Furthermore, Moralistic Therapeutic Deism might seem to be a helpful response to the question of religious socialization and reproduction. It is a faith much easier to pass on to youth than, say, faithful Catholicism or seriously observant Judaism. It is simpler and more commonsensical for this culture than all the old religious mumbo-jumbo about Torah, keeping kosher, sin, incarnation, grace, repentance, sanctification, the Hajj, Zakat, discipleship, etc. From a socially functionalist point of view, these are compelling arguments. But I can see two significant problems with them—the first sociological, the second more theological.

The first problem with thinking that Moralistic Therapeutic Deism can happily serve as a socially functional interreligious faith in U.S. society, I would argue, is that it is ultimately a *parasitic* religious faith. It cannot sustain itself as an autonomous living entity over time. Rather, as far as I can tell, it survives by feeding upon the degenerating bodies of other, particularistic religious faiths. Like a virus, Moralistic Therapeutic Deism needs the body of another living creature to sustain and perpetuate its own life. In the United States, it is the integral, historical religious traditions of Christianity, Judaism, Islam, and so on that serve as the "host body" that this parasitic religious faith colonizes, feeds upon, and decomposes. The problem here is that Moralistic Therapeutic Deism does not simply coexist with historic religious faiths—like remoras (shark suckers) attached to sharks. Rather, it seems to me, it eventually kills particularistic religious faiths. Moralistic Therapeutic Deism is not simply, for instance, an amusingly pathetic version of Christianity. It is not-Christianity. Most lethal biological parasites and viruses have enough host bodies in their environments that, even when they kill some, they can move on to live in or on others. Living religious faith traditions, however, are not so plentiful. There are only so many in existence that Moralistic Therapeutic Deism can continue to feed upon. And once their carcasses are infected and consumed, there may not be others to jump to. The question I am raising here, in other words, has to do with the cognitive, social, and moral sustainability of Moralistic Therapeutic Deism as a socially functional religious faith into the indefinite future. Teenagers today may glibly take it for granted. But, if it continues, will it be plausible and compelling to their children in 2025 and grandchildren in 2050 if the living historic faith traditions on which it feeds have been badly decomposed? I suspect not.

The second, more theological problem with taking Moralistic Therapeutic Deism as some kind of new socially functional interreligious faith for U.S. society consists of a different judgment based on my previous observation that it is not simply a pathetically deteriorated form of our main historical religious traditions. It is its own, distinct faith. So, it may in fact serve some important social functions for a pluralistic society. But from an historically orthodox or simply serious Christian, Jewish, or Muslim point of view, it is simply not the religious faith one ought to believe in, practice, and pass on to one's children. It is a rival religion.

Which brings us back to our original question: What are the prospects of success for religious communities in contemporary U.S. culture seeking to induct their youth into the beliefs, commitments, and practices of their historical faith traditions in ways that will both form the lives of their youth as individuals and carry on with significant continuity those collective faith traditions into the future? The sheer apparent pervasiveness of Moralistic Therapeutic Deism among U.S. teenagers of most religious stripes suggests that the prospects are not good. There are simply so many social and cultural forces stacked against the successful transmission of historical religious faith to contemporary youth. And for this reason I am prepared to take the suggestion of Thomas Luckmann, quoted above, more seriously today than I have in the past. Having researched the religious and spiritual lives of U.S. teenagers for four years, it does indeed appear to me that mainstream American religion—which now also includes evangelical Protestantism—reflects a process of *internal* secularization, whereby "the secular ideas of the American Dream"—namely, individually defined, subjective, therapeutic happiness—"pervade church religion" in the United States. And insofar as religious communities cannot reproduce what they themselves do not internally embody, it is difficult to see how historical religious faith traditions can succeed in their tasks of religiously educating and socializing youth without a significant change of approach to the task.

THOUGHTS TOWARD SUSTAINING INTEGRAL RELIGIOUS FAITH
TRADITIONS

Let us suppose, for a moment, that members of America's historical religious traditions do not want to fail in their project of religious education, socialization, and reproduction. Suppose that they have a will to resist and turn back the parasitic colonization of Moralistic Therapeutic Deism. And let us suppose further that such agents of religious socialization were to ask for friendly sociological advice about succeeding in their task. What might a sociologist prepared—probably foolishly so—to offer such advice have to say to them? Here I offer a few ideas that seem to follow from the foregoing. Specific communities of faith will have to decide what, if anything, of the following makes sense in and for their own situations.

First, as I have written elsewhere, a key way to get most youth more involved in and serious about their faith communities is to get their parents more involved in and serious about their faith communities.[5] This is contrary to stereotypes about widespread teenage anti-parent rebelliousness. But the sociological fact is that by far and away the best social predictor of the religious identities, commitments, and involvements of youth is the religious identities, commitments, and involvements of their parents. Whether recognized or not, parents of teens normally retain a great deal of influence over the religious outcomes of their children. Stated differently, every parent of teens *is in fact* always educating, forming, socializing their children religiously and spiritually. The only question is: in what way and to what effect? One of the best things that adults can do who are concerned about how teenagers' religious and spiritual lives are going to turn out is to focus attention on strengthening parents' religious and spiritual lives. Parents' default motto about teen religious outcomes should be, "We will get what we are." Hence, the challenge grows ever bigger.

It might also be helpful for U.S. religious educators to realize that the central problem most of them face is not teenage rebellion, but teenagers' benign "whatever-ism." In fact, large numbers of U.S. teenagers are currently in religious congregations and feel fine about them. Most teens expect to stay involved at some level and generally feel okay about the adults in their congregations. But religion simply does not make much sense to many of them or mean much of great depth. Again, there are exceptions to this rule. A minority of U.S. teens is religiously serious, committed, involved, and knowledgeable. But for most, religion is merely a nice thing that functions as "part of the furniture" in the background of their lives. Thus, the real challenge is not preventing teens from heading out the doors in droves. Rather, the challenge is to much better engage the teens who are already sitting in the pews and seats.

Along these lines, findings from the NSYR also suggest that religious educators need to work harder on articulation. For very many teenagers we interviewed, it seemed as if our conversation was the first time any adult had ever asked them what they believed. By contrast, the same teens could be remarkably articulate about other subjects about which they had been drilled, such as substance abuse and "safe sex." The philosopher Charles Taylor argues—rightly, in my view—that inarticulacy undermines the possibilities of reality.[6] If so, then religious faith, practice, and commitment can be no more than indistinctly real when people cannot talk much about them. Articulacy fosters reality. A major challenge for religious socializers of youth would thus seem to be helping teens to *practice talking about* their faith by providing practice at using vocabularies, grammars, stories, and key messages of faith. If we think of the language of faith in American culture as increasingly becoming a "foreign language" to many people, religious educators need, like "real" foreign language teachers, to have their students hear what the well-spoken language sounds like and help them practice speaking that other language of faith for themselves.

Part of what religious educators working with youth on the articulation of religious beliefs toward effective formation in faith will need to do involves being prepared—now hold onto your seats!—to tell youth that their existing religious views are not quite right and perhaps even flat wrong. Not every idea that teenagers verbalize can be affirmed. Now I realize that in our culture, in which individuals' personal experiences and feelings are self-authenticating, such that one person's view is purportedly as good as another's, this very proposal must seem authoritarian, dictatorial, and disrespectful of young people's creativity and self-esteem. (And then we wonder why it is hard to religiously educate youth into a historical religious tradition? Who is socializing whom?) But I relent not. It is simply elementary sociology to see that every plausible social group must set boundaries and specify normative beliefs and behaviors if it is to survive and function. Schools do this, as do sports teams, corporations, hobby clubs, neighborhood associations, and every other extant social group. As long as youth are free to accept or reject what they are taught as they mature as individuals, there is nothing inherently oppressive or disparaging about being very clear with young people regarding the identity and expectations of the religious tradition in which they are being raised. What actually *is* arguably unfair and disrespectful to youth is to *fail* as communities of faith to provide youth with the clear substantive belief content, defining identity boundaries, and moral expectations that they can then bounce around, digest, question, struggle over, and eventually personally embrace, revise, or reject. Agents of religious traditions will, of course, have to be prepared to be rejected. But, sociologically speaking, it is better to be clear to all and rejected by some, than to try to affirm all and so offer a definite identity and purpose for none. In any case, most youth, and indeed most adults, are plenty used to being told if and when they are thinking or doing something wrong—by teachers, coaches, instructors, bosses, celebrities, advertisers, and television programming. They can handle it. The question is: are religious educators willing to risk it?

Nurturing regular religious practices in the lives of youth also seems to be an important piece of the religious socialization puzzle. Interviewing teens, we found that very basic religious practices, like regular scripture reading, prayer, and intentional works of service and mercy, mark and pattern the lives of teenagers committed to faith—and do not for teens not committed to faith. Strengthening the faith lives of youth would appear to have to involve the formation of regular personal religious practices. That is, if youth are to be effectively socialized, they will need to be taught to *practice* their faith—and not only in the sense of acting it out, as when we say, "He is a practicing Catholic." They should also be taught to practice their faith in the sense of consistently working on habits, skills, and virtues that foster the movement toward excellence in faith—similar to the way musicians and athletes have to *practice* their skills. The available evidence suggests that youth educators will not get far with teenagers, in other words, unless regular and intentional religious practices become an important part of teens' larger faith formation.[7]

In all of this, it also seems to me that religious communities would do well to better attend to their own faith particularities. In efforts to be accessible and civil, it appears that many youth—and no doubt adults—are hearing the messages that historical faith traditions do not particularly matter, that all religious teachings are basically the same, that no faith tradition possesses anything that anybody particularly needs. This is not a recipe for successful religious socialization. It tends to produce a bland, "oatmeal" approach to faith, a view of religion as an optional lifestyle preference. For youth, this ends up offering little challenge or interest. Or it forms them into consummate religious consumers seeking primarily to meet their own felt needs and wants.

Finally, my last piece of sociological advice is to stop listening so much to the advice of sociologists, psychologists, and other experts of modernity and start paying more serious attention to and develop more confidence in the historical and theological wellsprings of one's own religious faith. Many religious educators—perhaps especially those in mainline Protestantism—it appears to me, lack confidence in what they are teaching. Admittedly, traditional religions have been battered by some centuries of Enlightenment-inspired attacks and rival worldviews. But in recent years many of modernity's grand claims have been judged wanting. The year 2005 simply looks and feels quite different from an integral faith perspective than did, say, 1790 or 1935. In any case, teens are well able to detect insecurity, hesitation, waffling, and disbelief in others. If adults want youth to embrace and carry on their religious traditions, they need first to be clear about their *own* commitments and convictions about religious faith, and then take that to youth no-holds-barred. Again, youth may choose to reject the faith, but at least they then have rejected something substantial that someone gave them a good shot at believing.

## CONCLUSION

The questions that this chapter addresses are immensely complex. Space limitations prevent a full analysis of the questions of religious socialization of youth, the possible internal secularization of American religion, the meaning of Moralistic Therapeutic Deism, and so on. The relative brevity and simplicity of this chapter should not be misread as suggesting that the questions involved are simple or easy. They are not. There is much more that needs studying, understanding, and discussing. But the present chapter needs to be brought to a close, which I do with a few final observations.

In her essay in this volume, Nancy Ammerman frames and focuses this book by asking about the possibilities for balancing the vibrant religious faiths of historical traditions with the good of civil tolerance learned as a benefit of modernity. Can we have both? Is a balance possible to strike? Our research on U.S. teenagers suggests clearly that the two are currently not in balance. Among most U.S. thirteen-to-seventeen-year-olds, at least, civil tolerance is the "winner," hands down. Most teenagers' primary concern today is to be nice, tolerant, inclusive, fair, happy, good-feeling, and successful in terms specified by the dominant culture. More substantive and particularistic religious beliefs and practices are not only being seemingly *neglected* when compared to these therapeutic goods. Religious faith itself appears to be being *transmuted* to essentially be about achieving these goods. For many U.S. teenagers, that is actually what religion *per se is*. Some Americans seem to worry that contemporary religion in the United States is an ever-present threat to civil peace and harmony. My observation to the contrary is that, at least among the vast majority of U.S. teenagers, the cultural force of civil tolerance—including as it is expressed in religious terms in Moralistic Therapeutic Deism—have significantly colonized and domesticated American religion.[8] American religion may indeed threaten civil peace on the margins, in extremist sectarian religious movements. But among and as reflected by most American adolescents, the idea that religion poses a threat to civil harmony is laughable. Of all the possible threats in this arena that a sociologist of religion might observe, the real threat seems rather to be to the project of sustaining the integrity of the substance of faith and practice of historical religious traditions. That is the project that seems most endangered.

What might this tell us about secularization as an alleged master social process of modernity? I do not believe that the NSYR findings about the religiosity of U.S. teenagers lend themselves to a wholesale endorsement of mainstream secularization theory. The reality "on the ground" seems more complicated than can be accounted for by most secularization-theory hypotheses and predictions. But—against the rather sanguine thinking of some critics of traditional secularization theory, myself included in prior years—I have come increasingly to think that much of American religion is indeed undergoing some kind of process of *internal* secularization, as suggested in the 1960s by Thomas Luckmann. Survey answers regarding belief in God and importance of faith may remain stable over time.[9] Meanwhile, however, it could very well be that the "God" in whom many Americans have come to believe, and the actual reasons for the importance that faith occupies in their lives, are gradually drifting toward something quite unlike those of the historical religious traditions with which most Americans claim to identify. When, for example, the Holy Bible is being packaged for teenagers by an Evangelical publisher to look just like *Cosmopolitan* and *Tiger Beat* magazines—in hope that perhaps more teens may start reading the Bible—one has to begin to wonder if religion is in fact not losing out to secular forces.[10] Not all religious change is desperate cultural accommodation.[11] But neither is it all creative, generative innovation.

Even in what would be American traditional religion's worst-case scenario, however, things are far from hopeless. For starters, none of America's traditional religions, by the dictates of their own worldviews, is permitted to lose hope. Beyond that simple theological position, however, there very well may be sound means by which communities of faith can more faithfully meet the challenges of the formation, education, and socialization of young members. I am a sociologist, not a religious educator. But I have tried here (and in the postscript of my related book) to "think out loud" about such possibilities. My ideas floated here and elsewhere may or may not be on target or useful for different communities of faith. But, whether they are or not, I do believe it is clear in any case that agents of religious socialization in U.S. historical faith traditions are now generally not succeeding in their tasks—and so are due for some hard soul-searching toward developing more confident and creative ways to educate and form youth in their religious traditions. Without such a change, American religious traditions may find their members increasingly embracing the Moralistic Therapeutic Deism described above—even as they cheerfully report in high numbers on surveys that they do believe in God and attend religious services regularly and that faith is indeed very important in their lives. In which case, secularization theorists may not have won the debate, but they certainly will enjoy the last laugh.

# The "Interior" Lives of American College Students: Preliminary Findings from a National Study

*Jennifer A. Lindholm*

"What is the meaning of college?" "What am I going to do with my life?" "How will I know I am going the 'right' way?" "What kind of person do I want to be?" "How is everything I've worked for up to this point going to contribute back to society?" "How am I going to leave my mark when I finally pass away?"

These were the life questions noted most frequently by the undergraduate students we interviewed recently as they reflected on what are currently the most salient "spiritual" issues in their lives. Indeed, for traditional-age college students, the undergraduate years are commonly characterized as an intensive period of cognitive, social, and affective development.[1] As they refine their identities, formulate adult life goals and career paths, test their emerging sense of self-authority and interdependence, and make decisions that will significantly impact their own and others' lives, young adults often grapple with issues of meaning, purpose, authenticity, and spirituality.

That students' religiosity generally tends to decline during the undergraduate years has been well documented empirically.[2] However, some researchers have found that commitment to spiritual growth among traditional-age students may actually increase during college.[3] While existing research sheds important light on the spiritual/religious dimension of college students' lives, there remains much to learn about students' spiritual development during their undergraduate years. Using qualitative and quantitative data collected as part of an ongoing national study on college-student spirituality, this chapter provides an overview of preliminary findings on the perspectives and practices of undergraduate college students within the United States today.

DEFINING SPIRITUALITY

The word *spirituality* originated from a merging of the Latin word for breath, *spiritus*, with the concept of enthusiasm, from the Greek *enthousiasmos*, meaning "the God within." The resulting word, spirituality, "captures the dynamic process of divine inspiration, or 'the breath of God within.'"[4] While the semantic interpretation of the word spirituality is clear, its meaning in operational terms is more ambiguous. Traditionally, the construct of spirituality has been closely aligned with religious beliefs and convictions. Current conceptions, however, are becoming much broader. Although for many, spirituality remains closely linked with religion, we are seeing today a growing number of individuals who identify their spirituality as either loosely or not at all associated with an established religious tradition.[5]

Whereas religion is characterized by "group activity that involves specific behavioral, social, doctrinal, and denominational characteristics,"[6] spirituality points to our interiors, by which we mean our subjective life, as opposed to the objective domain of material objects that one can point to and measure. In other words, the spiritual domain has to do with human consciousness—what we experience privately in our subjective awareness. Spirituality also has more to do with our qualitative or affective experiences than it does with reasoning or logic and relates to the values that we hold most dear, our sense of who we are and where we come from, our beliefs about why we are here—the meaning and purpose that we see in our work and our life—and our sense of connectedness to each other and to the world around us.[7] As Astin has explained, spirituality also encompasses aspects of our experiences that are not easy to define or talk about, such as intuition, the mysterious, and the mystical. Others have described spirituality as an energizing force; a source of inner strength; a way of being in the world; and a "dynamic expression" of who we truly are.[8]

Essentially, at its core, spirituality involves the internal process of seeking personal authenticity, genuineness, and wholeness; transcend-

ing one's locus of centricity; developing a greater sense of connectedness to self and others through relationships and community; deriving
meaning, purpose, and direction in life; exhibiting openness to exploring a relationship with a higher power that transcends human existence
and human knowing; and valuing the sacred.[9] While religious values
may be connected to these key facets, spirituality may well exist apart
from religion altogether.

Irrespective of the presence or absence of clearly defined linkages
between spirituality and religion, to ignore the role of spirituality in personal development and professional behavior is to overlook a poten-
tially powerful avenue through which people construct meaning and
knowledge.[10] Indeed, it is the spiritual component of human beings that
gives rise to questions about why we do what we do, pushes us to seek
fundamentally better ways of doing these things, and propels us to
make a difference in the world.[11]

## Examining the Intersections Between Spirituality and Higher Education

Within American society, the spiritual dimension of our lives has traditionally been regarded as intensely personal, an innermost component
of who we are that lies outside the realm of appropriate discussion or
concern within business and nonsectarian academic contexts. However,
in an era that some social and political scientists have characterized by
its spiritual "poverty," we have seen a growing societal quest for ways
of fostering spirituality and an associated hunger for spiritual growth.[12]
In 1998, for example, 82 percent of Americans expressed a need to "experience spiritual growth," up from 54 percent just four years earlier.[13]
In recent years, there has also been increasingly widespread recognition
of what seems to be an inherent disconnect between the dominant values of contemporary American society and the perspectives and practices that will enable us to respond effectively not only to our individual
needs but also to local, national, international, and global challenges.

While many of the core literary and philosophical traditions that
make up the liberal education curriculum are grounded in the maxim,
"know thyself," there is generally little attention paid in today's secular
colleges and universities to facilitating student development in the inner
realm of self-understanding.[14] Whereas spiritual aspects of student development were cornerstones of early American college curricula, En-

lightenment ideals, positivistic modes of thinking, and scientific worldviews, which began to exert a powerful influence on American thought in the late nineteenth century, have continued to dominate societal values and individual goal-orientations.[15] Rather than providing a developmental context characterized by self-reflection, open dialogue, and thoughtful analysis of alternative perspectives, many of today's college and university environments mirror instead the strong societal emphasis on individual achievement, competitiveness, materialism, and objective knowing.

Given the broad formative roles that colleges and universities play in our society, higher education represents a critical focal point for responding to the question of how we can balance the "exterior" and "interior" aspects of our lives more effectively. Existing research indicates that developing people's abilities to access, nurture, and give expression to the spiritual dimension of their lives impacts how they engage with the world and fosters within them a heightened sense of connectedness that promotes passion and action for social justice.[16] Spirituality has also been positively linked with physical, mental, social, and emotional well-being.[17] Consequently, some have argued that spirituality is an essential aspect of lifelong learning and, as such, that it should play a significant role in the teaching/learning process.[18]

Although we have witnessed an increasing interest recently in issues of meaning, purpose, authenticity, and spirituality within the higher-education community, relatively little empirical research has been conducted on these topics specifically within campus contexts.[19] In this chapter, we highlight selected findings from the 2003 College Student Beliefs and Values (CSBV) Pilot Survey and related interviews with eighty-two students who were sophomores, juniors, or seniors during the 2003–2004 academic year. Attention is focused primarily on how students conceive of spirituality, their levels of religious and spiritual engagement, their spiritual struggles, and their perspectives on addressing issues of meaning, purpose, and spirituality within the campus environment. Individual differences on selected dimensions of spirituality are also considered.

SPIRITUALITY IN HIGHER EDUCATION:
A NATIONAL STUDY OF COLLEGE STUDENTS' SEARCH FOR
MEANING AND PURPOSE

A team of researchers at UCLA's Higher Education Research Institute (HERI) is currently exploring the trends, patterns, and principles of spirituality and religiousness among college students, and how the college experience influences—and is influenced by—spiritual development. The study, funded by the John Templeton Foundation, and directed by Alexander Astin, Helen Astin, and Jennifer Lindholm, is designed to enhance our existing understanding of how college students conceive of spirituality and the role it plays in their lives. Subsequently, we will consider how colleges and universities can be more responsive in facilitating student development in this realm. We are guided in these efforts by a nine-member Technical Advisory Panel and an eleven-member National Advisory Board. This multifaceted, longitudinal project addresses the perspectives and practices of students as well as faculty. The student-centered aspect of our research is guided by the following questions:

1) How many students are actively searching and curious about spiritual issues and questions such as the meaning of life and work?

2) How do students view themselves in terms of spirituality and related qualities such as compassion, honesty, optimism, and humility?

3) What spiritual/religious practices (e.g., rituals, prayer/meditation, service to others) are students most/least attracted to?

4) How do spiritual/religious practices affect students' academic and personal development?

5) What is the connection between traditional religious practices and spiritual development?

6) What in the undergraduate experience facilitates or hinders students' spiritual/religious quest?

In spring 2003, third-year undergraduate students attending forty-six diverse four-year colleges and universities across the country completed the CSBV survey, which was designed in consultation with members of the project's Technical Advisory Panel. The four-page, 234-item CSBV Pilot Survey was designed as a longitudinal follow-up of a selected sample of twelve thousand third-year undergraduates who completed the Cooperative Institutional Research Program (CIRP) Freshman Survey when they first entered college in fall 2000.[20] Approximately 3,700 students ultimately completed and returned CSBV questionnaires.

Following the 2003 CSBV survey administration, the UCLA-based project team performed a number of analyses in order to determine the feasibility of developing "scales," which would combine several items with similar content. For these purposes, we relied on the technique of factor analysis, a procedure that examines the correlations among a set of variables (in this case, questionnaire items) with the aim of reducing the variables to a smaller set of more general "factors." In many respects, this was a trial-and-error process in which we sought to identify clusters of items that had consistent and coherent content and that simultaneously demonstrated a high degree of statistical internal consistency. In total, nineteen scales were established, twelve of which are addressed in this chapter. In subsequent analyses, we employed a multistage weighting procedure to approximate the results that would have been obtained if all third-year, full-time students at each of the forty-six participating institutions had responded to the survey.[21]

This phase of our quantitative research provided us with preliminary insights regarding the *what* of students' spiritual perspectives and practices. However, we were also interested in talking with students directly to understand better the *how* and *why* elements related to their beliefs and behaviors. Consequently, in association with the 2003 CSBV survey, we also conducted ten focus-group interviews at six institutions around the country to examine in greater depth how students conceive of spirituality, what role (if any) spirituality plays in their lives, how they perceive their campus environments and current life circumstances to facilitate or hinder their spiritual development, and what (if any) aspirations they have with respect to spiritual growth. The students we interviewed—all of whom had completed at least one year of college—attended a diverse group of institutions with respect to geographical location, size, type (universities, liberal arts colleges, religiously-affiliated institutions), selectivity (based on the average composite SAT score of the entering class), and control (public versus private). The information we have gleaned to date from these two components of our research is the primary focus for the remainder of this chapter. Future phases of the project and associated goals are also described. Subsequent to providing brief historical context using data collected as part of the Higher Education Research Institute's Cooperative Institutional Research Program, this chapter is specifically responsive to four questions:

1) What meaning does spirituality have in undergraduate students' lives?

2) How do students experience spirituality within the context of their daily lives?
3) To what extent does spirituality make a difference in students' lives?
4) Do undergraduate students perceive their college campuses as being responsive to their spiritual development needs?

NOTABLE TRENDS IN THE VALUES AND BELIEFS OF ENTERING COLLEGE STUDENTS

Each fall since 1966, the Cooperative Institutional Research Program (CIRP) has collected survey data to profile the background characteristics, attitudes, values, educational achievements, and future goals of new students entering colleges and universities across the United States. The trend data generated by these consecutive annual surveys not only reflect changes that directly affect higher education, but also can be viewed as indicators of how American society is changing.[22] Trends on selected items that have been included on the CIRP Freshman Survey over the years provide useful context for examining the spiritual/religious development of today's undergraduate college students.

For example, in examining data collected over the past thirty-eight years, we see contrasting trends in the respective emphasis that entering college students have placed over time on "being very well-off financially" and "developing a meaningful philosophy of life." The shifting emphasis on these two pursuits began in the early 1970s, crossed paths in 1977, and reached opposite extremes in the late 1980s (see figure 1). Since then, they have largely maintained their respective positions, with a slight increase in the "well-off financially" value and a slight decrease in the "philosophy of life" value. In fact, in 2003, the "philosophy of life" value reached an all-time low, with just 39 percent of incoming freshmen indicating that this pursuit is "very important" or "essential" to them, compared with an all-time high of 86 percent among the freshman class of 1967. By contrast, in 2003, "being very well-off financially" reached its highest point in thirteen years, with 74 percent of entering freshmen espousing financial success as personally "very important" or "essential."

Over the history of the survey, the number of students claiming "none" as their religious preference has also nearly tripled, reaching a

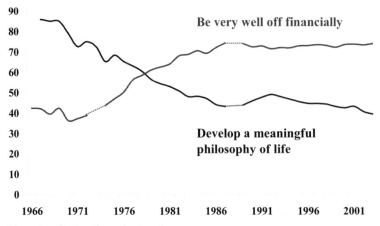

**Figure 1.  Contrasting value trends**
*Source:* Cooperative Institutional Research Program, Higher Education Research Institute, UCLA

record high of 17.6 percent in 2003 compared with 17.2 percent in 2002 and a low of 6.6 percent in 1966 (see figure 2). The percentage of students indicating that their parents have no religious preference also reached record levels in 2003, with 14 percent of fathers and 9 percent of mothers reportedly identifying with no religious preference. Since the survey began, there has been a twelve-point decline (from 92 percent in 1968 to 80 percent in 2003) in the percentage of freshmen who attended religious services "frequently" or "occasionally" in the past year. The 2003 figure represents the lowest in the history of the survey.

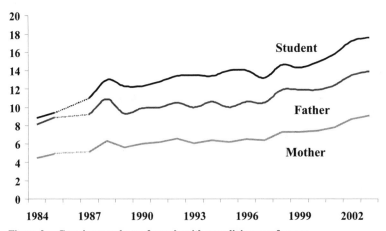

**Figure 2.  Growing numbers of people with no religious preference**
*Source:* Cooperative Institutional Research Program, Higher Education Research Institute, UCLA

Nonetheless, with 80 percent of incoming freshmen still indicating that they attended services during their last year in high school at least occasionally, it is clear that overall levels of religious service attendance among the country's high school students still remain high.

Related trends are also evident with respect to students' engagement in prayer/meditation and their self-rated spirituality. For example, since 1996, the first year an item querying the time students devote to prayer or meditation was added to the survey, the percentage of entering freshmen who engage in such activity on a weekly basis has declined from 67 percent to 64 percent. In 2003, the percentage of incoming freshmen who rate their level of "spirituality" as "above average" or "highest 10 percent" among their peers dropped for the fourth consecutive year to 38 percent, compared to a high of 46 percent in 1999 (this item was also added to the survey in 1996).

SPIRITUALITY AND RELIGIOUSNESS IN THE LIVES OF TODAY'S COLLEGE STUDENTS

Despite declines over time in the religious/spiritual inclinations of the country's entering college freshmen, we find that the majority of 2003 CSBV survey respondents—all of whom were third-year undergraduate students at the time they were surveyed—indicate an awareness of, and connection with, the spiritual dimension of their lives. For example, 77 percent agree that "we are all spiritual beings"; 71 percent "gain spiritual strength by trusting in a higher power"; and 58 percent indicate that integrating spirituality into their lives is "very important" or "essential." Moreover, substantial numbers of students (upwards of 84 percent) report that they have had what they consider to be a spiritual experience (e.g., while witnessing the beauty and harmony of nature, listening to beautiful music, etc.). While students' survey responses indicate that spirituality likely plays an important role in their lives, the question remains of what, precisely, they mean by "spirituality."

*Defining Spirituality*

The students we interviewed, all of whom had completed at least one year of college, commonly conceived of spirituality in terms of people's "ultimate beliefs," "morals," or "philosophy of life"; it is regarded as a core "part of who you are" and the "values that you live by." As one man shared: "[Spirituality is all about] why we're here, what we should be doing with our lives, and what's right and what's wrong." Inherent in most students' constructions was a largely self-focused element, a sense that spirituality is an "individual thing" with strong components of "self-reflection" and "internal conversation." Others conceptualized spirituality in terms of "what you're experiencing from the world and how you process that and send that back out into the world."

While an individualistic theme was prominent, there was also a strong, commonly expressed sentiment that one's individual connection with his or her spirituality has important implications for connecting with others. Equally prevalent was the notion that spirituality is heavily process-oriented and tightly linked with "asking questions about who you are and what you believe." For many students, the time and energy expended on getting to know oneself better is linked inextricably with one's ultimate capacity to better understand others. As one woman shared:

> I think one aspect of [spirituality] is just really learning how to interact with people and respect people and another aspect is really learning the meaning of your life and what you were placed here for and the ability to put everything into the correct perspective, including yourself . . . you know, putting yourself in perspective with everyone else around you.

How do students perceive the relationship between spirituality and religion? For a few of those we interviewed, the two constructs are largely inseparable. In the words of one woman,

> For me, [spirituality] has always been religion-based or focused. I personally feel spiritual when I'm praying, or if I need to call on God for myself . . . that's when I would feel spiritual.

However, the vast majority perceive distinct differences between spirituality and religion and viewed the relationship between the two as highly variable. As one man explained:

> When I first think of spirituality, I usually connect it with thinking about the way you were raised . . . with some kind of religious background . . . but there are a lot of people who consider themselves to be spiritual without a religious affiliation.

Regardless of their religious faith, or lack thereof, students tended to view spirituality as an integral, "everyday" part of one's life that encompasses "emotional feelings" and an "individual connection" to "an intangible something larger than yourself," a "power beyond man." Religion, on the other hand, was commonly perceived as focusing more on "group concerns" and "doctrinal points" and conjured up for many students the image of a place where people may go to worship on a regular, or occasional, basis. Nearly all participants across institutional types agreed with the sentiment that people can be spiritual without considering themselves religious. As one man said:

> I think a lot of people have some involvement with spirituality without adhering to any particular religion. There are a lot of people out there who are just kind of into the spirituality thing. Just [being] connected outside yourself and caring for your own soul, your own spirit . . . I think a lot of people these days are realizing that is an important thing to do.

Another woman shared similar sentiments:

> Spirituality doesn't necessarily mean religion to me, it means that you believe in a higher being than yourself. Spirituality to me is my hope and my faith and it's something that keeps me sane and keeps me going and reaching a specific and a higher goal for myself.

For some students, like this woman, the link between spirituality and religion is tenuous at best:

> [When I hear the word "spirituality"], I don't really think of religion that much. I [think more of] being out in nature, away from society and all the worries in the world. . . . You just feel free . . . and I don't really think that has anything to do with religion at all.

Generally speaking, today's college students tend to be fairly tolerant of divergent perspectives. For example, 88 percent of 2003 CSBV survey respondents agree that "nonreligious people can lead lives that are just as moral as those of religious believers" and 70 percent agree that "most people can grow spiritually without being religious." In fact, some students, like this woman, openly questioned why people *really* attend religious services and doubt whether spiritual growth necessarily occurs as a result of such attendance:

> Just because you participate in a religious service does not mean that you are a spiritual person. It could just mean that you're going through the motions. . . . It could be traditional reasons why you go to church. . . . It could be habit. The spiritual aspect is something that you have to seek out. It doesn't just happen because you go to church.

Interestingly, nearly without exception, participants reported having experienced a change in their perspectives on the association between religiosity and spirituality since entering college. In describing their views, many students, like this man, spoke of a change over time in how they define these two constructs and the relationship between them.

> I think [the distinction] is something unique to actually being at college. I never heard anyone distinguish between spirituality and religion when I was back home at my high school and junior high. They were always the same thing. Then I got to college, where you are allowed to be more freethinking or whatever. . . . That's when I started to see that there could be a difference between the two.

## Spiritual/Religious Engagement and Struggle

In conducting the 2003 CSBV survey and talking with undergraduate students, we were also interested to learn more about their levels of religious engagement. We find that although just 29 percent of respondents had attended religious services frequently during the past year, 78 percent said they discuss religion and spirituality with their friends and 77 percent indicated that they pray. Specifically with respect to discussing issues related to religion and spirituality with friends, those we interviewed overwhelmingly concurred that although they do reflect privately on this dimension of their lives—in some cases very often—actual conversations with others tend to take place only when "upsetting" things happen. As one man shared:

> For me, it's interesting because conversations with my friends don't start with anything really spiritual. But, you know, when

something bad happens, that's when you tend to talk about stuff. . . . You know, a relationship ends or somebody's relative dies or somebody gets severely injured or something. . . . That's when this talk tends to come up with me and my friends.

Indeed, albeit a minimally discussed aspect of many students' lives, their religious beliefs and spiritual considerations are often very important. For example, roughly three-quarters of CSBV survey respondents (74 percent) indicated that their spiritual and religious beliefs provide them with strength, support, and guidance. A similar percentage feel that their spiritual and religious beliefs have helped them develop their identity (73 percent), while two-thirds say that their beliefs give meaning and purpose to their lives (67 percent). One woman's remarks offer summative insight into how those we interviewed commonly contextualize their spiritual and/or religious beliefs:

I don't have any answers about how spiritual I am or how spiritual I should be or anything like that, but I still feel that regardless of what I believe, there has to be something or else, you know, we're all in trouble.

Among those we interviewed, there was also a recurrent theme of wanting to "figure out" personal perspectives in relative independence from any proscribed set of beliefs. One man stated his feelings very directly:

My spiritual ideologies are something that I want to acquire on my own, as opposed to either being given [them] or having them shoved down my throat.

While many undergraduate students forego regular engagement in structured religious activities, findings from the 2003 CSBV survey revealed that a notable proportion of third-year college students are nonetheless actively struggling with what they consider to be spiritual issues. For example, two-thirds (65 percent) of those surveyed report that they question their religious/ spiritual beliefs at least occasionally (18 percent frequently), while 68 percent indicated that, at least "to some extent," they are "feeling unsettled about spiritual and religious matters." Moreover, 76 percent say they have "struggled to understand evil, suffering, and death" at least occasionally and 46 percent have, at least occasionally, "felt angry with God." One-third (38 percent) feel "disillusioned with my religious upbringing" at least "to some extent."

Indicative of the spiritual struggles that some college students are experiencing was what one woman shared with us:

> I think I have a hard time believing in God or a Higher Power because you see so much suffering everywhere. You wonder if someone is in charge and, if so, why would He . . . or She . . . do this? Why would some people be suffering while other people have all the riches in the world? Why am I fortunate, but they're not? But at the same time, I feel I'm not fortunate because I have feelings that other people don't. I think it's just a big cycle that gets you . . . at least it got me . . . into disbelieving that there's something out there.

Some of the students we interviewed were also struggling with reconciling the teachings of their religion with their own evolution of beliefs, particularly because, as one woman noted, "once you're exposed to [other beliefs], you can't really ignore them." Indeed, for many students, exposure to "the other" and resulting realizations that what they once believed to be the absolute, unquestionable "truth" about some aspect of their own or others' lives is not necessarily the only "right" way prompts much questioning and self-reflection. As one man explained:

> Somebody says, "So do you think I'm going to be damned because I'm an atheist? And then you think, "Well, I don't know." I really don't know how to respond. I am thinking in my religion, [the answer] is "yes," but I really don't feel that way.

Some of the doubts the students we interviewed have experienced are very profound, as were this man's:

> I'm praying to God and at the same time, I'm questioning whether He even exists. I'm a scientist first and so [those beliefs] directly contradict my religious beliefs. My belief in God . . . I keep it there just in case . . . because nobody can tell me for sure how man was created. So I have a couple of options lying there, just in case.

A related struggle for many students is reconciling a perceived conflict between personal needs and faith expectations. Should issues of faith and doctrine always come first or does dealing effectively with the demands of everyday life need to take precedence? For students like this woman, the question is a source of conflict:

> I am not really thinking about how my life right now is going to help out the people in my religious community. I'm more worried about myself and my family and I think that in my religion, that's [viewed as being] selfish. . . . You are supposed to look out for everyone else. Well, I am caring about myself and my family. In my religion, they're always talking about how God comes first, but I just don't see that happening in my life. That's somewhere below school and my family and paying the bills. . . . Then I can go to church, when those things get done.

Not surprisingly, the most prevalent struggles voiced by participants relate to deciding what they want to do with their lives after graduating, considering what kind of people they hope to become, and determining how they should best go about creating a life that is personally meaningful, professionally rewarding, and that, ultimately, contributes to society. For many, like this woman, thinking about these issues perpetuates constant questioning and related self-doubt:

> Most of the time, I'm questioning myself, like, "What's the point of life?" or "What is my mission in life?" I've been raised that everybody has a mission in life. But most of the time, [I'm] like, "What is my mission?"

Others, like this man, talked more explicitly about specific issues they are wrestling with and expressed frustration that their soul-searching has not yet led them to find definitive answers:

> I'm just trying to figure out what the next stage in my life is. I really don't know what the hell I should be doing or what I shouldn't be doing. What I am actually doing is just going to school right now. I have no idea whether that's the right thing to do and spirituality isn't really helping me and neither is religion.

Some students struggling with self-described "big" questions also found themselves reflecting often on the meaning of their education and life after college. One woman described her experience in grappling with the specific goals of college attendance:

> A question I've been dealing with [that is] kind of indirectly related to spirituality is the point of college. Like the fact that we're

paying for this education so that we can make money later in life. . . . What does that have to do with the grand scheme of things? Is that really important when you compare it to the meaning of life . . . of love . . . of friendship . . . of all these higher ideas? Like, "What are we doing here?"

A man at a different institution shared similar sentiments:

A lot of times, I find myself wondering why are we in class . . . why are we in school . . . why do I want to have a job? What would I have accomplished if I died tomorrow . . . going to school for three years? Just going through it, as opposed to actually living and spending time with my family or my friends. . . . I feel like sometimes I miss out on connections because I'm too busy getting all wrapped up in society and the world I'm supposed to live in, and my culture, and all the junk that I'm supposed to get done before I graduate when I feel like I should really be spending my time with my friends . . . or just making connections.

With respect to long-range spiritual goals, most interview participants aspired to establish a more readily accessible connection with their spirituality and to build lives in which they balance well their multiple, and sometimes seemingly conflicting, roles and responsibilities. One man's remarks capture well a sentiment commonly expressed by his peers:

I'm still at the point where it's a conscious effort sometimes to observe some of the values that I do really want to embody and my hope is that, with time, those actions will become more natural. . . . I won't have to consciously think about doing them.

While the majority of those we surveyed and interviewed indicated their interest in, and engagement with, the spiritual/religious dimension of their lives, we would be remiss to overlook the significant minority of students who are less spiritually and religiously devoted. Approximately 25 percent of students evidence a high degree of religious/spiritual skepticism as indicated by their agreement with the following statements: "It is futile to try to discover the purpose of existence" (31 percent); "whether or not there is a Supreme Being is a matter of indifference to me" (27 percent); "I have never felt a sense of sacredness" (24 percent); "believing in supernatural phenomena is foolish" (22 percent); "in the future, science will be able to explain everything" (21 percent); and "the universe arose by chance" (19 percent). Moreover, 12 percent of CSBV respondents indicated explicitly that they do not consider themselves to be on a spiritual quest.

## Spirituality, Religiousness, and Well-Being

In conducting the CSBV survey, we were also interested to learn the extent to which students' spirituality/religiousness impacted their physical and psychological well-being. Overall, undergraduates' sense of personal well-being was found to decline significantly during the college years. Fully 77 percent of the college juniors who responded to the 2003 CSBV Survey reported feeling depressed either "frequently" or "occasionally" during the past year, compared to 61 percent when they first entered college. During the same three-year period, the number of students who rated their emotional health as either "below average" or in the "bottom 10 percent" relative to their peers doubled (from 6 to 14 percent), and the number who frequently "felt overwhelmed by all I have to do" also increased (from 33 to 40 percent). Roughly one student in five reported seeking personal counseling since entering college.

Relative to their more nonreligious peers, however, those who are highly involved in religion are less likely to experience psychological distress (e.g., feeling overwhelmed by all they have to do or that their lives are filled with stress and anxiety) and less likely to report poor emotional health. For example, compared to nonparticipants, students who frequently participate in religious services show much smaller increases in frequently feeling overwhelmed between their freshman and junior years (+2 percent versus +14 percent). Similarly, students who do not attend religious services, compared to those who attend frequently, are more than twice as likely to report feeling depressed frequently (13 versus 6 percent) and to rate themselves "below average" or in the "bottom 10 percent" in emotional health (21 versus 8 percent). Moreover, only 20 percent of highly religiously involved students reported high levels of psychological distress, compared to 34 percent of students with low levels of religious involvement—indicated by the reading of sacred texts; attendance at religious services; attendance at a class/workshop or retreat on matters related to religion/spirituality, etc. Similar findings emerged with respect to religious commitment—characterized, for example, by their seeking to follow religious teachings in their everyday lives, finding religion to be personally helpful, and gaining spiritual strength by trusting in a higher power. Only 23 percent of highly religiously committed students reported high levels of psychological distress, compared to 33 percent of students with low levels of religious commitment.

Spirituality (e.g., believing in the sacredness of life, seeking out opportunities to grow spiritually, believing that we are all spiritual beings), on the other hand, appears to have a mixed relationship to psychological health. Highly spiritual students, for example, are prone to experience spiritual distress (e.g., questioning one's religious/spiritual beliefs; struggling to understand evil, suffering, and death; feeling unsettled about spiritual and religious matters): 22 percent of highly spiritual students reported high levels of spiritual distress, compared to only 8 percent of students with low scores on spirituality. Highly spiritual students are also slightly more likely than students who score low on spirituality to report high levels of psychological distress (26 versus 21 percent). On the other hand, spirituality is positively related to both self-esteem (e.g., intellectual self-confidence, social self-confidence, self-rated courage) and feelings of equanimity (e.g., feeling good about the direction in which one's life is headed, feeling at peace/centered, seeing each day as a gift). While self-esteem and equanimity are also positively associated with both religious commitment and religious involvement, the associations with spirituality are stronger.

In addition to declines in self-perceived psychological health during college, students show a net decline in their self-rated physical health: the number who rate their physical health as either "above average" or in the "highest 10 percent" drops significantly between college entry and the end of the junior year (from 57 to 45 percent), while the percent rating their physical health as either "below average" or in the "bottom 10 percent" doubles (from 5 to 10 percent). Declines in self-rated physical health may be attributable, at least in part, to the fact that students tend not to be as physically active after they enter college. For example, the number of hours per week devoted to exercising or playing sports declines substantially during the first three years of college. Those devoting more than ten hours per week to such physical activity decreases by more than half (from 35 to 14 percent), while the number devoting less than six hours per week increases from fewer than half (44 percent) to two-thirds (68 percent). For traditional-age college students, spirituality and religion do not appear to have much impact on physical health.

Attendance at religious services, for example, shows little relationship to self-rated physical health, nor does spirituality. Similarly, religious and spiritual involvements bear little relationship to exercising or participating in sports.

Students also show marked increases in the frequency of alcohol consumption during the first three years of college. While only 17 percent of 2003 CSBV survey respondents reported drinking beer "frequently" when they entered college as freshmen, the rate of frequent beer drinking increases to 29 percent by the end of the junior year. Similarly, the number of students who report drinking wine or liquor frequently more than doubles (from 11 to 24 percent) during the first three years of college, while the number who abstain from wine or liquor declines by more than half (42 to 19 percent).

Being religiously involved, however, appears to decrease the likelihood that nondrinkers will become involved with alcohol during college. Among students who abstain from drinking beer prior to entering college, three-fourths (74 percent) continue to abstain during college if they are highly involved in religious activities. By comparison, fewer than half (46 percent) continue to abstain if they have little or no involvement in religious activities while in college. Similar differences relating to degree of religious involvement occur among students who abstain from drinking wine or liquor prior to college. Alcohol consumption is also less likely to occur among students who are highly spiritual and religiously committed, but the negative relationship to beer drinking was found to be strongest among the religiously involved: only 9 percent of highly religiously involved students reported drinking beer "frequently" during college, in contrast to 41 percent of those who had little or no religious involvement. The rates of total abstinence from beer drinking for the two groups were 60 percent and 18 percent, respectively.

Overall, our findings reveal that religiousness appears to have a readily discernible relation to select dimensions of undergraduates' well-being. In particular, relative to their less religious peers, students who are highly religious are less likely to report poor emotional health and to experience psychological distress. Compared with students who score low on spirituality, highly spiritual students also tend to indicate high levels of self-esteem and equanimity. Perhaps reflecting their active engagement in questioning and refining their beliefs, highly spiritual students are also comparatively more inclined than their less spiritual peers to experience both spiritual distress and psychological distress. Finally, neither spirituality nor religiousness were found to have a broad impact on physical well-being. Highly religious students, however, were more likely than their less religious counterparts to abstain from drinking.

## Individual Differences

Thus far, this chapter has focused on how undergraduates, as an aggregate, view spirituality and its role in their lives. How does spirituality differ across various student populations? Here, we highlight selected key distinctions divided by gender, academic major, and political orientation/engagement. Future analyses that our project team plans to conduct will focus, in greater depth, on the origins and outcomes of these differences. We will also examine additional dimensions of individual differences, including race/ethnicity and religious affiliation.

*Gender* Overall, and in keeping with the results of previous studies,[23] we find that college women exhibit greater commitment to spirituality and religion than men. Among CSBV survey respondents, 37 percent of the women and 25 percent of the men were high scorers on religious commitment. Women are also more inclined than men to view themselves as being on a spiritual quest (defined by having goals such as attaining inner harmony, searching for meaning/purpose in life, and becoming a more loving person) and to classify themselves as highly spiritual. However, our behavioral measure of religiousness—religious engagement—evidences less gender differentiation, with 22 percent of women and 18 percent of men scoring high on this scale. Men, however, show higher levels of religious skepticism overall—on the order of one in five men being highly skeptical, relative to one in ten women. Women are also more likely than men to experience spiritual and, especially, psychological distress, with about one-third of the women surveyed (32 percent, compared to only 20 percent of the men) reporting high levels of psychological distress during their third year in college. Finally, high levels of charitable involvement—performing volunteer work, participating in community food and clothing drives, participating in community action programs—are shown by 21 percent of the women, compared to only 8 percent of the men. By contrast, 33 percent of the men and only 12 percent of the women show little or no charitable involvement.

*College Major*   With respect to differences between students majoring in various fields, we see that students in the fine arts and humanities are about three times as likely as physical-science and computer-science majors to report high levels of spirituality. Interestingly, fine arts and humanities majors are also more likely than other majors to be highly engaged in a spiritual quest (43 percent and 42 percent respectively) and to express high levels of spiritual distress (27 percent and 31 percent). By contrast, students in the physical sciences (19 percent), computer science (23 percent), engineering (23 percent), and business (24 percent) are the least likely to show high levels of engagement in a spiritual quest, while especially low percentages of computer-science (10 percent), engineering (11 percent), business (15 percent), and education (17 percent) majors report high levels of spiritual distress.

Close to half of education majors reported high levels of religious/ spiritual growth during their first three years of college. This contrasts sharply with just one in five among physical and computer science majors and one in four among history and political-science majors. Students majoring in journalism, health professions, engineering, and psychology fall in between, with about one in three reporting a high level of religious/spiritual growth during college.

We also find that the highest levels of religious commitment— finding religion to be personally helpful, gaining spiritual strength by trusting in a higher power, seeking to follow religious teachings in everyday life, etc.—occur among students in education (53 percent) and the fine arts (48 percent). The lowest levels of religious commitment, on the other hand, are found among students in biological science (32 percent), history or political science (31 percent), computer science (30 percent), sociology (30 percent), and the physical sciences (30 percent).

*Political Orientation and Engagement*   Not surprisingly, students who are highly engaged religiously differ from their less religious classmates in their attitudes about a number of social issues. The largest gap is in views about casual sex, with only 7 percent of highly religious students (compared to 80 percent of the least religious students) agreeing with the proposition that "if two people really like each other, it's all right for them to have sex even if they've known each other for only a very short time." The most and least religious students also differ markedly in their rates of agreement with legalized abortion (24 percent versus 79 percent) and legalization of marijuana (17 percent versus 64 percent). Highly religious students are also much more likely to support "laws prohibiting homosexual relationships" (38 percent) than are the least religious students (17 percent).

A very different pattern emerges, however, when it comes to attitudes about gun control and the death penalty. More of the most religious students (75 percent) than of the least religious students (70 percent) agree that "the federal government should do more to control the sale of handguns," and the most religious students are substantially more likely than the least religious students to support abolition of the death penalty (38 percent versus 23 percent).

Students who identify themselves as politically "conservative," compared to those who self-identify as "liberal," are noticeably more likely to show high levels of religious commitment (50 percent versus 18 percent) and religious engagement (37 percent versus 10 percent), and are also more likely to demonstrate high levels of equanimity (35 percent versus 23 percent) and self-esteem (37 percent versus 29 percent). Liberal students, by contrast, are more likely to express high levels of religious skepticism (23 percent versus 7 percent) and to be engaged in a spiritual quest (33 percent versus 27 percent).

Political engagement—defined by such characteristics and behaviors as voting in student elections, frequently discussing politics, wanting to influence the political structure, and participating in student government—was found to be only weakly related to religious engagement and unrelated to religious commitment. However, students who are highly engaged politically, compared to politically unengaged students, show much higher levels of charitable involvement, social activism (e.g., aspiring to influence social values, and helping to promote racial understanding), growth in global/national understanding (i.e., self-change during college in understanding global issues, problems facing our nation, and local community problems), and self-esteem. They are also much more likely to be engaged in a spiritual quest.

Taken together, our findings to date suggest that, by and large, undergraduates are indeed engaged both spiritually and religiously. Moreover, there are notable differences in students' perspectives and practices based on individual characteristics. To be sure, our preliminary analyses of the CSBV survey and related interview data generate a wide range of questions for further research. The findings also raise questions about an often overlooked aspect of the undergraduate experience: how students perceive their campus environments with respect to promoting or hindering their spiritual development.

## MEANING, PURPOSE, AND SPIRITUALITY IN THE CAMPUS ENVIRONMENT

Given the questions, struggles, and contradictions college students deal with, it is critical to understand how the college experience adds to or detracts from students' spiritual development. What are the opportunities in college for students to pursue their spiritual quests? To search for answers to their spiritual questions? To grow spiritually? Do students discuss the spiritual issues and questions they have with others on campus? Do they talk about spirituality in any of their classes? Would they welcome more opportunities for such discussions?

Indeed, we find that considerable numbers of students are searching for meaning and purpose in life (75 percent), discussing spirituality with friends (78 percent), and discussing the meaning of life with friends (69 percent). However, more than half (56 percent) said that their professors never provide opportunities to discuss the meaning and purpose of life. Similarly, nearly two-thirds (62 percent) said that their professors never encourage discussions of spiritual or religious matters. Moreover, while 39 percent said their religious or spiritual beliefs have been strengthened by "new ideas encountered in class," 53 percent reported that their classroom experiences have had no impact on this dimension of their lives. Overall, just 55 percent are satisfied with how their college experience has provided "opportunities for religious/spiritual reflection."

Echoing the sentiments of CSBV survey respondents, the students we interviewed had mixed experiences dealing with spiritual/religious topics on campus. The majority of students at one of the religiously affiliated institutions, for example, felt that their spirituality has been strengthened because of the culture and practices of the institution. However, there were also some students within the same institution who felt that being in an environment where everyone is of the same faith has its limitations, in that there are essentially no challenges to their existing beliefs and thus, no growth. As we heard from many students across different types of institutions, it is the diversity of faith and beliefs within the campus environment that they feel most contributes to their spiritual growth. As one man explained,

I like having that diversity. I enjoy being able to have debates or arguments during lunch with my friends. I think questioning everything and trying to understand the other side helps me to be a lot more spiritual . . . in understanding what I really believe in . . . because, at the end, I might not agree with them at all. It helps me grow more by questioning. . . . It really helps me see why I believe what I do.

While many students were inclined to have discussions about religious/spiritual issues with their peers, we heard from them recurrently that they are "cautious" both about how they approach these conversations and with whom they engage in such dialogue. In part, these apprehensions stem from a feeling that the spiritual dimension of one's life is inherently personal. Understandably, students often do not feel comfortable "exposing" such aspects of their experience within environments where they are not secure that their perspectives will be heard without judgment and that their sentiments will be respected or, at the very least, will not be ridiculed.

Students also held diverse perspectives about whether the spiritual realm of personal development could be addressed effectively in classroom settings. Overall, with respect to their experiences discussing religion and spirituality within the classroom, while some students recalled classes that challenged them to "think outside the box" and "evaluate my own values, morals, and beliefs," most students concurred with one woman, who explained:

> We don't really talk about anything controversial. [The professor] will just basically tell us the facts and what we need to learn.

While students were often aware of topically relevant courses they could take on their campuses, such as those offering perspectives on various religious faiths, the general consensus was that, in the words of one woman, "there's no class that talks about spirituality as a whole with an unbiased point of view." One student noted her perception— particularly in her biology classes—that spirituality is "kind of in the air" in certain class discussions, but that professors tend to steer the conversation away from topics that are controversial. Another woman concurred:

> [Professors] have that look that says, "Don't even go there." I know some people just want to jump out of their seats and say,

"How do you know?" and "I don't believe it." I've actually had people tell me from previous years that have graduated that teachers used to actually lower their grades if they even tried to argue with them. So there's this thing where, you know, you'll see people look at each other and you'll see the wheels turning in everyone's head, but nothing is really said because everyone's just like, "Okay, let's just get through this because I know it's going to be a fight anyway."

Others, such as this man, shared a more positive classroom experience:

I find that when teachers just briefly touch on the significance [of something] in terms of how things are in general, that helps me. It doesn't happen very often and I know it doesn't really work with all the subjects, but just touching on it a little bit is helpful. I think if it's forced, it won't work. If we have like forced discussions where people are sort of made to divulge what they think about [spiritual] things, it doesn't really [work], but just touching on it can be helpful.

Some students at nonsectarian institutions felt that discussions about religion, whether in class or not, are generally frowned upon and that people are "afraid" to broach associated topics. The hesitancy in raising religious/spiritual issues expressed by one man was shared by many of his peers:

The taboo of bringing up religion . . . it's a bad thing. . . . There's a sense that you shouldn't bring up God in the academic setting. When you start bringing up religion, you show your assumption that there is a God and people try to play on that and you feel attacked and that's the reason I feel uncomfortable bringing up religion in the academic setting.

Indeed, while students were generally open to the idea of engaging in conversations about the spiritual aspect of their lives within campus settings in which they felt comfortable, there was widespread agreement that the process of opening communication lines for such exchanges could be challenging. This was particularly true given what students perceived to be the "prevailing assumptions" within academe. In reflecting on how existing norms might be altered most effectively, one woman's sentiments captured well the perspectives of her peers:

I think the one thing I would change is professors. They're almost, like, scared they're going to offend somebody. I mean, it's rare that you get a professor to actually sit there and show you what they [believe]. I've never seen a professor actually involved in a real debate with students.

## FUTURE DIRECTIONS

Spiritual growth has been described both as "complex and multifaceted" and as "contingent and universal."[24] Moreover, different trajectories have been evidenced for men and women and there is evidence from our preliminary work that meaningful dimensions of difference in process, practice, and perspective may also exist among students from different racial/ethnic backgrounds and faith traditions. Developmental paths have also been viewed as responsive to sociohistorical context. As Stokes has elaborated, changes in how people make meaning of their lives also tends to occur more intensively during times of crisis and transition than during periods of calm and stability.[25] To be sure, preliminary findings from the "Spirituality in Higher Education" study support these assertions and raise new questions.

Recently, we completed the first phase of data collection for a larger longitudinal study of college students' spiritual development that we believe will provide more comprehensive insight into the spiritual development of undergraduate students. Based on findings from the 2003 CSBV survey and related interview research, some of which have been highlighted in this chapter, we developed a revised two-page, 128-item version of the CSBV survey. That survey was administered in summer and fall 2004 to a diverse sub-sample of 2004 CIRP Freshman Survey participants. The sub-sample comprised approximately 120,000 entering freshmen at 240 colleges and universities. These students completed a special six-page Freshman Survey, which is intended to serve as a "pretest" for a longitudinal follow-up survey to be conducted in spring 2007 that will make it possible for the UCLA research team to track changes in students' spiritual development during their undergraduate years.

A related component of this 2004–2007 longitudinal student study is aimed at discerning how college and university faculty view the intersections between spirituality and higher education, examining how faculty beliefs and behavior may influence students' spiritual development, and exploring how faculty view their own spiritual expression within the context of their academic careers and institutionally based work. The following questions are among those that provide direction for this aspect of our work:

1) What role do faculty believe spirituality should play in the undergraduate experience?
2) How do faculty view their responsibility for helping students achieve a greater sense of meaning and purpose in their lives?
3) To what extent do faculty view themselves as potential facilitators of students' spiritual/religious development?
4) To what extent do faculty engage their students in curricular activities that can promote inner development such as reflective learning, journaling, and community service?
5) How might life-stage and/or generational differences affect how students and faculty differentially define and experience their spirituality?
6) What are the contextual (i.e., cultural and structural) aspects of campus life that faculty perceive as facilitating or hindering their own and/or their students' spiritual expression and development?

Our preliminary analyses (beginning in spring 2005) of faculty data will focus on creating national norms based on the weighted responses of approximately 75,000 faculty at 520 institutions nationwide. Subsequently, we will conduct a series of more in-depth analyses involving data collected from students and faculty at the 175 institutions that are participating in both the 2004 CIRP/CSBV Freshman Survey *and* the 2004 HERI Triennial Faculty Survey.

The importance of including faculty data in our analyses of students' spiritual growth and development during their undergraduate years is underscored by the fact that faculty attitudes and behavior are known to have important implications for student development. The actions of faculty both within and outside the classroom impact the learning and development of future teachers, lawyers, physicians, and policymakers, not to mention their very own academic successors and the thousands of others whose work affects our lives. Interpersonal interaction with faculty enhances a wide variety of student outcomes and, as Terenzini, Pascarella, and Blimling have shown,[26] is one of the most influential sources of undergraduate student learning.

As the primary adult agents of socialization within the college environment, faculty have the ability to impact student experiences and outcomes both positively and negatively. Beyond influencing students' intellectual and career development, interacting with faculty has been shown to enhance students' personal identity awareness and moral development.[27] In addition, student-outcomes research shows that informal (i.e., out-of-class) interaction between students and faculty increases faculty influence on undergraduate students' values, beliefs, and behaviors[28] and positively affects students' intellectual curiosity, interpersonal skills, and maturational development.[29] Faculty mentoring has also been positively associated with student inclinations toward humanitarian behavior.[30] To date, however, there has been no empirical research that focuses specifically on how faculty values, attitudes, beliefs, and actions affect the spiritual growth and development of undergraduate students.

One of the most critical questions posed by the "Spirituality in Higher Education" project is how spirituality affects other aspects of college students' development, including their academic performance, psychological and physical health, sense of personal empowerment, civic responsibility, empathy, racial/ethnic awareness and tolerance, religiousness, and satisfaction with college. While definitive answers to these questions must await the longitudinal study currently underway that will conclude in spring 2007, data collected thus far has enabled us to gain some preliminary insight about college students' spirituality. Ultimately, the aim of this work is to promote public awareness of and attention to the spiritual development of American college students. Moreover, we hope that the insights, understanding, and dialogue generated through this research and related efforts will provide a broad foundation for associated student, faculty, and institutional development initiatives that are aimed at facilitating this important and too-often-overlooked aspect of college student development.

# Congregations That Get It: Understanding Religious Identities in the Next Generation

*Tobin Belzer, Richard W. Flory, Nadia Roumani, and Brie Loskota*

## Introduction

Organized religion in the United States is on the threshold of a seismic shift. Today, religious and community leaders are witnessing a crisis in the transmission of religious memory, practice, and tradition to the next generation. In major urban centers across the United States, there is a generalized perception that individuals in their twenties and early thirties constitute a "black hole" in congregational life. Members of the young-adult population are simply missing from most churches, synagogues, and mosques. Religious and community leaders are given to lamenting about the throngs of young people who are "spiritual but not religious" as a way to explain young people's absence from organized religious life.

This study does not attempt to understand the behavior of the majority. Instead, this research explores the experiences and attitudes of young adults who are exceptions to the norm—namely, those who are actively participating in congregational life. Congregations with significant programs for young adults in their twenties and thirties are valuable sites for investigation to qualitatively examine the changing nature of religious identity. Based on qualitative interviews and participant observation, the research team constructed profiles of Jewish, Christian (Protestant and Catholic), and Muslim congregations. To explore the intergenerational transmission of faith, we analyzed individuals within an institutional context and the institutions themselves. This research highlights the similarities and differences among and between individuals and congregations across four faith traditions. This research is based at the Center for Religion and Civic Culture at the University of Southern California, in connection with Hebrew Union College, the Institute for Advanced Catholic Studies, and the Omar Ibn Al Khattab Foundation. It was generously supported by the Lilly Endowment.

## METHODS

Over the course of one year, the research team visited congregations in Los Angeles, Chicago, Detroit, New York, and Washington, D.C. The intent was to focus on urban areas where large populations of each religious faith are strongly represented. We identified congregations through exploratory conversations with young adults, religious leaders, and professionals working in religious institutions in each city. Within each religious tradition, we chose congregations to represent the broad theological spectrum, from conservative to progressive. Each congregation was also selected because of the intergenerational participation of its members.

With the aim of having an insider's perspective, and the awareness that outsiders can frequently identify issues that may be overlooked by insiders, we formed a research team with members who represent the three faith traditions. The team spent several weeks collecting data at each congregation. We conducted approximately one hundred interviews with congregational leaders, lay leaders, and young adults in fifteen congregations. In many instances, the entire research team conducted the congregational visits and interviews. Interviews were audio-recorded and many were also videotaped. We also videotaped other aspects of congregational life, including religious services and young adult programs.

## YOUNG-ADULT CONGREGANTS

Young adults across faiths and geographic locations shared several demographic characteristics. They also possessed numerous similarities in their motivations and desires surrounding congregational involvement. In this sample, young adults who are involved in congregational life are largely American-born, college-educated, from middle-class to upper-middle-class backgrounds, and are emerging into their professional identities.

The individuals interviewed do not necessarily feel compelled by tradition to affiliate with a specific denomination or attend a religious service or event, as did members of previous generations. Instead, their motivations to affiliate varied considerably. Some had negative experiences with religion, religious leaders, and communities, which still color their perceptions about religious institutions. For others, curiosity and interest in their own religious identity was sparked by their secular education and exposure to other religions and forms of spirituality. Others still view their religious identity as an ongoing journey, and can articulate a coherent narrative of their path. Many feel they do not have a strong foundation of knowledge about religion, especially with regard to religious texts and liturgy.

Many young adults said that they do not believe that organized religion is the only way to access the Divine. Involvement in congregational life is, for some, just one of many ways they experience the sacred in their lives. They do not want to confine or compartmentalize the spiritual dimensions of their lives to congregations or to specific times and places. They are interested in finding holiness in the world in general, not only within the context of their religion. Young adults described having religious experiences in numerous ways: through worship, through work, through relationships with peers, and through service.

Young adults' relationships with their congregations are complicated. Most are wary of their congregation as an institution, but are attracted to it as a community. The hierarchical, bureaucratic, political, and fiscal aspects of institutions tend to put them off. They are skeptical about spirituality, religion, and institutions in general, and are acutely aware of others' skepticism as well. Yet rather than reject religious affiliations outright like so many of their peers, the young adults interviewed purposefully sought out congregations where they feel comfortable.

Despite their active participation, many young adults interviewed said that they do not feel integral to congregational life. The ubiquity of events for singles has sent a strong message that single young adults are not as valuable participants as they are. Many individuals explained that programming to their age cohort in most congregations is aimed at ensuring that they find others in their religious group to marry. Consequently, they believe that most communal leaders are more interested in the quantity of people who show up than in the quality of their religious experience. They spoke of such congregations with disdain, and identified the varied and dynamic opportunities for involvement at their congregations as outside the norm.

Many people also described the financial aspects of religious life with distaste. Before they found their current congregations, some young adults said they felt alienated by the style and approach of religious leaders. Most religious leaders, they reported, do not care whether they are involved, except if they are able to make a financial contribution.

Young adults have come of age in an increasingly pluralistic and global society, and have little patience for anyone who tries to claim that their path is better than that of others. They are put off by interreligious and intrareligious prejudice and divisiveness. While they have chosen to engage with a particular congregation, young congregants do not feel as though they, or their peers, have found "The Way." Instead, they believe they have found a way that works for them at the moment.

The young adults we interviewed exercised typical American individualism as they decided about associating with religious communities, sometimes participating in more than one simultaneously. When becoming members, they were more often choosing a specific community, rather than committing to a larger movement or denomination. They tended to make such choices based on a number of factors such as interpersonal relationships, worship style, geographic location, opportunities for involvement, and accessibility of leadership.

Individuals also decided how often to attend and the extent of their participation. They chose how much of the official teachings to accept and how much ritual observance to practice. They chose how to balance their individual authority with their identity as members of a community and religious tradition. They sought communities where there is both flexibility and structure, enabling them to establish their personal boundaries. Most young adults interviewed were critical of the "show up and watch" style of religious participation.

The success of interpersonal connections played a very strong role in young adults' desire to affiliate as members of a congregation. Within every congregation studied, participants wished to associate with people who express and explore their religious identities in similar ways. Relationship building was a fundamental aspect of young adults' congregational experience.

## CONGREGATIONS THAT GET IT

Congregations that "get it" are far from uniform. The characteristics of the congregations in this study varied considerably in terms of size, date founded, budget, and theological approach. We found congregations large and small, progressive and conservative, old and new, that are engaging young adults in a variety of ways.

### Protestant Churches

The Protestant churches included in this study were chosen to represent a range of theological, political, and cultural perspectives, from liberal mainline to conservative Evangelical. Three churches were identified for this research: First Evangelical Free Church in Fullerton, California; Fourth Presbyterian Church in Chicago; and Marble Collegiate Church in New York City.

First Evangelical Free Church, known as "EV Free" to its members, is a large conservative Evangelical church in Fullerton, California, with upward of six thousand members. The church has been active in Southern California for more than fifty years. Four services are offered each Sunday, in addition to numerous educational programs that are organized around members' ages and life-stages. The young-adult group is one of many smaller communities within the larger congregation, each of which is led by a pastor dedicated to that group. The pastor of the young-adult group also leads a service oriented toward younger worshippers on Sunday evenings. At the "contemporary" worship service, young adults participate in all aspects of the service, including leading the congregation in contemporary Christian music.

The young-adult group at EV Free is called "The Interior," a name that reflects its emphasis on spiritual growth through teaching, discipleship, outreach, and community. The group meets following the Sunday evening service for a discussion of the sermon. At these weekly meetings, volunteer leaders make announcements about upcoming events, welcome visitors, and facilitate group discussions. Around seventy-five to one hundred young adults typically attend these meetings. A casual atmosphere functions to bring young adults together socially and contributes to a sense of community among the group's members.

The Interior's social, service-oriented, and spiritual events are all planned and implemented by young adults themselves. Outside of the Sunday meetings, they engage in Bible studies, retreats, service programs, and social activities. Some activities are primarily social, like a beach trip with optional surf lessons. Other events, such as retreats and mission trips, focus on faith and spirituality. Whether the focus is spiritual or social, every event includes aspects of both characteristics. At EV Free, the coupling of the spiritual and social is fundamental to the success of the young-adult group.

Fourth Presbyterian Church, located on Chicago's "Magnificent Mile," has been a liberal Protestant standard-bearer for many years. "Fourth Church," as it is known, has a vibrant five-thousand-member congregation. Its worship is in the style of a traditional Protestant service, complete with pipe organ, choir, and hymns. The themes of the church's many ministries range from music and arts to religious education to social services. More than two thousand people attend the church's four Sunday services, with the morning eleven o'clock service largely populated with young adults.

The young-adult group at Fourth Church includes about one hundred people and is led by a staff minister specifically hired to serve that population. Like the young adults at EV Free, the Fourth Church group meets each Sunday after the worship service. Approximately 20–30 people usually attend these discussions led by the young-adult minister. Conversations are based on sermon themes, and generally incorporate ideas about emotional and spiritual growth within the Fourth Church's liberal Protestant tradition. The group also participates in Bible study, retreats, and various social-justice programs. Social events include dinners in local restaurants, volleyball on the beach, or Cubs games. The mission of the group is threefold: to help young adult congregants develop their spiritual lives, to provide ways for them to participate in the life of the larger congregation, and to socially connect with one another.

Marble Collegiate Church in New York City is probably best known for its former pastor Norman Vincent Peale's concept, "the power of positive thinking." Marble Church is a congregation in the Reformed Church in America with approximately three thousand members. One of the pastors described Marble as a liberal Evangelical church that offers both traditional Bible teaching and an affirming environment for people to pursue their spiritual lives. The congregation celebrates a diverse set of beliefs and lifestyles within a context of a fairly traditional

Protestant presentation of scripture and liturgy. This environment is exemplified by the activities of "Connection," Marble Church's ethnically and ideologically diverse group of young adults.

During a discussion called "Bagels and Bibles" following the Sunday morning service, themes from the sermon are considered in a wide-ranging conversation that includes questions from the young congregants. The staff minister and participants respond to one another supportively as the discussion flows between the theological and the personal. Following the discussion, many young congregants organize themselves to socialize informally over lunch.

In addition to the Sunday meetings, the group offers various service opportunities, like cleaning up parks or distributing food at city shelters. Social and spiritual activities include book groups, retreats, meditation services, and Bible studies. As with each of the other two Protestant churches, many of the young-adult congregants participate in the life of the larger congregation by serving on committees, singing in the choir, or participating in service activities organized by the church.

*Catholic Churches*

The Catholic congregations included in this study—St. Monica's Catholic Church in Santa Monica, California; St. Clement's Catholic Church in Chicago; and Holy Trinity Catholic Church in New York City—are directed by Diocesan clergy (i.e., not run by religious orders like Franciscans or Dominicans), and thus represent a mainstream Catholic approach to theological and cultural issues. The three churches have similar approaches to young-adult congregants. Differences between the congregations result from variations in how the groups are organized and how long they have been functioning.

The churches all serve large congregations and have several hundred young-adult congregants. In each parish, young adults are involved in activities unique to their group and are also well integrated into the larger community. The inclusion of young adults in the larger life of the congregation is a prominent goal at these Catholic churches. Young adults are encouraged to take on leadership roles of all kinds. At all three Catholic churches, we met young adults who serve on organizing committees for the young-adult groups, and also participate in committees and boards within the larger parishes.

Each of the Catholic churches has developed a contemporary approach to the Mass that is oriented to young adults. Individuals both participate and direct the service, choosing and leading the liturgical music and serving as Eucharistic ministers, scripture readers, musicians, and ushers. The young-adult Mass in each city fills the sanctuaries with worshippers every Sunday evening and includes contemporary liturgy.

The churches provide young adults with numerous opportunities to cultivate relationships and further their understanding of Catholicism by offering multiple points of entry. Each helps individuals cultivate a relationship between religious values and everyday life. Weekly Mass is complemented by other religious and spiritual activities like retreats, Bible study, book groups, and service opportunities. Social activities—baseball games, volleyball, movie nights, wine tastings, and dinners at fine restaurants—create a sense of community. Some social events are combined with service activities, such as a fundraiser for a parish ministry. Sometimes, multiple types of events are offered on the same night. During the summer, for example, the "Contemporary Roman Catholics" (CRC) at Holy Trinity hosted a kickball game in Central Park followed by a fundraising event at a restaurant and bar to support a mission in the Dominican Republic. The CRC publicizes their numerous social, spiritual, and service-oriented events through an events calendar frequently updated on their Web site.

The churches strive to create an atmosphere where young adults can learn about their faith without feeling shame about their lack of knowledge. For example, St. Monica's provides a variety of learning opportunities for congregants, ranging from spiritual retreats to discussions like "finding Jesus in the Movies." After Mass on a typical Sunday evening, there are as many as five different activities, each oriented to various interests among the young congregants, and all oriented toward engaging young congregants with issues of faith and life. We found adult learning opportunities at each church that are directed specifically to young congregants' needs, backgrounds, and interests.

*Mosques*

The mosques identified for this research in Los Angeles, Detroit, and Washington, D.C., were chosen to demonstrate the ethnic and socioeconomic diversity of the Muslim community in America and to represent various schools of Islamic thought. Although the mosques vary considerably in structure, facilities, demographics, and programming, they possess many similar characteristics that enable them to connect with young adults.

The Islamic Center of America (ICA) in Dearborn, Michigan, reflects the Twelver Shiite practice of Islam, or Jaafaris. The mosque community varies in economic makeup, but includes predominantly middle-income households. The forty-two-year-old, Iraqi-born imam Sayed Hassan al-Qazwini has been the leader of the mosque since 1997.

ICA hosts the Young Muslim Association (YMA), which focuses on developing the spiritual identities of young adults. The YMA boasts almost seven hundred members. The group is an integral part of the ICA community, offering activities like fundraisers for the mosque, evening programs and lectures, community-service activities, and celebrations for Ramadan (the holy month of fasting) and Ashura (a Shiite holiday commemorating the martyrdom of Hussein, the Prophet Muhammad's grandson).

On any given Friday evening, approximately two hunded young adults attend the YMA program. The events typically begin with the *maghrib* (sundown) prayer followed by a lecture by Imam Qazwini. After the lecture, there is an open group discussion. Occasionally, during the Friday program, an individual will make a brief presentation on issues related to work, activism, or religious experiences. During one Friday session, for example, a YMA member discussed her experience as an intern in a congressional office on Capitol Hill. The session always closes with the evening prayer, *isha*. Following the prayers, chairs are cleared away and the lecture hall is transformed back into a gymnasium. Many of the male participants linger for a game of basketball.

Young adults also attend discussions and seminars that are open to the entire mosque community. Some are informative, covering topics such as marriage and religious practice, while others are provocative, such as a debate that was held between two Muslim scholars and two atheists. Often a scholarly lecture is followed by a discussion led by an American-born young adult.

A dynamic and active group, the YMA is led by the Leadership Council, known to the congregants as the "L Council," who work together to organize and lead programming. Members of the L Council also sit on the thirty-three-member board of the mosque. An advisory group that includes Imam Qazwini and three middle-aged, American-born Muslims, oversees the L Council. Some of the young adults we interviewed said that the imam and his advisors are extremely approachable; they felt comfortable broaching questions they would not otherwise ask. Many felt that Imam Qazwini has played a critical role in the YMA's success by simultaneously giving young adults space to lead and providing assistance from advisors.

At most mosques in America, the leadership tend to be in their fifties and sixties. At All Area Dulles Muslim Society (ADAMS) in Washington, D.C., one of the largest mosques on the East Coast, however, all four executive officers are men and women in their thirties. The leader of the community, Sudanese-born imam Mohammed Magid, has been integral to the process of empowering young leaders. His goal is to build a large pool of dynamic young adults who can ultimately take over the leadership of the mosque, thereby ensuring organizational consistency. The president of ADAMS, thirtysomething Rizwan Jaka, has been a part of the mosque since he was twenty-five. At twenty-eight, Jaka founded the "Playing and Praying" program, which organizes competitive sports like tennis and badminton for men and women. The director of the Saturday-school program is a twenty-five-year-old woman who grew up in the mosque community.

The ADAMS center, a predominantly Sunni mosque, serves a community of approximately ten thousand people in Washington, D.C., and Virginia. Rather than functioning as a traditional mosque that opens for the five daily prayers, the ADAMS center is run like a community center, offering a wide range of programs geared toward various age-groups and interests throughout each day and evening.

Young adults are attracted to the center's vibrant energy. They take full advantage of the many educational opportunities. There is typically a Qur'an class and a class for new Muslims. A martial-arts class meets on the lawn outside the mosque. Seminars and workshops focus on themes relevant to young adults' identities as both Muslims and Americans. They discuss issues surrounding courting and marriage, learn how to more deeply connect with Islam, and talk about the importance of voting. Topics focused on women in Islam typically attract a large young-adult presence. They are also drawn to Imam Magid's lectures, responding to his accessible style, humor, and ability to relate religious lessons to young adults' daily lives. Friday-night lectures, although open to the larger community, are particularly targeted toward young adults. Most sessions tend to attract between 100 and 150 participants.

As at ICA, each lecture is followed by discussion among the entire group.

Southern California contains an array of congregations that are successfully connecting with American-Muslim young adults. The congregations highlighted below do not represent the only congregations in Southern California successfully connecting with this generation, but represent a range of approaches taken in and around Los Angeles County aimed at connecting with Muslim young adults today. In the heart of Koreatown near downtown Los Angeles, the Islamic Center of Southern California (ICSC) has been one of the most dynamic centers attracting young adults since the 1970s. Two retired Egyptian-born medical doctors, Maher and Hassan Hathout, are among the founding members of this predominantly Sunni mosque. The congregation is extremely ethnically diverse, as exemplified by its nine-person board that includes members who are Pakistani, Bosnian, Sri Lankan, Egyptian, Turkish, Syrian, and Lebanese. Like the ADAMS center, ICSC has a number of young-adult board members. The board also includes four women, which is uncommon in mosques in America. In general, ICSC tends to favor more gender egalitarianism than most mosques. For example, some women don a headscarf only at prayer, choosing not to wear such a covering during other ICSC events.

The mosque has sparked the creation of a number of institutions that have helped to shape American Muslim identity. The institutions include: New Horizon School; the Muslim Youth Group; the Muslim Public Affairs Council (MPAC); the *Minaret* magazine; Elevate; Muslim Women's League (MWL); and Muslims in Action. Each of these programs emerged from the mosque's mission to promote Muslim American identity using various methods and emphasizing unifying principles that connect all Muslims.

For the past six years, Maher Hathout, a leader of ICSC, has opened his home every Sunday to young adults from the center for a Qur'anic study group. Each week, they gather to examine and discuss a selected text. Maher Hathout's approach to engage young adults is to meet individuals where they are, "not where we think they should be." He urges young people to interact and engage with texts, even if they do not read Arabic. These attitudes imbue the mosque's lecture series. "Qur'an for the Common Person" and "Islamic History," led by prominent Los Angeles–based scholars, were two series that proved particularly attractive to young adults.

Opportunities for activism also attract young adults who wish to use their religious faith to create positive social change. The leadership at ICSC has been effective at integrating dynamic young adults into these organizations. For example, Ahmad Younis, a twentysomething Egyptian American, returned to the mosque after completing law school and is now National Director of MPAC in Washington, D.C. One of the preeminent American Muslim nonprofit organizations, MPAC focuses on integrating American Muslims into the American civic and political systems.

Elevate, an organization founded in 2000, comprises people in their twenties and thirties who have graduated from the Youth Group and want to continue to engage in local activism in the Los Angeles area. Through social, educational, and religious programs, the group addresses issues relevant to young adults. Some members of Elevate take on leadership roles in the Youth Group, facilitating educational programs and organizing an annual retreat.

Founded in 1986, Masjid Ibaddilah is a two-room, one-story building on busy Jefferson Boulevard in South Central Los Angeles. It does not have the domed-mosque-style grandeur that is common in mosques around the country, yet the community exudes vibrant energy. Unlike the congregations described earlier, African Americans make up approximately 90 percent of Masjid Ibaddillah's population. Most congregants at this mosque are working-class, and approximately 60 percent have not attended college.

The mosque most successfully engages young adults through the ILM Foundation, which was co-founded by Assistant Imam Naim Shah and Imam Saadiq Saafir. The ILM Foundation, situated a few blocks from the mosque, focuses on integrating Islamic principles with activism by combining education and community-service opportunities. ILM's mission to "teach life skills to replace social ills" is served by offering local domestic-relief services. "Go Beyond the G.A.M.E." is a foundation program that promotes the principles of *G*ratitude, *A*ttitude, *M*otivation, and *E*ducation through recreational activities like sports camps, arts and cultural events, and youth conferences. The program's community-service component includes feeding the homeless, cleaning the neighborhood, and helping the elderly. Educational support is provided through homework assistance, entrepreneurial project training, college preparation workshops, and tours of colleges and corporations. Other programs include the Voter Registration Rally for Muslim Youth, food drives for the Eat Right to Think Right Free Food Program (through the Los Angeles Regional Food Bank), and the Partnerships for Humanity Inter-Faith Program.

The majority of volunteers at the foundation are American-born Muslim young adults. Most of the core volunteers regularly attend the classes taught by Imams Shah and Saafir. To build confidence among young adults, the courses focus on basic concepts of Islam, emphasizing the importance of religious practice. Basic life-skills are also taught. In these courses, Imam Saafir stresses the importance of self-knowledge as well as awareness of other religions and American society more generally.

Imams Saafir and Shah recognize that young adults need a comfortable environment where they can discuss issues and engage with their peers. A Young Adult Rap Session focuses on strategies to help young Muslims maintain their religious identities and practices while engaging with mainstream American society. Muslims in Action is another group that emerged from the mosque (in conjunction with ICSC), and is led by the young adults who organize educational opportunities and community events for Muslim young adults in Los Angeles.

The green dome of Masjid Omar Ibn Al Khattab has a strong architectural presence on Exposition Boulevard near downtown Los Angeles. Located next to the University of Southern California campus, Masjid Omar is part of the Omar Ibn Al Khattab Foundation. The predominantly Sunni mosque, built in 1994, hosts five daily prayer services, activities during Ramadan, and Sunday programs offering adult continuing-education courses and Qur'an and Arabic reading programs. Included in the Sunday program is an "Introduction to Islam" class in Spanish offered to the growing community of Latino converts by Latino Muslims.

The mosque also serves as a vibrant community center for both Muslims and non-Muslims in the Los Angeles community. The lecture hall and classrooms are often used as meeting places for local Muslim and non-Muslim nonprofit groups. Groups that frequently use the facilities include the Muslim Artists in LA, the ILM Foundation, and public agencies such as the Los Angeles Unified School District. Additionally, the mosque houses the Impact Community Center, which provides social and health services to low-income families and individuals, as well as foster-care placement. Furthermore, "Islam in the Curriculum" is a professional development workshop offered by the mosque for teachers, education administrators, and school staff.

The Omar Ibn Al Khattab Foundation, affiliated with the mosque, began its programming in 1986, focusing on empowering American Muslims and encouraging more active participation in civic life. The foundation focuses primarily on empowerment through education and outreach. Libyan-born Dafer Dakhil oversees the foundation's programs, specifically the extensive outreach programs with the non-Muslim community in Los Angeles. Resident-scholar Fathi Osman heads the foundation's educational outreach program, which distributes informational articles about issues pertaining to Islam in America.

The foundation oversees the Omar Scholars program, which provides a network for rising American-born Muslim scholars pursuing Masters or Doctoral degrees in the social sciences, humanities, and communication. Scholars are selected based on promise in their field and their ability to integrate Islamic perspectives into their work. The program is founded on the premise that emerging American-born Muslim scholars can contribute a contemporary Islamic perspective to the discourse on social and economic issues in America. Within the tradition of Islam, the program encourages a range of opinions and points of view, in support of a vibrant and diversified discourse that strengthens the community, advances intellectual development, and provides possible solutions to social ills. In the next phase of the program, the foundation is preparing to build a library and an institute for its scholars, providing them with an institutional base to do writing and research. This institute, the Center for the Study of Civilizations, will promote contemporary Islamic thought and disseminate their work particularly to young Muslims. It will encourage the cross-pollination of ideas among scholars within the community. The institute would also encourage young scholars to work with non-Muslim groups addressing communal social, economic, and political issues in pursuit of feasible solutions.

The task of negotiating American and Muslim identities animates a great deal of both thought and action among young adults in all of the Muslim congregations. These congregations are exemplary in their willingness to include young adults in the processes of leadership. They also actively navigate the numerous and complex layers of class, gender, and ethnic difference in their communities.

*Synagogues*

The Jewish congregations chosen for this research in Los Angeles, New York, and Chicago represent three denominations: Reform, Conservative, and Modern Orthodox. The thriving young-adult communities within each of these very different congregations highlight the fact that there is no single formula, but there are numerous opportunities for successfully engaging members of this population.

The young-adult population at Steven S. Wise Temple (SSWT) is a thriving subcommunity within a large, wealthy Reform congregation in Bel Air, California. With a large annual budget and a magnetic young staff, SSWT's "Young Congregation" typically attracts thirty to fifty people to its bimonthly programs. Congregation Bnai Jeshurun (BJ), on New York's predominantly Jewish Upper West Side, is known for its raucous Shabbat services that attract an intergenerational crowd of hundreds on Friday nights. At BJ, the normally staid worship service characteristic of the Conservative movement is infused with the energy of a four-piece band, rhythmic drumming, ecstatic dance, and charismatic rabbis who emphasize issues of social justice in their sermons. At Anshe Sholom B'nai Israel, located in a gentrified Chicago neighborhood, young adults make up the majority in their Modern Orthodox synagogue. Every Friday night, after services led by a highly respected young rabbi, the congregants host Shabbat dinners in their homes, carefully ensuring that each of the fifty or so attendees has a place to dine.

Individuals at each congregation express their Jewish identities through a variety of actions. Young adults across denominations spoke about the importance of attending religious services, performing home-based rituals, participating in volunteer opportunities, engaging in social events, pursuing education, and cultivating personal relationships with peers and congregational leaders. The relative import that individuals bestowed on these activities tended to fall along denominational lines.

The majority of congregants at Anshe Sholom B'nai Israel described their lives as revolving around their synagogue community. They spoke about the role of God in their daily lives. Individuals sought opportunities to focus on their personal religious commitments in a communal context. Most attend religious services on both Friday evenings and Saturday mornings and regularly have Shabbat meals with community members. They maintain Jewish dietary restrictions and follow behav-

ioral laws and customs in their daily lives according to a widely articulated community standard. Some also attend classes and lectures,
participate in volunteer opportunities, and are members of committees.
Most of the young adults in this community are newly married couples,
although there is also a small group of single people. Almost every congregant lives within walking distance of the synagogue (so they can attend services while adhering to the Jewish law that forbids travel on
Shabbat).

At Bnai Jeshurun, large numbers of young adults attend Friday evening services regularly, while far fewer participate on Saturday mornings. Many congregate independently to share Shabbat meals. Once a
month, five hundred or more young adults attend a "Singles Oneg," a
mixer with cookies, following the Friday evening service. This event
has a reputation as a "meat market" and tends to attract individuals
outside of the core community of young adults. The size of the core
community is much smaller; approximately thirty individuals regularly
take part in volunteer opportunities, enroll in classes, and serve on committees. Members of this core group spoke of the importance of their
relationships with congregational leaders. They have proactively
formed a monthly gathering with the young female rabbi. These individuals spoke about the importance of finding God in their lives. Some
young adults live close to the synagogue, while others travel a great
distance to attend.

Religiosity is not a priority for many of the members of Steven S.
Wise Temple's Young Congregation. During the interviews and at
events, neither God nor religious practices typically emerged as topics
of interest or concern. These young adults only celebrate Shabbat spo-
radically, and few adhere to dietary laws. Because of the location of the
synagogue and the nature of traffic in Los Angeles, the Friday evening
service at six thirty is virtually impossible for working young adults to
attend and very few do. Yet some Young Congregants drive as far as
forty miles to participate in other SSWT events.

Instead of ritual observance, the emphasis of the group is on community building. Young adults show their commitment by taking on
leadership roles within an elaborate organization of boards and committees. Every month, the group offers at least three events: a cocktail
party at a fashionable bar, an opportunity to volunteer, and an educational program. Both single and married people are always invited, re-

flecting members' apprehensions about gaining the reputation as a "singles" group.

At each synagogue, members found creative ways to facilitate regular intergenerational communication between congregational members, staff, and leadership. At Bnai Jeshurun, for example, new members are assigned mentors who help to integrate them into the community. At each event organized by SSWT's Young Congregation, committee members are given the responsibility of welcoming and integrating prospective members. After religious services at Anshe Sholom B'nai Israel, new people are encouraged to return to a member's home for a Shabbat meal.

Young adults at each congregation felt empowered to assert their ideas and make them manifest. At SSWT, Young Congregants formed an education committee, designed a learning series called "Everything You Never Learned at Hebrew School," and found a teacher for the course. At ASBI, a group of individuals started an alternative worship service, where they experiment with emerging forms of Orthodox feminist practices. At BJ, an informal group of young people organized and formed an affinity group called a *havurah*, which meets monthly for social and educational purposes.

Whether young adults are in the majority as they are at ASBI, integrated into an intergenerational congregation as they are at BJ, or represent a subgroup within a larger congregation, as at SSWT, each Jewish congregation was conscientiously focused on helping young adults feel welcome.

LESSONS LEARNED

This research was designed to be both descriptive and proscriptive. It is a response to congregational leaders who are concerned by the lack of organizational affiliation among young adults, and who are interested in engaging members of this population. Rather than questioning people with no affiliation about their lack of interest, we sought to investigate exceptional individuals and congregations. In this section, we summarize our findings in terms of lessons learned.

*Young adults want to feel that their presence is valued.* Those who are interested in congregational life are aware that they are exceptional—they know that the majority of young adults are not interested in religious affiliation. As such, those who participate want to be acknowledged for their unusual commitment and interest. Every congregation we studied recognized that young adults make an important contribution to congregational life.

Young congregants expressed the value of having a physical space within the place of worship for young-adult programs and the importance of having specifically designated funding. Some congregations in this study underwrite the activities of the young-adult group as a way to acknowledge the importance of continuity based on the participation of the next generation. When applicable, congregations reduced fees for activities and memberships, and had a policy of turning no one away for lack of funds.

Many congregations have a staff person who is specifically hired to coordinate young-adult programming. We found that funding a charismatic young person, whose role is dedicated to cultivating community, is a very effective way to acknowledge and engage young adults.

*Young adults want a sense of ownership in their congregations.* They value opportunities to assume leadership roles within their peer group and welcome chances to move into leadership roles in the larger congregation. While they comfortably seek guidance from the elders in the community, they appreciate the responsibility and autonomy to determine their group's future. We found that congregations engendered a sense of ownership by enabling young congregants to create and plan their own events. Leadership positions were made available to young congregants both within their peer group and within the larger congregation. Active participants were appreciated frequently for their contributions and their continued involvement was encouraged. Most of the congregations also purposefully hired young congregants to serve as staff members and educators as a way to engage them in numerous aspects of congregational life.

*Young adults' interests in religion are multifaceted.* For some, their deep sense of belonging comes from being a part of a community. They want to connect with others who are also articulating a sense of self. Some young adults desire emotional support and guidance. Some want their religious group to be a place where they can develop their professional and social networks. Many single young adults participate in congregations in the hope of meeting a life-partner. Despite that, most actively deplore and avoid specifically "singles" oriented events (even when they are single and looking for a relationship).

Many young adults want to learn about increasing their practice of tradition and rituals. Some seek to deepen their relationship with God. Some approach religion through the intellectual study of modern socio-historical texts or the religious canon. Others value the opportunity to effect social change with a group of people who share their values. Still other congregants seek a space for creative religious expression through music, art, writing, or dance.

The congregations we examined offered multiple points of entry, and in doing so created numerous arenas for young congregants to reflect upon and articulate their own religious identities. Many also organized affinity groups so that young congregants can find like-minded peers. Each offered opportunities where young adults can sometimes engage as participants and other times take on the responsibilities of leading.

*Young adults thrive when they are "met where they are."* They do not want to feel judged for their level of religious practice or knowledge. When they do not have a strong base of knowledge, they do not want to feel ashamed. Some said that they were not interested in debating the minute details of observance or tradition, which they asserted is often implicitly about judging others. Instead, they want to approach religious practice focused on meaning and intention.

The young adults interviewed did not tend to measure the intensity of their religious identity based on the extent of their religious practice or knowledge. They acknowledged that their level of interest and participation waxes and wanes. While respecting the religious standards of the congregation and their religion at large, many took pride in making their own choices based on personal factors such as: level of knowledge, peer group, and religious upbringing. Each of the congregations effectively took young adults' differing commitments to religious observance and levels of religious education into account.

*Young adults welcome opportunities to feel emotionally affected.* They want to feel moved by music, a connection to their history, a sense of cultural heritage, and nostalgia. Congregants described their positive reaction to worship services in which the leaders created space that enabled them to be emotionally affected. They spoke of the importance of feeling like a participant, rather than an audience member. Both peer- and clergy-led services effectively engaged the young adults we interviewed.

Congregational leaders who are accessible and engaging are especially attractive to young adults. Many young adults look to congregational elders as role models whom they wish to emulate. Some turn to religious leaders for personal and religious guidance. They seek leaders who show genuine interest in them as individuals. They want to be greeted and to feel welcomed. They respond to knowledgeable teachers with whom they share mutual respect and who do not speak to them in an excessively dogmatic or condescending manner.

Across faiths, young adults are seeking religious relevance in their daily lives. In their congregations, they want an environment that encourages questioning and provides learning opportunities. They desire honest discussion and appreciate when topics are relevant to their daily lives. They want an accessible atmosphere that is consistent with the religious standards of the congregation.

*Young adults respond to a theoretical and practical balance between the particular and the universal.* Every individual interviewed acknowledged that there are many ways to believe in God and to live a religious life. Young adults appreciate when leaders and members refrain from disparaging other religious traditions and denominations. At the same time, they are attracted to congregations in which they are free to think critically and analytically.

Young adults appreciate an acknowledgement of the existence of individual differences such as class, race, gender, and sexual orientation. They do not want to feel cloistered from the outside world. Instead, they want to be able to share their spiritual interests with peers of different faiths. Through the articulation of similarities and differences, they deepen a sense of self as a member of their own faith.

While they differ organizationally, congregations that are successfully attracting young adults share numerous characteristics in terms of approach. Across geographic locations, the Catholic, Jewish, Protestant, and Muslim young adults in this study share more in common than they differ in terms of their religious needs, desires, and values. We found that generational similarities surpass religious differences. As a result, congregations would do well to look across traditions for lessons about engaging young adults in congregational life.

# Section Three

Passing on the Faith to the Next
Generation of Jews

# BJ: A PORTRAIT OF A REVITALIZED SYNAGOGUE

*Rabbi J. Rolando Matalon*

I am pleased to be here to talk about the work that my congregation, located on the Upper West Side of Manhattan in New York City, has been doing for the past eighteen years. Congregation Bnai Jeshurun (BJ) was founded in 1825. Until then, the only synagogue in New York City was a Spanish-Portuguese synagogue, which observed Judaism according to the customs of Sephardic Jews. In 1825, there were enough Eastern European Jews to permit the founding of their own synagogue, where they could observe Judaism according to their own customs. Originally Orthodox, this active and prominent community was eventually served by rabbis belonging to the three major religious movements in Judaism: Orthodox, Reform, and Conservative.

In the 1970s and early 1980s, Bnai Jeshurun suffered a severe decline and was faced with having almost no members, a beautiful but decrepit building, and almost no life. In 1985, a remarkable rabbi was invited to revitalize this community: Rabbi Marshall Meyer, who was my teacher and mentor. He had been a disciple of Rabbi Abraham Joshua Heschel, one of the great Jewish thinkers and activists of the twentieth century. Rabbi Meyer had spent twenty-five years in Argentina, creating new Jewish life, including a new-paradigm synagogue and a rabbinical seminary that trained rabbis who eventually spread throughout the continent, attracting thousands of Jews to an exciting and relevant Judaism, especially young people who brought their parents to a meaningful Jewish religious life. Rabbi Meyer was very active in the struggle for human rights in Argentina from 1976 to 1983 during the years of the military dictatorship that caused the disappearance and the murder of thousands of people. He incorporated into religious life what is known as spiritual activism. After twenty-five years in Argentina, Rabbi Meyer accepted the challenge of reviving Bnai Jeshurun and returned to New York in 1985.

I had the privilege to work with him almost from the beginning and he was a great mentor and teacher. I shared the spiritual leadership of BJ with him until his untimely death at the age of sixty-three in 1993. This community, which regenerated itself in 1985, experienced rapid growth, particularly a few years after its new beginning. BJ's sanctuary was very pretty but it had been abandoned and was damaged. The sanctuary was filled with pews, was dark, and had a very high podium: it was not conducive to an uplifting communal spiritual experience. In 1991, a large section of the plaster ceiling collapsed and the synagogue building had to be closed. Two blocks away, a Methodist Church with which we had been in conversation about sharing some social-justice programs invited us to gather in their large sanctuary. We all thought it would be for just a few months and we moved into the Church of St. Paul and St. Andrew, whose congregation welcomed us with generous hospitality and tremendous warmth. That was the beginning of a wonderful and fruitful cooperation between the church and the synagogue which continues today.

From the time we moved into the church in 1991, our growth became geometric: every week more and more people came. Several years later our own sanctuary was repaired, the high bimah was removed, and the pews were replaced with chairs so we could rearrange the space in any way we wanted. However, there wasn't enough space to accommodate the increasing number of people, so we were forced to hold two overlapping services, one in the synagogue and one in the church. Now the most salient point about this revitalized congregation is not the number of people but rather the level of commitment and involvement of the people who come. That is unusual, compared to other liberal Jewish congregations. The number of people who report that BJ is central to how they organize their lives and the way they define their identity is high, and includes people who decided to remain in Manhattan, some under financial pressures and others with expanded families in small apartments, so as to be able to remain part of the BJ community. A number of families decided to move out but commute in from West-chester or New Jersey; among those there are some that moved back to the neighborhood for the sake of living in proximity to the community. Another striking feature of our community is its inclusiveness and di-versity in terms of age-groups represented: there are singles and fami-lies, straight people and gay people, members with different levels of income, and people in the congregation who grew up with very strong Jewish backgrounds as well as those who are completely new to an ac-tive Jewish life and to any type of serious commitment to Jewish learn-ing and Jewish involvement.

Our community became a model for many around the country, and people started to come and try to learn something from our experience that they could take to their own congregations and apply to their own settings. We have tried to understand what principles are operative at the core of our community. We did so anecdotally for a number of years and at some point it became clear that we needed to engage in a study that was more than anecdotal in order to uncover those principles, so they could be shared with other congregations and enable them—not to copy or emulate our methods, but rather to apply and adapt our insights freely to their own congregations as they try to revitalize their own syn-agogues. A cultural anthropologist, Ayala Fader, and an ethnomusicol-ogist, Mark Kligman, were engaged to conduct the study, mounted in partnership with the Righteous Persons Foundation and Synagogue 2000. The study began in September 2000 and concluded in May 2001, involving extensive interviews with me and my colleagues, the presi-dent and members of the Board of Trustees, members of the staff, and a variety of members representing different constituencies within the congregation. This was not a sociological study but an ethnographic study. The overarching conclusion of the study is that BJ is driven by a vision of Judaism that sees Jewish life as a continuous search for a con-nection to the divine or to a life lived in the presence of the divine: through prayer, through observance, through the study of Torah and our sacred texts, through *gemilut hassadim*—acts of loving-kindness per-formed for others—and through social justice. A large percentage of our congregation has adopted this vision as their own.

The study identifies four elements that are at the core of our identity as a congregation and our experience:

1) The centrality of the experience of the divine.
2) The expectation of an engaged participatory membership.

3) An approach to Jewish practice in which existing materials are used and combined in a way that creates something new and unexpected.

4) A rabbi-led congregational structure.

## 1) The Centrality of the Experience of the Divine

Essential for us is to experience the divine, not just to talk about God. We strive for this through prayer, Jewish observance, study, and acts of kindness and social justice.

### Prayer

Our community is organized in such a way that the experience of prayer is at the center. Friday evenings and Shabbat mornings find our community gathered together to pray and to celebrate. During the week the community is fragmented in the pursuit of many different activities. There are those who participate in our classes, those who visit the sick or comfort those in mourning, those who volunteer in our homeless shelter, those who tutor children in public school, and those who come to volunteer in our office. The community is active but fragmented, and on Shabbat the whole community comes together and that becomes the central experience of the community. I see it as a flower with many petals that join at the center: the center of the flower is our Shabbat.

Our experience of prayer focuses on the emotional and personal meaning of prayer. It is not prayer by rote, it is prayer that is engaged. It is, as Rabbi Heschel says, "prayer that matters." Our prayer service is not a gimmick to bring people to the synagogue. It is not a gimmick for Jewish continuity so that there will be Jews in the next generations, or a gimmick for social purposes—to create a venue for people to meet and to generate social bonds. All these are by-products. For us prayer is "prayer that matters" as an experience in and of itself. We are very happy about all the by-products of our prayer services, but our goal is to generate an experience of prayer that is transformative, touches the soul, and is engaging. Our members are often moved by the experience and they want to come again, and eventually they engage in other Jewish activities that are important as well, such as study and observance, doing for others, and so on.

In many synagogues, because people feel so uncomfortable and inadequate when faced with Jewish prayer, the rabbis turn the service into a class. We have classes on Jewish prayer during the week to uncover the meaning, history, and theology of the prayers, but we don't teach prayer during prayer. We pray during prayer. In our synagogue, the spiritual leaders are involved in prayer ourselves, which should be obvious, but unfortunately is not. We make every effort to pray, and when we are not praying we're struggling to pray, we're praying that we may be able to pray. We often tell people that we need a long service in order to get just a few seconds of real connection, of real prayer, of real opening of the soul. We view prayer services as the exercising of our spiritual muscles to be able to get there for just a little bit.

One of our models and great teachers is Rabbi Abraham Joshua Heschel, who wrote a book about prayer entitled *Man's Quests for God*, now reprinted as *Quest for God*. I recommend it equally to Jews, Christians, and Muslims. It is a profound book and I want to quote just briefly from it: "An atmosphere of prayer is not created by ceremonies, by gimmicks, or speeches, but by the example of prayer, by a person who prays, you create the atmosphere not around you but within you. I am a congregant," he says, "and I know from personal experience how different this situation is when the Rabbi is concerned with prayer instead of how many people attend the service, the difference in a service in which a rabbi comes prepared to respond to thirty centuries of Jewish experience, and the one in which he comes to review the book of the month and the news of the day."

Our prayer has some ecstatic moments or ecstatic elements, where people clap and rise from their seats and dance. We are very aware of the dangers that predictability and rote repetition pose to genuine prayer. It is not unusual to see people who are singing very loud, and clapping, and standing, and in some cases crying, whether tears of pain or tears of joy. People know that it is permitted to let the spirit flow, to let the soul go wherever it needs to go and be touched, we hope, by the presence of God or by the presence of community, or, at other times, by somebody who puts an arm around the person who is in need of a hug. One day my colleague and I were explaining our vision of prayer, and it was at the end of a service and we were trying to get people to that place where everything flows, and we were quite passionate about it. When the service ended a person approached us and said, "You really believe this stuff, don't you?"

*Jewish Practice*

Another element in this first principle of the centrality of the experience of the divine is Jewish practice. We are a progressive community and, at the same time, we are fairly traditional in that we are committed to highlighting the relevance of Jewish observance and practice as an opening to the experience of God. There are members who are not knowledgeable or who are not familiar with the language of ritual or observance; yet we urge them to try to reclaim our symbolic language of ritual and practice as a vehicle to search for God's presence. We invite people to learn and to consider taking on practices, to consider experimenting. Our members know that they find themselves in an atmosphere of tolerance where individual differences and choices are respected. They know that not everyone is in the same place and that we don't expect everybody to be in the same place. We don't expect everybody's experience of Shabbat to be the same, but we want everybody to try and to struggle with its meanings and its possibilities. We ask people to demand much of themselves and to push themselves.

We strive to create an environment where questions about Jewish observance and Jewish law are fostered and valued; we don't believe that people must blindly obey the rules of Jewish law. At BJ people can bring their questions and share them. At times, we have had support groups, for instance, for people who are taking on the discipline of the Jewish dietary laws. People enjoy discussing with others who currently are or have been on the same path. What unites us at BJ is not that our observance is identical and uniform, but rather that we are willing to struggle and to consider climbing to the next level. We are all climbing together. There is a movement toward a more committed, more responsible Jewish experience. It is essential for us to move beyond the details of religious behaviorism: Jewish observance is not just about observing, but about experiencing God in the observance, in the walking. The word for Jewish law is *Halakhah*, which comes from the verb *to walk*. As we walk, meanings open up; as we walk, transformations happen. Our goal is not just to observe in a behavioral way, but to observe in a way that involves the heart and the mind.

*Study*

Our experience of study is similarly oriented in that we ask people to take upon themselves a serious commitment to study as an avenue to the experience of God. Study has for us a number of different goals. First, to know: to be acquainted with our history, our texts, and our traditions. To know also in order to expand our awareness: the more we know, the more we expand our awareness of God's work in the world. Second, to know what to do and how to act: Judaism is a path, a practice, and therefore we have to learn in order to know what to do. Jewish law is intricate and complex; we have to learn in order to know what is essential and what is secondary, where we can be flexible, where we shouldn't be flexible. And third, to study, as an act of devotion. When we study, engaging both our minds and our souls, there comes a moment when our intellects and our souls become aligned. In devotional study we meet God through text, reflection, and discussion. We can therefore have an experience of the divine not just through prayer and not just through observance, but also through our study. When our souls and our minds open, there is insight. God flows in to our minds and our souls, and there is an experience of growth and transformation through study. Although we are not at all anti-rationalists, at BJ our predilection is for texts that engage the intellect at the same time as they open the heart and the soul. We call these devotional texts.

*Social Responsibility*

Another area where we experience the presence of God is in the exercise of social responsibility, that is, through social justice and social action. We tell our members that for prayer to be of consequence, our lives have to be devoted to doing God's work in the world. We are in God's presence not just within the walls of the synagogue and at the time of prayer or study. Our prayer has to have a consequence in the way in which we live our lives. We therefore ask people to commit to acts of loving-kindness toward other people in the community, toward people who are in need of support at times of personal difficulty, such as illness or recovery or loss. We are a large community and there are always people who face challenging circumstances. We ask members to do for others in the community and also to do for others outside our own community whether it be at our shelter for the homeless, our weekly soup kitchen, or elsewhere. BJ has in place a serious social-justice program that involves hundreds of volunteers in advocacy and action concerning issues such as homelessness, poverty, healthcare, children at risk, women's rights, and the environment.

## 2) The Expectation of an Engaged Participatory Membership

Our mission statement at BJ is summarized in the words "To Inspire and To Require." We often remind people not to expect the rabbis to do the praying for them: the rabbi's role is to lead, to show the way, to excite the congregation about the possibility of prayer, but each member has to make his or her own efforts at prayer. People are reminded that if they attend services but remain passive, they deprive the whole community of the fruits of their struggle to pray. A sacred community is created when every person participates in it. Not just in prayer, but in all other areas people are urged to jump in, to involve themselves personally, to be responsible Jews. But a synagogue community is not a free-for-all.

At the same time we acknowledge that there are those who are not ready or able to participate, and that is fine. There may be people who are not able to actively participate because of a life situation in which they need to receive and are not in a position to participate, whether spiritually, emotionally, or financially. We believe that a community, as opposed to the market, must make room for asymmetric exchanges: at any given time some receive more than they give while others give more than they receive. Years ago, people who wanted to join as members of BJ were asked to fill out a membership form and to submit it with a check to cover the required membership fees. That is the traditional way to do it. It became clear to us that this impersonal system was antithetical to our vision of community: we didn't know who the new members were and what motivated them to join us, and they didn't necessarily know the values of the community and the spiritual requirements of membership. So we created a membership orientation process that consists of three sessions led by staff and members of the congregation, which presents our history, our philosophy, our programs, and is careful to welcome personally and integrate new members into the larger community. Now people know that being a BJ member is not just showing up occasionally, paying membership dues, and being entitled to a series of services. Rather, members pay for the privilege of serving. We remind them that they come to BJ to do something that is completely counterintuitive: you don't pay to be served, you pay for the privilege to serve. And people love that!

Tze'irim (Hebrew for "young people") was formed to galvanize the community of people within their twenties and thirties (singles and couples) at Bnai Jeshurun. Time and time again it became clear, through conversations and meetings, that this group of people was looking to "find each other" in the midst of the larger community. Continually, people in this age group voice the desire to participate in activities with each other (Shabbat, learning, social-justice work) as long as they can be within a group of people of a similar age. Over the last couple of years, the main focus of Tze'irim events has been creating Shabbat dinner opportunities—in more intimate settings as well as larger communal settings. This year, the group has committed to holding one event a month whether a Shabbat dinner (at home or at BJ), a hike, or a *havdalah* to ritually mark the end of the Shabbat with song, study, and celebration. The group is also trying to take on the responsibility of cooking for our five-night-a-week shelter for the homeless on a monthly basis. This year we began a listserve for Tze'irim and now we have over 150 members.

## 3) Approach to Jewish Practice

Our approach to Jewish practice consists of combining existing materials from different traditions within Judaism. Old customs join with new ones, North African traditions with Eastern European ones. We practice what is known as *bricolage*. We bring all these pieces together to create something new and unexpected. At BJ there is an expectation of innovation and freshness. We creatively borrow from here and there. The best example is our approach to liturgical music: we utilize melodies from different parts of the Jewish tradition, historically and also geographically, and we also borrow from other traditions. We are very fond of taking spiritual chants that are meaningful in other faith traditions and adapting them to our own needs. These melodies or chants are already infused with spiritual meaning within another tradition. We believe that, in this era of globalization, this type of creative borrowing links us and places us into dialogue with other faith traditions.

## 4) A Rabbi-led Institutional Structure

Such a structure is definitely not normative within the American Jewish Synagogue. Rabbis are hired and fired by boards who run the affairs of the synagogue and tell the rabbi what to do. By contrast, BJ is a rabbi-led institution. While the rabbis, the board of trustees, and the community enjoy a partnership and a fruitful exchange, the rabbis are clearly the guides and they are trusted to put forth the vision and to lead the congregation. At BJ, the rabbis actively participate in all board meetings; BJ doesn't have a ritual committee that makes decisions regarding liturgy and synagogue practice. What stifles many Jewish congregations in America is the fact that rabbis are dictated to by their boards.

Each of these four core principles represents the bridging of categories that are usually seen as being mutually exclusive:

authenticity and innovation
responsibility and choice
tradition and change
authority of the rabbis and democracy

By holding together these polarities, or by riding out the tension between them, BJ creates a unique culture and ethos of creativity, restlessness, and transformation. Creativity, restlessness, and transformation, together with passion and joy, are the foundations of a meaningful religious life.

# CURRENT EXPRESSIONS OF AMERICAN JEWISH IDENTITY: AN ANALYSIS OF 114 TEENAGERS

*Philip Schwadel*

This chapter explores the characteristics of 114 American teenagers' Jewish identities using data from the National Study of Youth and Religion (NSYR).[1] The NSYR includes a telephone survey of a nationally representative sample of 3,290 adolescents aged 13 to 17. Jewish teenagers were over-sampled, resulting in a total of 3,370 teenage participants. Of the NSYR teens surveyed, 141 have at least one Jewish parent and 114 of them identify as Jewish. The NSYR also includes in-depth face-to-face interviews with a total of 267 U.S. teens: 23 who have at least one Jewish parent and 18 who identify as Jewish. The following analysis draws upon quantitative data from the 114 teens who identified themselves as Jewish in the face-to-face interviews.

## EXPRESSIONS OF JEWISH IDENTITY

The Jewish research participants expressed their Jewish identities predominantly through their Jewish communal participation or civic involvement. Relationships with other Jews are extremely important to the teens surveyed. They tend to value the concept of "the Jewish community." Based on their understanding of the importance of performing *mitvot* (good deeds) and facilitating *tikkun olam* (repair of the world), many Jewish teens articulated their Jewish and non-Jewish civic involvement as an expression of their Jewish identities. Few Jewish teens, however, conveyed their Jewish identities in what are generally considered traditional forms of religious expression.

These findings were discerned by asking teens how important or unimportant religious faith is in shaping how they live their daily lives.[2] Only 16 percent of Jewish teens surveyed said religious faith is very or extremely important in shaping their daily lives, compared to 41 percent of the Catholic teens and 65 percent of Protestant teens (table 1). During an interview, one Jewish teen explained: "I don't even think about religion often." This was a common sentiment among those interviewed. Another Jewish teen said: "I don't feel really religious. . . . I'm only like a part-time believer type thing." Still another explained that

Table 1   Traditional religious beliefs and activities, ages 13–17 (percentages)

|  | Jewish | Catholic | Protestant | All teens |
|---|---|---|---|---|
| Faith is very/extremely important in shaping daily life | 16 | 41 | 65 | 51 |
| Faith is very/extremely important in shaping major life decisions | 24 | 41 | 63 | 50 |
| Definitely believe in God | 70 | 85 | 93 | 85 |
| Unsure about belief in God | 27 | 14 | 6 | 12 |
| God is a personal being involved in the lives of people today | 37 | 66 | 77 | 68 |
| God is not personal, but something like a cosmic life force | 36 | 15 | 9 | 15 |
| Definitely believe in the possibility of divine miracles from God | 25 | 55 | 74 | 61 |
| Pray alone a few times a week or more | 11 | 49 | 63 | 53 |
| Read the scriptures alone once a week or more | 8 | 13 | 35 | 26 |
| Attend religious services at least once a month | 33 | 58 | 65 | 60 |
| Okay to pick and choose religious beliefs | 76 | 55 | 40 | 47 |
| Okay to practice other religions | 76 | 59 | 43 | 53 |
| N | 114 | 819 | 1,792 | 3,370 |

Source: National Study of Youth and Religion 2002–2003.

being Jewish is "important in the fact I meet friends and like I meet people I can talk to but I don't think it's like very important in the fact that I'm like always praying all the time." Other Jewish teens expressed a disbelief in religion in general, such as a thirteen-year-old boy who said that religion is "not important . . . because it's all made up." Compared to the Christian teens surveyed, Jewish teens are less likely to hold conventional religious beliefs or to participate in congregations. Some Jewish teens even articulated antipathy toward religion.

Regardless of their geographic location, their Jewish education, or their parents' denominational affiliation, most Jewish teenagers surveyed are not particularly interested in what they consider the religious aspects of Judaism. Most said that religious faith is neither a daily source of inspiration nor a vital aspect of their decision-making about major life issues. Only 24 percent of the Jewish research participants said religious faith is very or extremely important in shaping their major life decisions, compared to 41 percent of Catholic teens and 63 percent of Protestant teens (table 1). As one Jewish teen put it: "I say I'm Jewish, but it's not like I live every day like I'm Jewish."

The Jewish teens surveyed expressed a strong sense of religious individualism. More than three-quarters of the Jewish teenagers said it is okay to pick and choose religious beliefs. The same number would approve of practicing religions other than Judaism (table 1). One Jewish boy said that "no one" influenced his ideas about religion. He explained that he is solely responsible for his religious beliefs and his relationship with the supernatural. A sixteen-year-old Jewish girl believes that it is okay to pick and choose religious beliefs "because like if you don't agree with something then you shouldn't have to follow it." In contrast, far fewer Christian teens expressed such internally driven authority: 55 percent of Catholics and 40 percent of Protestants say it is okay to pick and choose religious beliefs, and 59 percent of Catholics and 43 percent of Protestants say it is okay to practice other religions.

The Jewish teens surveyed were considerably less likely than the Christian teens to regularly attend religious services. One-third of Jewish teens attend synagogue at least once a month, whereas 58 percent of Catholic teens and almost two-thirds of Protestant teens report monthly church attendance (table 1).[3] Jewish teens reported that their synagogue attendance declined further after their bar or bat mitzvah ceremony. Twenty percent of the sixteen- and seventeen-year-old Jewish teens surveyed said they never attend religious services, while only 6 percent of thirteen-, fourteen- and fifteen-year-old Jewish teens never attend. One Jewish teen justified his lack of synagogue attendance in this way: "I mean I think I could communicate with God without having to go [to synagogue] every Saturday and doing specific prayers. Like I feel like I have a connection without being organized in this group."

While Jewish teens are not very likely to adhere to traditional religious beliefs or to participate in synagogue, they strongly value their Jewish identities. Jewish teens are New Yorkers, Californians, Texans, and proud residents of every other state. They are jocks, nerds, geeks, freaks, and popular kids. They are also Jewish, and most consider their Jewish identities to be central to their perception of themselves.

## CENTRALITY OF JEWISH COMMUNITY

Many of the Jewish teens surveyed participate in Jewish programs and events. For most of these Jewish teens, their involvement is focused on in-group social networks. The majority of Jewish teens surveyed are active in organized Jewish activities: 55 percent of Jewish teens say they have taken classes in the last two years to study Hebrew, Jewish history and traditions, or modern Jewish life. Approximately one-third are currently involved in Jewish youth groups (table 2). About one-half of the Jewish teens have also been campers at Jewish summer camps (table 2). Many Jewish teens who are not interested in religiosity have vibrant informal and formal Jewish affiliations. This attitude is exemplified by a Jewish teen who feels that religion is "not very important." Despite that opinion, she had a bat mitzvah, is highly active in a Jewish youth group, and said being Jewish is important to her.

For the Jewish teens surveyed, religious observance is not the focus of their Jewish involvement. A girl who is highly active in a Jewish summer camp explained that her camp is "a secular camp and it's a lot of culture, a lot of Jewish culture, so I feel . . . like more part of the culture and not of the religion." Participation in formal and informal Jewish education is more common among teens than attendance at worship services. Jewish teens closely resemble non-Jewish teens in their patterns of enrollment at Sunday school, youth-group participation and summer-camp attendance, yet the meaning they give to those experiences may differ.

Most of the Jewish teens in the sample had Jewish educational experiences that included a bar or bat mitzvah. Barry Kosmin notes that the bar or bat mitzvah "is one of the most significant ways parents can publicly affirm their identity as Jews at this life stage."[4] Eighty-one percent of the Jewish teenagers publicly affirmed their Jewish identities in that way (table 2) and, since some of the teens are only thirteen-year-olds, it is likely that more than 81 percent will eventually have a bar or bat

**Table 2  Religious activities revisited, ages 13–17 (percentages)**

|  | Jewish | Catholic | Protestant | All teens |
|---|---|---|---|---|
| Had a bar mitzvah or bat mitzvah | 81 | — | — | — |
| Regularly practice Jewish traditions observing the Sabbath | 48 | — | — | — |
| Taken classes in last two years to study Hebrew, Jewish history, traditions, or modern Jewish life | 55 | — | — | — |
| Attended a religious Sunday school a few times a month or more in last year | 39 | 38 | 61 | 47 |
| Currently involved in any religious youth group | 34 | 24 | 52 | 38 |
| Ever been a camper at a summer camp run by a religious organization | 48 | 24 | 50 | 39 |
| Celebrated Chanukah in last year | 100 | — | — | — |
| Celebrated Passover in last year | 98 | — | — | — |
| Celebrated Rosh Hashanah in last year | 89 | — | — | — |
| Celebrated Yom Kippur in last year | 91 | — | — | — |
| Celebrated Simkhat Torah in last year | 42 | — | — | — |
| Celebrated Sukkot in last year | 54 | — | — | — |
| Organized volunteer work or community service occasionally or more often in last year | 52 | 34 | 31 | 33 |
| Involved in any political activities in last two years | 30 | 8 | 12 | 11 |
| N | 114 | 819 | 1,792 | 3,370 |

*Source:* National Study of Youth and Religion 2002–2003.

mitzvah. A bar- or bat-mitzvah ceremony was very meaningful for some teens in the sample. A girl recalled, "I loved my bat mitzvah. . . . I had to work really hard and did my whole Torah portion and I did some Haftorah. . . . I loved the service, even though I was really nervous." For other Jewish teens, the significance of the event centered on family and community, rather than on the performance of religious tradition. The focus on family was a motivating factor for one girl who speculated: "If I didn't do it I don't think I would have been devastated but I guess maybe it was important for my family." Whatever the focus of the ceremony, most Jewish teens in the sample participated in this rite of passage; even the thirteen-year-old boy who believes that religion is "all made up" had recently had a bar mitzvah.

One-half of Jewish teens in the sample said that they observed Shabbat (the Sabbath) (table 2). Most observe Shabbat at home, rather than through synagogue attendance. As with their bar- and bat-mitzvah ceremonies, the focus of Shabbat for most of the teens is on family rather than religious observance. One teen explained that he does not attend synagogue more than a few times a year and does not consider himself to be a religious person, but on many Friday nights his family has a Shabbat dinner and his father "tries to get like Jewish philosophical discussions going."

The Jewish holidays are also significant events for the Jewish teens in the sample. Almost all celebrate Chanukah and Passover, and the vast majority of them also celebrate the High Holy Days—Yom Kippur and Rosh Hashanah (table 2).[5] About half of the teens surveyed celebrate Simchat Torah and Sukkot (table 2). For many Jewish teens surveyed, the celebration of holidays marks their only Jewish engagement after their bar- or bat-mitzvah ceremony. Many of these holidays are traditionally centered at home. Consequently, some teens who never attend synagogue still observe the Jewish holidays.

Most of the Jewish teens see Jewish holidays as significant family gatherings rather than expressions of religious observance. One teen explained: "For Chanukah or Passover we light candles . . . or we have a seder or dinner . . . and probably get together with family." This teen, like many others, did not mention the religious significance of the holiday. Instead, she focused on the importance of being with her family. Many other Jewish teens expressed the importance of celebrating the holidays with family and friends—even those who feel little connection to religiosity. One girl talked about how Jewish holidays help bring her family together. She said,

> Religious holidays [are] always a time to see . . . extended family. So it's always nice. So like for Passover, we would go to our cousins' house and that's like a time to see everybody. So it's always nice, it's like having Thanksgiving all the time.

Many of the Jewish teenagers spoke of the holidays as secular, celebratory events, akin to Thanksgiving or the Fourth of July.

The significance of Jewish family and friends is also evident in Jewish teenagers' discussions of their future family plans. Many Jewish teens in the sample expect to marry other Jews and to raise their children Jewish. Even those teens who do not consider themselves religious spoke about the importance of the Jewish family and of having Jewish friends. One teen explained that she is generally more comfortable around Jews. She said, "I feel like the Jewish ones are more understanding." While she does not consider herself to be a religious person, she talked about her desire to marry a Jew.

A number of Jewish girls reported that their mothers advised them to marry a Jew because it would be "easier." One indicated that her mother would prefer that she marry "a nonreligious non-Jew [rather] than a really religious Jew." This specificity demonstrates how the importance of shared ethnic ties, rather than religious beliefs, were the focus of that mother's advice. Some Jewish boys also spoke about the importance of the Jewish family. One boy hoped to raise his children as Jews, but felt that if they "didn't believe in it by the time they were you know in their teens it wouldn't necessarily bother me." The desire to marry Jews and raise Jewish children emerged as a significant expression of Jewish identity among the teens surveyed.

Jewish teens repeatedly mentioned the centrality of Jewish friends, family, and the Jewish community in the articulation of their Jewish identities. When asked about the importance of being part of the Jewish religion, a sixteen-year-old Jewish girl from Queens explained the centrality of community with these words: "I think it's important because . . . it makes you closer . . . to people and it makes you bigger, but then again it doesn't necessarily have to do with religion." This teen explained that her closest friends (whom she considers "brothers and sisters") were made through her involvement in a Jewish youth group. When she was younger, her family attended synagogue to celebrate the

High Holy Days. At the time of the interview, she said that she rarely attends religious services, even on the major holidays. She explained: "I'm Jewish, but again I'm not religious at all." As with many of the teens surveyed, relationships with other Jews make up the primary expression of her Jewish identity. The majority of teens interviewed consider being Jewish "important," but claim that "it doesn't necessarily have to do with religion."

## CIVIC ACTIVITY AND HELPING OTHERS

In addition to the significance of relationships with other Jews, the Jewish teenagers surveyed emphasized the importance of helping others as part of their understanding of what it means to be Jewish. They are highly active in civic organizations and many consider their voluntary activity and community service to be an expression of their Jewish identities. The NSYR survey shows that Jewish teenagers are particularly likely to participate in civic activities. More than one-half of Jewish teens said they did organized volunteer work or community service in the previous year (table 2). Conversely, only about one-third of Christian teens reported volunteering or doing community service. Jewish teens are also politically motivated, with 30 percent of Jewish teens having been involved in political activities (not including student government) in the previous two years, compared to 8 percent of Catholic teens and 12 percent of Protestant teens (table 2).

When asked directly, many Jewish teens said their voluntary activities have little to do with their Jewish identities. Instead, they claimed that their sense of responsibility to help others was based on their socioeconomic status.[6] This reflects the fact that most of the Jewish teens surveyed had middle- and upper-middle-class backgrounds.[7] A more complex dynamic emerged when the teens were asked how they became involved in their voluntary activities and with whom they volunteer—Jewish organizations played a large role. For example, one Jewish girl explained that she volunteers because she is "a lot more fortunate . . . than like the lower class." She clarified that she does not volunteer out of a sense of religious obligation. Nevertheless, her primary form of community service is to volunteer in her synagogue's gift shop. Another girl, who rarely attends synagogue and does not consider herself a religious person, has been an active member of a Jewish youth group for five years. As a member of the group, she has attended antiwar protests and performed volunteer work. Additionally, she plans to volunteer as a counselor for the youth group. Yet she too explained that her volunteerism is not performed out of a sense of religious obligation.

Other Jewish teens were more direct about the connection between volunteerism and their Jewish identities. For some, helping others clearly takes on religious significance. Rather than praying or attending synagogue, they focus on performing *mitvot* (acts of loving-kindness) and *tikkun olam* (repair of the world) as an outlet for their religious beliefs and values. One girl asserted that people have an obligation to volunteer. "I guess it's what I've been taught. . . . Volunteering and helping people," she explained, is "one of the main aspects" of Judaism. She spoke about "acts of loving-kindness" and described helping others as "one of the pillars" of Judaism (a fact that impresses her about the Jewish religion). Another Jewish teen said that being Jewish explicitly motivates her voluntary activity. She described the many "talks in Hebrew school about helping others out, doing good deeds." Another Jewish teen explained that her voluntary activities revolve around her synagogue's work in a soup kitchen. She was required, as part of her bat mitzvah training, to do community service. Other Jewish teens also mentioned working to help the poor or homeless through their synagogues. One girl, for example, cooked for the homeless in a synagogue-organized activity. She said, "I did it because for school they wanted you to do a mitzvah project and it just seemed like . . . a good thing to do for a mitzvah project." For many Jewish teens, voluntary activity and community service are important expressions of their Jewish identities.

Many Jewish teens in the sample equated being "a good Jew" with "being a good person." One teen explained, "There's a large Jewish belief about doing mitzvahs or doing good . . . just being like that, being helpful, being nice all the time . . . you know, a good person." Many other Jewish teens echoed these sentiments, such as a teen who explained that "for me Judaism is more of like how you live your life, like how you be a moral person." Jewish teens repeatedly focused on being a good person and helping others as primary aspects of their Jewish identities.

## CONCLUSION

Only a small minority of Jewish teens in the NSYR sample regularly performs religious rituals or attends worship services. Most say religion has little effect on their daily lives. A substantial number of the Jewish teens surveyed are unsure about the existence of God. Some were indifferent or even antagonistic toward religion in general.

Most take a pluralistic and individualistic approach to their religious beliefs and practices. They approve of exploring and practicing other religious traditions and feel entitled to adapt Jewish traditions to suit their needs. Some Jewish teens foresee greater religiosity in their futures. A sixteen-year-old boy who stopped attending synagogue shortly after his bar mitzvah speculated, "I'll probably end up doing [religious activities] again as I get older, just 'cause that just seems the way things work in life." At the time of the survey, most Jewish teens in the sample did not feel obligated by Jewish doctrine.

Instead, the majority of Jewish teenagers in the survey expressed their Jewish identities through formal and informal communal membership. Many Jewish teenagers said that it is essential to have Jewish friends. They expressed the intention to raise their children as Jews. Many of them, especially the girls, hope to marry a Jew. Large numbers belong to Jewish community groups, attend Jewish summer camps, and participate in Jewish youth groups. Jewish holidays are celebrated with a focus on familial connection. Jewish teens expressed a strong connection to the Jewish community.

Jewish teenagers participate in many voluntary and community-service activities, which they often regard as an expression of their Jewish identities. They speak about the importance of helping others and many equate those actions with being "a good Jew." The concept of a mitzvah, or a good deed done out of religious duty, is central to Jewish teenagers' consciousnesses.

Jewish identity is ever changing: Expressions of Jewish identity wax and wane throughout an individual's life. Teens' observance of Shabbat, participation in Jewish organizations, and celebration of Jewish holidays, etc., will be transformed as they grow older. Whether observance of religious rituals will play a greater or lesser role in Jewish teens' futures remains to be seen.

# Section Four

Passing on the Faith to the Next
Generation of Christians

# A Spiritual Crossroads of Europe: The Taizé Community's Adventure with the Young

*Brother John of Taizé*

I stand before you today with a mixture of gratitude and apprehension. Gratitude, because the organizers of this conference saw fit to include the Taizé Community in their program, ostensibly as a "model that retain[s] religious traditions in non-reductive ways while at the same time bridging in an open and dialogical way the ever-increasing religious pluralism of the contemporary world." It is quite something to be considered, even remotely, such a model. So on behalf of my community I thank the organizers for this show of confidence in the life we have been attempting to live for the past sixty-plus years.

At the same time I feel apprehension, because we are constantly aware of the huge gap between what happens around and through us and our own conscious efforts. I am reminded of Brother Roger's audience with Pope Paul VI in 1972. The pope very generously said to the founder of the Taizé Community, "If you have the key to understanding the young, please tell me." Brother Roger immediately replied that he would like to have that key but did not have it, and never would. In one way or another, including through this very conference in which we are now participating, the pope's question continues to be put to us. And Brother Roger's answer more than thirty years ago still expresses our spontaneous reaction today. I would be very happy to give you the key to understanding the spiritual quest of young people at the beginning of this new millennium, but this is far beyond my powers. I will be glad, however, to reflect with you on our attempts to welcome young adults and to share our life with them, in the hope that this will confirm some of your own views and spark in some of you insights to put into practice in your own life and work with the younger generations.

BACKGROUND

Let me give some background to my reflections by briefly recounting something about Taizé. On this side of the Atlantic, many people consider Taizé a type of singing: short phrases, often in Latin, repeated over and over again. Others use the word "Taizé" to refer to a style of communal prayer using these chants, and Scripture readings, in an atmosphere of silence and peace. When these people say "I went to Taizé last night," they mean that they attended a service of this sort, not that they hopped on a plane and spent the previous evening in France.

In Europe, on the other hand, and increasingly now in the United States, Taizé is known as a place of pilgrimage primarily for young adults. Every week throughout most of the year, hundreds and often thousands of visitors—between two and five thousand in the summer months—generally between the ages of seventeen and thirty, visit a tiny village in Burgundy, France, named Taizé, for an experience of prayer and community life. They come from all over the world, spend a week together with many others, and then return to their own homes to continue their own Christian and spiritual journey, each in his or her own way.

While all this is part of the story, what is lacking is the center that unifies these diverse impressions. At the heart of life in the village of Taizé, and the source of the worship and music now known across the world, is a monastic community of just over one hundred brothers from many different countries and from different Christian traditions. In August 1940, with France cut in half by the Nazi invasion, a young man from Switzerland named Roger came to the village of Taizé, first of all to welcome refugees, particularly Jews, who were fleeing the invaders. With his sister, he spent two years together hiding refugees and helping them cross the border into neutral Switzerland. But Roger's reason for coming to Taizé went beyond the immediate political situation: he was motivated by the dream of a community that would be a sign of reconciliation among divided Christians and, as a consequence, become a ferment of peace in a war-torn world.

After two years, Brother Roger was forced to leave Taizé and returned to Switzerland. There he met three other young men who shared his vision. As soon as it became possible, the four men returned to Taizé and began living a life inspired by the great monastic tradition of Western and Eastern Christianity: praying three times a day, working to support themselves, and offering hospitality. In the immediate postwar years, this meant taking in a group of orphaned boys (for whom Brother Roger's sister became the surrogate mother) and visiting a German prisoner-of-war camp located in the vicinity. In 1949, the first seven brothers committed themselves for life to celibacy, material and spiritual sharing, and making their decisions in common.

In the 1950s, Taizé was a place of prayer, work, and hospitality that welcomed clergy and laity concerned about the ecumenical vocation, the search for visible unity among the divided followers of Christ. At the same time, brothers went out to live in small groups in areas of poverty and social division. At that time, the community was already made up of brothers from different Protestant backgrounds. Following the Second Vatican Council, it became possible for Roman Catholics to join the community as well. Today the hundred or so brothers come from some twenty-five different countries; most of them live in Taizé, though there are also small groups located in Brazil, Senegal, South Korea, and Bangladesh.

TAIZÉ AND THE YOUNG

One thing should already be clear from this brief historical overview: Taizé did not begin as a place of meeting for the young; the brothers have never had any formal training in youth ministry. By the late 1950s, some work camps and other gatherings were occasionally organized for young Christians, but it was really the sociocultural changes we associate with the 1960s that gave the impetus to Taizé's adventure with young adults. In the course of the late sixties and early seventies, the numbers of these young adults who visited the hill of Taizé mushroomed. Their motives were incredibly diverse, but they were all searching: searching for a better world, for peace and justice, for a deeper and more relevant faith. They were trying to find their place in society, looking for others with a common vision, perhaps desiring above all to be listened to and to be taken seriously. They came to Taizé as they came to many places, perhaps attracted more specifically by the countercultural ethos of monasticism. They came, went away again, told their friends, and came back in larger numbers. By the early 1970s, during the Easter vacations there were already thousands of young people arriving in this out-of-the-way village in the middle of Burgundy, far from cities and the amenities of modern life.

This sudden influx of the young to a monastic community in rural France, however intriguing in itself, is not to my mind what is most interesting and significant concerning the question that interests us here. Such a phenomenon is not unknown, and in general it disappears as quickly as it arises. The fascinating thing about Taizé is that today, over thirty years later, the coming and going of young visitors shows little or no signs of abating. Those who would explain it by simple so-ciological factors, by a kind of fortuitous match between the tastes of the young and the characteristics of a particular place, will have to re-fine their arguments to take into account the changes over time. The youth of 2004 are not those of 1970, nor indeed those of 1985. If I may hazard a generalization, particularly perilous in this domain, today's young people seem to be less ideological than their predecessors, more fragile, harder to grasp or to subsume under overarching categories; they are less a mass of dough and more a heap of sand. And yet, whether dough or sand, they keep coming to Taizé.

An equally interesting and significant element, not unconnected to the one just mentioned, is the response of the community of brothers to the influx of the young. As already stated, they had no particular train-ing or preparation for youth ministry. In some ways, they were as sur-prised as anyone at the growing number of visitors. And yet they felt it was necessary to respond, to do all that was necessary to offer hospital-ity to those who came knocking at their door. This sometimes required significant and demanding changes in their life. An event that took place at Easter 1971 is often mentioned in this respect. In 1962, a new, larger church had been built for community worship, since the twelfth-century Romanesque church in the village was sometimes filled to over-flowing. Less than ten years later, with three thousand young people expected for Easter, the new church had become too small in its turn. So the brothers knocked down the back wall of their new church and attached a circus tent so that all the worshippers could fit inside. This step was an eloquent sign of Taizé's readiness to place the welcome of the youth over material considerations, a sign that clearly had a great impact on those who came.

Why did the community make welcoming the young such a priority? First and foremost, hospitality is an important human, Christian, and monastic value. In the stranger, Christ himself is welcomed. Second, beginning in the 1960s, the gap between generations was widening as never before. Parents and children found, sometimes with surprise, that they were speaking entirely different languages. In the older generations, fear of the young was often palpable. A conference like this one would have been unthinkable back then. In such a climate, it seemed all the more essential to listen to the younger generations, to allow them to realize that they had a place in society and in the Church. And finally, Brother Roger saw the search of the young, and even their protests, as a "sign of the times" that should be listened to. At a time when the ecumenical movement, after its first flowering, was running the risk of settling down into mere peaceful coexistence, he felt that by listening to the intuitions of the young the entire Church could be helped to find a way forward toward greater authenticity.

Perhaps we can already draw a provisional conclusion from what we have seen so far. Taizé's "success" in attracting young people was not the result of an explicit plan of action, an agenda set out in advance; it was rather a response to their arrival and their aspirations in a way consonant with the life and faith of the community. It was precisely because the adventure with the young was and is seen as meaningful by the brothers in terms of their own understanding of their vocation, that it could also be meaningful to the young visitors. These visitors did not have the impression that they were the "targets" of a conscious and intentional strategy. Instead, they were asked to take part in a joint undertaking that had meaning first of all for the brothers themselves.

PRAYER AND COMMUNITY

Let us now look at some of the aspects of the welcome of the young in Taizé, which may afford further insight into the way the next generation views its religious identity. The experience offered to the young visitors (and the not-so-young: it should be mentioned that although 85 percent are between fifteen and thirty years old, there are also adults and families with children) in Taizé is essentially the core of the brothers' own life—prayer and community.

First of all, prayer. Three times each day the bells start ringing and everything stops. Everybody—permanent residents and visitors—heads for the Church of Reconciliation for a time of common prayer lasting about forty-five minutes. In the evening, the worship is prolonged by meditative singing which can last, for those who wish, until the early hours of the morning. Worship in Taizé is based on the age-old monastic tradition. The services are classical in form, made up of psalms, Scripture readings, intercessions, and, at the center, a long period of silence. When the numbers of visitors began to increase, the community reflected seriously on how to make the prayer more accessible to them, while maintaining the sung, biblical, and meditative quality that has always characterized it. One solution we came up with was the short refrains sung over and over again, first in Latin and then gradually in other languages as well, now associated throughout the world with the name of Taizé. More accessible and shorter scripture readings were chosen, and read in different languages. Instead of entire psalms sung in French, verses are sung in different languages by soloists to which everyone responds with a simple antiphon such as "Alleluia."

If the worship was intentionally and willingly made more accessible to the young, it nonetheless remains the prayer of a monastic community. The young visitors know that it is not a prayer crafted especially for them but that, whether they are present or not, day in day out, the brothers will be in the church praying. To their minds, this gives it a certain authenticity. At the same time, we have discovered that there is often a tendency to underestimate the ability of the younger generation to enter into a form of prayer that may be quite demanding. For example, at the heart of every service in Taizé there are eight or more minutes of total silence—a time to rest in God, to let the words listened to and sung penetrate one's being, a way of keeping worship from becoming routine. In the summer months, when five thousand visitors, mostly young, are in the church, you can still hear a pin drop during this period of silence. The experience never fails to affect people deeply, and it alone should keep us from selling the young short. When they grasp the significance of a spiritual practice, we have found that they are ready and willing to take part.

One misgiving sometimes expressed by those who hear about the prayer style of Taizé is the concern that it plays on the emotions and offers a superficial "high" rather than a deep encounter with the divine. It is true that in Taizé, we have always believed that worship is not just a cerebral process but involves the whole being. As during most of the Christian centuries, and still today in the Eastern Church, liturgy attempts to involve the whole being in a relationship with the Source of all life. In our community, using very simple means (candles, icons, soft lighting, some bricks and some cloth), we attempt to create a space that facilitates attentiveness and inner silence. The prayer is sung and, as in many religious traditions, the repetition of the words sung helps one to go beyond superficial rationality and come closer to the core of being.

On the other hand, prayer in Taizé makes no attempt to appeal specifically to the emotions. It is, in fact, rather low-key. Its quiet, meditative atmosphere has little in common with many prayer styles that are consciously employed to try and attract the young. In fact, many of the participants need a day or two to enter fully the rhythm of the prayer. They are not used to sitting in silence for almost ten minutes, to repeating words in different languages. While there may be an immediate fascination with the style of worship, it usually takes a little time for them to feel fully at home there. Is this not because a meditative prayer calls out to a deeper level of their being where they are not accustomed to dwelling? They are challenged to discover a part of themselves often covered over by the busyness of contemporary society. They are forced to work a little bit to get to a place where they discover that they are more fully themselves, but not to expend so much effort that they become discouraged and abandon the search. Whether conscious or not, behind the prayer of Taizé there is thus a pedagogical intention in the deepest meaning of that term. A good teacher always starts where the pupils are at, using what is accessible to them to lead them beyond their prior unreflective understanding of life.

This type of worship is often described by saying that it implicitly communicates a sense of mystery. Our modern or postmodern consumer and technological society, for all it has achieved in the mastery of the universe, has often led to an appalling superficiality, to a reduction of life to what can be measured, bought, and sold. Entire dimensions of existence once familiar to our ancestors have become buried in the rubble of our toys, the products acquired today and broken tomorrow as we move on to other equally desultory activities. Is there any wonder that people are hungering, most often largely unconsciously, for a rediscovery of the depths of life? Is not an important role of our churches and religious institutions to help people rediscover these depths in a way made authentic by millennia of experience, so that they are not enticed by modern counterfeit encounters with the sacred? Perhaps what some people consider "emotional" is simply anything that does not correspond to a detached and superficial rationality, and it is our notion of the intellect that needs in fact to be reframed.

A word often used by the young themselves to characterize the prayer of Taizé is freedom. "The prayer here is so free," they not infrequently say. At first, these comments left me perplexed. Our prayer is at the opposite extreme from what is usually called "free prayer." Each service is crafted in advance; the order of worship does not change and there is little improvisation. Upon reflection, I came to realize that what they mean by "free" is the creation of a space which leaves room for body and soul to breathe. First of all the body: there are no pews in Taizé; most of the participants sit on the floor in a variety of postures. After the service properly speaking, especially in the evening, the singing goes on and one can come and go as one wishes. One can sing or simply listen to the others chanting, in an atmosphere particularly conducive to inner discovery. The time of silence offers a more explicit space of freedom which one can fill as one chooses, provided of course that one does not disturb others. Paradoxically, perhaps, the set organization of the prayer favors the creation of an open space where body, mind, and heart are liberated; we discover that structure and freedom need not be mutually opposed, but that, correctly understood, the former can make the latter possible. This, I might point out, is another truth kept alive by the monastic tradition.

It is often assumed that contemporary Westerners, particularly the young, are impervious to liturgical symbolism. In our day the vestments, signs, postures, and gestures used in the public prayer of the historical churches often seem to many a closed book. Our experience in Taizé is rather that such forms of symbolic expression still speak to people, provided they are kept simple and when necessary explained (though outside of the service itself). For example, for years we have celebrated a "weekly Easter" during our Friday evening and Saturday evening services. On Friday evening, a large icon of the cross is brought to the middle of the church and laid on some bricks. All are invited to come up to the cross if they wish for a moment of silent prayer while the meditative singing continues, perhaps placing their forehead on the wood of the cross. It is explained earlier that this can be a way of entrusting their lives to Christ on his pilgrimage through death to life, as well as committing to him all those near and far who are undergoing difficulties in their own lives. We have found that this prayer is very meaningful to all kinds of people, both those with an explicit liturgical background and those for whom such forms of expression are new. Similarly, on Saturday evening everyone is given a taper, a symbol of the light of the risen Christ. These candles are lighted by the children present in the prayer at the end of the service, and then everyone passes the flame to his or her neighbors. Such simple but basic symbols seem to give people access to a dimension that remains alive within them, even when it has been almost smothered by a culture that privileges other forms of communication.

## A UNIVERSAL COMMUNITY

In addition to offering an experience of prayer that is both meditative and accessible, the other important aspect of life in Taizé always mentioned by its young visitors is that of participating in a kind of universal community in microcosm. In the summer months, there can be young people from up to eighty countries present, from all the major Christian traditions and even beyond (there are always some Muslim students from Africa, and a few Jews, who make their way to Taizé). It is not rare for a young North American to be in a discussion group with Romanians, Swedes, Russians, perhaps a young man from Chile and a young woman from the Philippines. Fortunately, now most European students speak at least a bit of English and are often fluent in more than one language, which generally makes Americans feel a bit ashamed of their limited linguistic skills. Every day, these groups meet to discuss questions that follow from the Bible introduction given by one of the brothers. Sharing important questions with people from a great diversity of backgrounds and experiences, discovering that beyond the differences there is often a common aspiration, is an experience that has a deep impact on people. It gives concrete and specific content to expressions like "the planetary village" or "one human family." Born in a society where worldwide communication is taken for granted, young people today have an innate sense of the universal. Through discussing, working and praying together with people their own age from across the world, this universalism no longer remains abstract but takes on specific names and faces.

One of the aspects of the meetings in Taizé often emphasized by the young is the *trust* they sense is placed in them. Simply on a practical level, it would be impossible to welcome so many visitors if the brothers, along with the communities of sisters who work with us, had to do everything. So everyone is given as much responsibility for the ongoing life in Taizé as they can handle. When people arrive, they are welcomed and given an orientation not by the brothers but by other young people like themselves. The small-group discussions are likewise led by facilitators chosen from among those who arrive for the week. If this lack of trained staff means that the sharing is sometimes less smooth and more open-ended, the young people are appreciative of the fact that they are given the opportunity to express what is in them freely. They don't feel constrained to give the "right answers." The practical work too is organized by and with the young people. At any given time, there are about fifty young men and women who remain for a longer time in Taizé as volunteers. They take on a lot of the responsibility for organizing life on the hill.

This responsibility extends beyond Taizé itself. At the end of each year, the community organizes a five-day-long "European meeting" in a large city. Approximately sixty thousand young adults come to take part from throughout Europe and beyond. Participants are offered hospitality by parishes and congregations in the area. Such a meeting obviously requires a great deal of local preparation, many visits and explanations. Supported by a team of brothers and sisters, the young volunteers undertake most of this preparation. Without perhaps realizing it, they are receiving priceless training in pastoral ministry. I remember that after the meeting we held in Paris some years ago, I accompanied to a follow-up meeting at the Sorbonne the young German woman who had been given responsibility for churches and communities in that part of the center of Paris, a very significant area that included some of the most prestigious churches on the Left Bank. I was impressed by how well this young woman was able to facilitate contacts and get people to work together. Not only was she of Protestant background with very little or no previous experience in doing such work, but her French was rudimentary to the point of being almost nonexistent! Her sense of responsibility, practical intelligence, and good will nonetheless accomplished miracles, and perhaps her lack of expertise even helped ensure her a warm welcome.

So, our discovery about the young is that when given responsibility, they very often rise to it. They do not simply want to be the passive recipients of programs tailored to them; they appreciate being invited to take part in an ongoing search to which they have something vital to contribute.

## SIMPLICITY

When you ask young people what strikes them about the experience of Taizé, the word "simplicity" often comes to their lips. Life in Taizé is simple first of all because that is the only way that we can welcome so many people. With no sources of funding beyond the contributions of the participants and the work of the brothers, the material side of life must be kept basic. The young sleep in cabins with bunk-beds or in tents; the food is wholesome without being fancy. There are few distractions outside of the worship and the group meetings. And yet this simplicity of life seems to offer a refreshing change to young people who come from societies that are drowning in excess, where nothing ever stops, where there is no time to just *be*, and be together. They discover that it is possible to be happy without an overabundance of consumer goods; they have a good time together without being burdened by expectations to meet or schedules to follow. Although a lot happens during the day in Taizé, there is no sense of rushing from one thing to the next, no deadlines to meet. The Italians have a good word to express this simplicity; they call it *essenzialità*, which can be loosely translated as "focusing on what really matters."

Perhaps in part because there is time to breathe, young visitors to Taizé are also struck by the atmosphere of acceptance and friendliness. Coming from cities characterized by anonymity and the fear of strangers, many are astonished the first day to see that everyone says hello and people speak to one another while waiting in line for meals! In such a climate of trust, it is easy to make friends and to open up to others. "I was surprised," said Rodica, a young woman from Romania in Taizé this summer, "to see that a discussion in Taizé can be at the same time quite ordinary and quite profound. It is not rare during a discussion, despite language problems, to speak about personal questions almost without realizing it, sometimes even intimate subjects."

In Taizé there is no gap between the public and the private spheres, and this too offers a significant contrast with life in contemporary society. There is, instead, time for solitude and personal reflection, and time for working and sharing with others. But it is obvious that these dimensions are both part of an underlying unity. Many young people, like their elders, are searching for this unity in their life, not a unity imposed from without, but one that springs from a common source that is able to unify the myriad aspects of life. To put it another way, many are looking for a faith that is one with their life. As a young man from Senegal who spent two months in Taizé put it, "My experience at Taizé shows me that religion and life are not two separate and independent spheres set side-by-side. At Taizé, you can be 100 percent young, listen to the music other young people do, dress like they do, and yet make your life a fully Christian life."

## To the Sources of the Faith

Something should now be said about the daily Bible introductions given to all those who take part in the international meetings in Taizé. Until the late 1970s, there was no systematic attempt to teach those who came; the accent was placed on sharing and searching together. Then, more and more, the young people themselves asked for some direction to help them discover the wellsprings of the Christian faith and the Bible. Our experience has been that, across the board, there is an ever greater ignorance in recent years concerning the basic teachings of religion; for many, the Bible is a closed book. At the same time, a significant minority of the young is deeply committed and eager to deepen their knowledge of their faith. So for both these populations, it seemed important to provide input that would help them to discover and deepen their understanding of what Christians believe.

Each morning, participants in the meetings hear one of us explain a biblical text or topic for approximately forty-five minutes. At the end, the brother gives some questions, which are usually followed by a time of personal reflection and then sharing in small groups. The questions try to help participants to understand the text better, but also to relate it to their daily life. Naturally, through only six talks in the course of a week, it is impossible to provide a comprehensive introduction to the Bible. Perhaps the most important thing we can do is to give people a taste for such reflection, to help them see that the Bible is not an outdated and incomprehensible book irrelevant to their concerns, but rather that it sheds light on the questions that they themselves ask about their existence and its meaning. We also look for topics that are central to the Christian faith, that enable us to touch upon basic themes and teachings. For example, this past summer one group spoke about the story of the disciples of Emmaus (Luke 24:13–35) and another about the first four chapters of Genesis.

In one sense, the ignorance of many of the young works in our favor because, unlike their predecessors, they are not prejudiced against the Christian faith. For some of them, indeed, Christianity is almost as exotic as Buddhism! This enables them to discover the teachings of the Bible and of Jesus as if for the first time. This of course involves a great challenge for us; we are called not simply to repeat tried-and-true phrases but constantly to reinvestigate the meaning of what we ourselves believe. It is a truth known by all teachers that it is impossible to interest one's students unless one is captivated by the material oneself. In this sense, one always preaches first of all to oneself.

If the Bible introductions in Taizé seem relevant to the young, whereas in religion classes in parishes or universities this is not always the case, it may also be because the teaching is situated in a context where the Christian life is being lived in a way that embraces all of existence. The young people join the brothers for prayer in the church three times a day; they participate with them in a life of community, simplicity and service to others. Thus the words spoken and the ideas discussed are in harmony with the rest of the day. The brothers are not just teachers; their life has sign-value as well. As Pope Paul VI put it in his Apostolic Exhortation *Evangelii Nuntiandi* (December 8, 1975, no. 41): "Modern man listens more willingly to witnesses than to teachers, and if he does listen to teachers, it is because they are witnesses." Or to quote Cardinal Walter Kasper: "Following Christ's example we must be personally involved in this transmission [of the faith] and make ourselves a gift for others. . . . Christian tradition means giving oneself. It comes about through witnesses who are personally involved, whose entire life is a sign."[1] In the final analysis, and at the risk of seeming simplistic, Taizé's relationship with young adults seems to be a fruitful one because it is rooted in mutual *trust*. Where trust is absent, fear and suspicion gain the upper hand in encounters with others, even if they are clothed in seeming indifference. Trust on the other hand permits each party to benefit from the gifts and intuitions of the others. It gives rise to the conviction that together we can achieve far more than each one can do by themselves.

How is such trust engendered? Certainly not by a conscious strategy. One is trusted because one trusts, and one can trust because one knows that one is trusted. The young people sense that the brothers trust them; they also realize that they are not being manipulated but are simply invited to enter a common life. The life of the community itself is built on mutual trust, and this mutual trust is rooted in a God who is trustworthy. In the words of the late philosopher Paul Ricoeur, a frequent visitor to Taizé for fifty years, "At times I have the impression that, in the kind of patient and silent meticulousness that characterizes all the acts of the members of the community, everyone obeys without anybody giving orders. This creates an impression of joyful service, how can I put it, of loving obedience, yes, of loving obedience, which is the complete opposite of submission and the complete opposite of an aimless meandering. This fairly narrow path between what I have just referred to as submission and meandering is broadly marked out by the life of the community. And we, the participants (not those who attend, but those who participate), as I feel myself to have been and to be here, benefit from it. We benefit from this loving obedience that we in our turn exercise with respect to the example that is given. The community does not impose a kind of intimidating model, but a kind of friendly exhortation . . . a shared peacefulness."[2]

So many young and not-so-young people, even (or perhaps especially) those without much religious formation, are still burdened by the image of a God who condemns, who loves conditionally, that is, as long as we follow certain rules and regulations. What many find in Taizé is simply the heart of the Gospel of Jesus Christ—the revelation that "all God can do is love," to quote some words Brother Roger is fond of using to characterize the teaching of Saint Isaac of Nineveh, a seventh-century Syrian Christian. When they are invited to pray around the cross on Friday evenings to entrust their burdens to Christ, they discover a God who accepts them as they are, with all their limitations, and this discovery in many cases can lead to radical changes in a person's way of relating to him- or herself and to others.

Our community's deepest aspiration is to make accessible the sources of trust, so that people, especially the young, can live lives rooted in this trust. In a world where fear and mistrust seem to reign more and more between individuals and nations, is this not the best way the great religious traditions of humankind can show their perennial value, by allowing a mutual trust between humans, one rooted in the

Absolute, to define the parameters of life in society? It is not for nothing that for years now, the name we have given to our endeavors with the young is that of a "pilgrimage of trust on earth."

I would like to conclude by recounting a small experience that many of us brothers have had when speaking to the young pilgrims. In some ways, although minor in itself, it sums up what we have been talking about these days at this conference. So many times, when they return to see us, sometimes after an interval of several years, these words come spontaneously to their lips: "Returning to Taizé is like coming home." Coming from a generation raised on all the creature comforts to the *n*th degree, from young people who take for granted their own room, their own bath, their own electronics warehouse, their own car, these words have something stupefying about them. In Taizé they sleep in tents or cabins; the food is nourishing but far from gourmet, or even Burger King; they are expected to attend religious services three times a day; there is no television, movies or popular music . . . and yet they feel at home! Are these words not an eloquent testimony to the fact that "human beings do not live on bread alone," that there is a longing in us that is not stilled by the good things of this world? Do they not attest to the fact that even the excesses of a consumer society built on a growing worldwide gap between rich and poor cannot uproot this longing from people's hearts and that, when they find a place where it can be expressed together with many others, their hearts can breathe at last and they feel that they have at last arrived at their spiritual homeland? If they say that they feel at home in Taizé are they talking about a village in Burgundy? Are they not really saying that there they have touched, however briefly, their true identity, the mystery at the core of existence, what the Bible calls the "heart"? In that case, the place in Burgundy would be a "sacrament" that makes this other dimension accessible. It seems to me that this reaction of the young helps us glimpse the true calling of our churches and other religious institutions: to offer a space where people's deepest longing for Reality can be liberated and begin to breathe, to point beyond the short-lived attractions of a culture built on sand to the true Home for which human beings were created and where they are meant to live, wherever in fact they may be.

# Religious Identity and Belonging Amidst Diversity and Pluralism: Challenges and Opportunities for Church and Theology

*Peter C. Phan*

The four realities referred to in the title of my essay—namely, identity, belonging, diversity, and pluralism in religious matters—when combined together and placed in the North American context, present both challenges and opportunities for the Christian church and its theology. To understand how religious, and more specifically, Christian identity and belonging are shaped in this context, I begin by briefly describing the four realities mentioned and then outline the main challenges as well as the opportunities they present to the process of forming Christian identity. Next I elaborate a series of theological insights that I hope will help the church meet these challenges and exploit these opportunities for building Christian identity. I conclude by suggesting a variety of ways to construct and develop Christian identity, especially in young people, in our increasingly religiously diverse and plural world. My perspective is mainly that of a Roman Catholic theologian, though I will also make use of recent sociological studies on religious belonging in the postmodern world, especially in the United States.

## Being a Christian in a Religiously Diverse and Plural World

Perhaps the challenges to and opportunities for the process of forming Christian identity in our religiously diverse and plural world are best summed up in the now common slogan: "Spiritual but Not Religious."[1] Depending on the tone of voice, the catchy phrase can be a confident declaration of the superiority of one's way of relating to God or, more generally, to the transcendent and sacred Reality, over various organized religions with their officially prescribed dogmas, codes of ethics, and modes of worship, and also an implied criticism of a way of life that is religiously correct but allegedly not genuinely spiritual. At the other extreme, it can be a limp apology for having abandoned the religious traditions in which one had been brought up and an expression of a sincere and anguished quest for something-as-yet-undefined to fill one's religious void. Whether it is one or the other or any of the variegated hues and shades in between, the claim of being spiritual but not religious is both the by-product of religious diversity and pluralism and a new way of defining religious identity and belonging.[2]

## Religious Diversity

Religious diversity here means the mere fact that today, more than ever, thanks to migration, globalization, and the technologies of communication, people have a sharper awareness of the multiplicity and diversity of religious faiths and practices and of the competing exclusive claims of truth and value that many if not all religions make for themselves. In the United States, thanks to the "new immigration" spurred by the 1965 Immigration and Naturalization Act, Catholics, Jews, and Protestants now rub shoulders daily with Buddhists, Hindus, Muslims, Sikhs, Jains, and the followers of many other lesser-known religious traditions.[3] The presence of these religiously diverse immigrants cannot but raise troubling questions about religious boundaries and church membership which have hitherto been taken as clear-cut by mainline Christians.

## Religious Pluralism

Religious pluralism is the philosophical and theological response to this empirical fact of religious diversity. Philosophically, religious diversity brings back to the forefront the question of whether it is possible to establish an epistemological foundation for the knowledge of the transcendent and sacred Reality. Answers to this question range from theism to deism, agnosticism, and atheism, with a new twist dictated by the pluralistic context. More specifically, religious diversity raises the question of whether it is logically coherent for a particular religious tradition to make an exclusive claim of truth for its own knowledge of the transcendent and sacred Reality and to reject the claims of all other religions as false or at least deficient. Again, answers to this question are varied and multifaceted, ranging from naturalism, which dismisses all religious affirmations as meaningless, to skepticism, which refuses to adjudicate such a question, to confessionalism, which appeals to the authority of one's religious tradition as the criterion of truth.[4]

Theologically, religious pluralism challenges the claims about a particular instance of God's self-revelation, and a faith's response to it, as universally valid and normative; about a specific historical mediator as the only savior for all humanity; about a sacred scripture as the binding and infallible word of God; and about a community of believers as the exclusive sign and instrument of salvation. These claims have been made in various ways and to different degrees by many religions, but among them no doubt Christianity has been one of the most explicit and adamant to make these claims for itself and is therefore the most threatened by religious pluralism. It comes as no surprise that Christian theologians are the ones to have developed the most elaborate answers to religious pluralism, which will be expounded in the second section of this essay.

*Religious Identity*

Religious identity answers the question "Who are you?" with reference to the transcendent and sacred Reality or God. Identity is understood here in the sense articulated by Erik Erikson: mainly as an unconscious process of adaptation, synthesis, and integration of the various constituents of one's ego and at the same time as an accrued condition of such a process. It is therefore viewed not as a static or fixed entity but as a dynamic and constantly evolving reality. Furthermore, identity is both personal and social; that is, it is constituted by the meanings one has of oneself as well as by the meanings one has of the others and the perceptions that others have of oneself. One's identity makes a person distinctive from others by his or her consistent pattern of physical appearance, attitudes, emotions and thoughts, and actions, and at the same time this internal coherence is recognized by others as indicative of that person.[5]

Chronologically, the question of identity emerges most strongly at the onset of adolescence when the young person seriously ponders the question "Who am I becoming?" and attempts to shape his or her identity by a conscious integration of elements from personal and familial experiences, as well as from the societal and cultural meanings of his or her group. Such a process of identity-formation is threatened by what has been called "negative identity." On the one hand, adolescents are sorely tempted to internalize the "dark side" or the "forbidden fruit," that is, the qualities their caretakers warn them against. On the other hand, they run the risk of adopting the stereotypical group identity imposed by dominant majorities upon marginalized minorities in terms of racial, ethnic, sexual, and religious self-definition (Erikson's notion of "pseudospeciation"). Adolescents feel pressured to separate themselves from and to disvalue their community of origin in order to achieve success in the mainstream society and as a result develop what W. E. B. DuBois calls "double consciousness."[6]

With regard to religious identity, again along with Erikson, it may be held that the ultimate guarantor of human identity is God.[7] Erikson points out the fundamental necessity of ideology for the formation of identity. People need a more or less integrated complex of meanings, beliefs, and values to make sense of their experiences and to guide their life-transforming decisions, and this worldview inevitably contains a reference to the Divine as the *Mysterium tremendum et fascinans*, to use Rudolf Otto's phrase. Needless to say, in our religiously plural world, this longing for the transcendent and sacred Other is fulfilled in ways not anticipated in the past.

*Religious Belonging*

Religious belonging is the other side of the coin of religious identity. The formation of religious identity is ineluctably connected with belonging to and feeling solidarity with a particular group, be it family, ethnicity, race, gender, class, profession, or religion. The questions "*Who* am I?" and "*Who* do I become?" are inextricably intertwined with the larger question, "*Whose* am I?" Moreover, religious belonging is much more than a matter of official membership in a religious organization and regular participation in its life and activities. Ideally and not rarely it culminates in a profound sense of commitment and vocation, especially after a spiritual crisis, whereby a person invests all his or her material resources, intellectual gifts, and spiritual charisma to serve the mission of the religious institution to which he or she belongs.

Once again, in the postmodern world, the boundaries separating various religious groups, even in the United States, have become porous and blurred, so that, together with religious identity, religious belonging has been seriously weakened.[8]

## Challenges and Opportunities to Church and Theology

Within the parameters of these definitions of religious diversity, pluralism, identity, and belonging, what are the challenges and opportunities in particular for American Christianity? From the various sociological and psychological studies offered at this conference and elsewhere, they may be schematized as follows.[9]

As far as *challenges* are concerned, the most fundamental ones are those posed by the widespread distinction between "being religious" and "being spiritual." Although, according to the National Study of Youth and Religion (NYSR), American teenagers' interest in practicing the spiritualities of other faiths or in being "spiritual but not religious" is small, and according to the study "A Portrait of Detroit Mosques" (PDM) by Ihsan Bagby for the Institute for Social Policy and Understanding, Detroit Muslim youths are less likely to accept the possibility of being spiritual without being religious, the Higher Education Research Institute's study "Spirituality in College Students" (SCS) reports that 70 percent of college students agree that "most people can grow spiritually without being religious." Again, NSYR reports that nearly all American youths have a very negative or at best a purely instrumental view of organized religion. For them religion is not "an external tradition or authority that makes compelling claims and demands on their lives" but simply "an optional lifestyle choice." Even though, according to SCS, a very high percentage of college students find "religious/spiritual beliefs" to be very important in the formation of their religious identity, there still lurks in the instrumentalist view of religion the vexed question regarding the role of beliefs/doctrines and ecclesial authority (for Roman Catholics, the Magisterium) and religious belonging in the formation of religious identity.

These sociological findings raise the theological question of what role should be assigned to beliefs, the church's teaching authority, and religious participation in the shaping of religious identity. Correlatively, what impact do dissent from the Bible and church teachings and the lack of a consistent religious practice have upon the formation of religious identity? This theological issue becomes more urgent if Christian Smith's thesis regarding contemporary American youth is true, namely, that their "Moralistic Therapeutic Deism" requires as a cure a clear and definite articulation and inculcation of distinctive Christian beliefs and practices.[10] For instance, among Roman Catholics, it is not the case that there has been lacking a clear, insistent, repeated, definite, and definitive articulation of what Catholics must believe and practice. Rather it is the fact that, in spite of such an articulation, some or even many of these teachings and practices, which the Magisterium regards as essential, do not, in the first place, appear to be convincing to the average Catholic. Their plausibility, tenuous as it is, is further undermined by the presence of other religions that present equally or more attractive alternatives. Ironically, it is the repeated enforcement of such beliefs and practices in the face of religious pluralism that jeopardizes the credibility of the teaching authority itself, an indispensable agent in the formation of religious identity.

With regard to *opportunities*, three may be mentioned. First, according to SCS, "significant numbers of students are experiencing challenges and struggles in their spiritual and religious development." How can the church and those responsible for Christian identity-formation use these "challenges" and "struggles," not as psychologically exploitable opportunities for proselytism, but as "teaching moments" for critical and in-depth reflection on the nature of Christian identity and belonging? Second, SCS enumerates various activities, including prayer, in which American college students have had "spiritual" experiences. How can these "spiritual" experiences be turned into "religious" experiences, that is, ones that develop the students' knowledge of their denominational traditions and strengthen their religious belonging? Can and should these spiritual activities not be expanded to include such other-directed activities as work for justice and peace? Third, SCS and Christian Smith note that the American youth's Moralistic Therapeutic Deism contains a "posture of civility" toward other believers and religions. Can this "substantial degree of religious tolerance and acceptance of non-believers" be made to go beyond the— ultimately intolerant—"live-and-let-live" attitude and be transformed into a willingness to learn from religious beliefs and practices other than one's own, even for the purpose of a "serious, articulate, confident personal and congregational discourse of faith" and a "respectful, civil discourse in the pluralistic public sphere"? In other words, is there an opportunity for a "double religious belonging" that remains genuinely Christian and yet honors interreligious dialogue as an indispensable factor in the formation of Christian identity in the twenty-first century?

## Religious Identity: Theological Presupposition

Responses to the challenges of religious pluralism to Christian identity must of course be rooted in and guided by the truths of the Christian faith, though psychological and sociological findings will have an impact on how these truths are understood today. From the perspective of Roman Catholic theology, at least three fundamental doctrines come into play in matters of religious identity, that is, the theology of revelation, Christology, and ecclesiology. In light of the challenges and opportunities outlined above, three questions arise: What is the nature of the faith that is transmitted in the formation of Christian identity? What is the role of the church in the transmission of this faith? How is the Christian claim about Christ as the unique and universal savior to be understood in the context of religious pluralism? A brief consideration of these three realities—faith, church, Christ—is necessary for a discussion of the formation of Christian identity in the pluralistic context.

### Faith as Trust and Assent

In reaction to Luther's insistence on faith (*fides*) as trust (*fiducia*), the Roman Catholic Church has emphasized faith as an intellectual assent to a body of doctrines and the external acceptance of the symbolic, ritualistic, and disciplinary elements of the church. In light of this theology of faith, Cardinal Robert Bellarmine (1542–1621), a celebrated anti-Protestant controversialist, defines a member of the Catholic Church—which he regards as the only true church of Christ—as one who is characterized by three visible elements: profession of the Christian faith, participation in the sacraments, and submission to the authority of legitimate pastors, especially that of the one vicar of Christ on earth, the Roman pontiff.[11] The First Vatican Council (1869–70) defines faith as "the full submission of intellect and will to God who reveals himself" and as "a supernatural virtue, whereby, inspired and assisted by the grace of God, we believe what he has revealed is true."[12] While the surrender of the will, that is, a personal commitment to God, is not neglected, clearly the emphasis in post-Tridentine theology of faith is on the intellectual assent to the doctrinal contents, eventually formulated in propositions, of God's revelation.

The Second Vatican Council (1962–65) redresses the balance between the two elements of faith—assent and trust. In its dogmatic constitution on divine revelation *Dei Verbum*, the council states: "By faith one freely commits oneself entirely to God, making 'the full submission of intellect and will to God who reveals,' and willingly assenting to the revelation given by God."[13] To put it in traditional terminology, faith is necessarily both *fides quae* (objective beliefs) and *fides qua* (the attitude of "obedience" with which the believer assents to the objective beliefs). Unfortunately, there is a widespread tendency in contemporary theology, in opposition to what has been called the doctrinal or propositionalist model of divine revelation, to overemphasize the fiducial dimension of faith and belittle the role of the intellectual assent to the doctrinal contents of faith. As far as the Christian faith is concerned, faith, as St. Paul reminds us, comes from hearing (*he pistis ex akones* [Romans 10:17]), and what is heard includes, besides the "inner word" (*verbum internum*) of the Spirit, an external word (*verbum externum*) proclaimed by the church.[14]

It is vitally important therefore to keep in mind this dual nature of the Christian faith as *both* assent and trust when thinking about Christian identity. This identity is not formed by a wholly inner "spiritual" experience, a private encounter between the individual soul and God, apart from the beliefs and doctrines of a particular religion as well as from the believer's sociopolitical, cultural, and religious contexts.[15] There is no naked faith, shorn of beliefs and unclothed in cultural forms. Christian faith, and any religious faith for that matter, is necessarily embodied in doctrines and expressed in cultural particularities. Indeed, faith as a personal act of total and absolute commitment to God (the *fides qua*) is always enfleshed in a threefold mode: expressed as an act of adherence to a set of beliefs (the *fides quae*), celebrated in particular forms of community worship and prayer, and lived according to concrete moral norms. There is not an inner "core" of faith that can be detached from its historical embodiments and its doctrinal contents, as the seed-and-husk metaphor may suggest. Indeed, just as the successive layers of the onion that, when peeled off to reach the inner core, reveal nothing, so when the Christian faith is removed from its context-dependent doctrines, ways of worship and sacramental celebrations, and moral teachings, there is no Christian core to be found at all.[16]

In light of this theology of faith, Christian Smith's point is well taken when he says that "what actually *is* arguably unfair and disrespectful to youth is to *fail* as communities of faith to provide youth with the clear and substantive belief content, defining identity boundaries, and moral expectations which they can then bounce around, digest, question, struggle over and eventually personally embrace, revise, or reject." The vexing question, of course, is how this communication should be done effectively in the context of religious pluralism.

## The "Ecclesiality" of Religious Identity

As is pointed out above, identity formation is a process both personal and social. Identity is constituted by not only the meanings one has of oneself but also the meanings one has of others and others' perceptions of oneself. Indeed, the personal and social dimensions of identity are deeply intertwined and mutually condition each other. Another way of making this point is to say that Christian identity is essentially church-related or ecclesial. This "ecclesiality" of Christian identity follows upon two basic theological truths. First, humans are intrinsically social animals who can develop only within intercommunications with others, and therefore, even in their relationships with God, they can become who they want to be only by being and becoming with others. *Who* they are and become depends on *whose* they are. Religious *identity* cannot be divorced from religious *belonging*.

Secondly, God's self-revelation, to which faith is a response, is given primarily to a community and not to an individual *qua* individual. Therefore, Christianity as church is much more than a social organization for religious purposes in which an individual can flourish; it is not a club that believers of the same religious inclination and experiences establish in order to foster their religious growth and receive God's blessings. Rather, the individual receives faith, grows in it, and forms his or her Christian identity in and through the ecclesial community. This church exists prior to and independently of one's spiritual experiences; it is constituted by God's will and call and not because of my religious impulses and needs. Of course, the church must do what it can to serve the spiritual needs of its members, and these needs, if genuine, do not contradict the nature and mission of the church. But, as the German theologian Karl Rahner (1904–84) puts it so clearly, the church is "something that obliges me, and which forms a point around which I can orientate myself, but which is not present only when I begin to be religious with my own subjectivity. . . . Christianity is the religion of a demanding God who summons my subjectivity out of itself only if it confronts me in a church which is authoritative."[17]

Hence, the "instrumentalist" view of religion among American youth, as reported by Christian Smith, represents a serious misunderstanding of the nature of the church. It is no doubt the child of the therapeutic individualism and mass-consumer capitalism prevalent in our culture. This instrumentalist view also breeds the distinction between "spiritual" and "religious" and reinforces the possibility of being one without being the other. One can therefore only applaud Smith's proposal to promote "regular personal religious practices" among youth, since it is only through practice that one achieves excellence, in faith as well as in any other endeavor. However, this does not mean that any and all practices of the church should be urged on youth today, nor does it mean that *only* practices of one's own religious tradition should be recommended. Within our pluralistic religious context, such an approach is no longer feasible nor even desirable. The crucial question then is how to promote Christian identity and belonging with a frank acknowledgment of the church's errors and sins and without excluding other religious traditions. This non-exclusion cannot be limited to a "posture of civility" toward religious differences, but rather includes a positive regard for and a willingness to learn from the beliefs and practices of other religions.

## Christ the Universal Savior and Religious Pluralism

A positive regard for non-Christian religions in the context of religious pluralism seems to go against the common profession of Christ as the only and universal savior. As mentioned above, it is Christian theologians who have developed elaborate theologies of religions to deal with the challenges of religious pluralism. Following Paul F. Knitter, these theologies of religions and religious pluralism may be divided into four main types.

The first, called "the replacement model," summarized in the slogan "Only One True Religion," holds either that non-Christian religions are unbelief and must be totally replaced by Christianity or that they contain some truths but cannot offer salvation and must be partially replaced by Christianity. The second, called "the fulfillment model," with the slogan "The One Fulfills the Many," holds that non-Christian religions possess elements of truth and grace and can therefore be called "ways of salvation." However, because only Christianity possesses the fullness of truth and grace, other religions are fulfilled in it and therefore their adherents can be called "anonymous Christians." The third, called "the mutuality model," with the slogan "Many True Religions Called to Dialogue," holds that all religions, including Christianity, are called into a conversation with one another for mutual enrichment, since none of them, though true, possesses the whole and complete truth. The fourth, called the "acceptance model," with the slogan "Many True Religions: So Be It," holds that each religion has its own aim and its particular ways of achieving this aim so that no common ground exists among these diverse religions. However, as a Christian, one must maintain that salvation is attained only though Christ and should not attempt by means of grand theological theories to solve the question of whether and how non-Christians will be saved.[18]

From the Roman Catholic perspective, the third model, which was proposed mainly by Karl Rahner and is now embraced by a large number of Roman Catholic theologians, seems, with some significant amendments, to be the most adequate means to meet the challenges of religious pluralism and at the same time to remain in harmony with the Christian faith. An expanded version of this model is briefly summarized here to serve as a basis for discussing religious identity and belonging.[19]

1) The fact that Jesus is the unique and universal savior and that baptism is required for salvation does not exclude the possibility of non-Christians from being saved.[20]

2) Nor does this fact exclude the possibility of non-Christian religions functioning as "ways of salvation" insofar as they contain "elements of truth and of grace."[21]

3) These two possibilities are realized by the activities of both the Logos and the Holy Spirit. The Logos, though identical with Jesus of Nazareth, is not exhaustively embodied in him, who was spatially and temporally limited and therefore could not exhaustively express the divine saving reality in his human words and deeds. There is a "distinction-in-identity" or "identity-in-distinction" between the unincarnate (*asarkos*) Logos and Jesus Christ. Hence, the activities of the Logos, though inseparable from those of Jesus, are also distinct from and go beyond Jesus' activities, both before and after the Incarnation.

4) In addition, the Holy Spirit, though intimately united with the Logos, is distinct from him and operates salvifically beyond him and "blows where he wills" (John 3:8). Thus, God's saving presence through God's Word and Spirit is not limited to the Judeo-Christian history but is extended to all human history and may be seen especially in the sacred books, rituals, moral teachings, and spiritual practices of all religions. In this way, what the Holy Spirit says and does may be truly different from, though not contradictory to, what the Logos says and does, and what the Logos and the Spirit do and say in non-Christian religions may be truly different from, though not contradictory to, what Jesus did and said.

5) Religious pluralism then is not just a matter of fact but also a matter of principle. That is, non-Christian religions may be seen as part of the plan of divine Providence and endowed with a particular role in the history of salvation. They are not merely a "preparation" for, "stepping stones" toward, or "seeds" of Christianity and destined to be "fulfilled" by it. Rather they have their own autonomy and their proper role as ways of salvation, at least for their adherents.

6) This autonomy of non-Christian religions detracts nothing from either the role of Jesus as the unique and universal savior or that of the Christian church as the sacrament of Christ's salvation. On the one hand, Christ's uniqueness is not exclusive or absolute but *constitutive* and *relational*. That is, because the Christ event belongs to and is the climax of God's plan of salvation, Christ is uniquely constitutive of salvation. Jesus' "constitutive uniqueness" means that he and only he "opens access to God for all people."[22] Moreover, because the non-Christian religions themselves are a part of God's plan of salvation of which Christ is the culminating point, Christ and the non-Christian religions are related to one another. On the other hand, because the non-Christian religions possess an autonomous function in the history of salvation, different from that of Christianity, they and Christianity cannot be reduced to each other. However, being ways of salvation in God's plan, they are related to each other. Autonomy and relatedness are not mutually contradictory.

7) There is then a *reciprocal* relationship between Christianity and the other religions. Not only are the non-Christian religions complemented by Christianity, but also Christianity is complemented by other religions. In other words, the process of complementation, enrichment, and even correction is *two-way* or reciprocal. This reciprocity in no way

endangers the faith confession that the church has received from Christ as the fullness of revelation, since it is one thing to receive a perfect and unsurpassable gift, and quite another to *understand* it fully and to *live* it completely. It is therefore only in dialogue with other religions that Christianity can come to a fuller realization of its own identity and mission and a better understanding of the unique revelation that it has received from Christ. Conversely, other religions can achieve their full potential only in dialogue with each other and with Christianity.

8) Furthermore, despite the fact that Christian faith proclaims that Jesus Christ is the fullness of revelation and the unique and universal savior, there is also a reciprocal relationship between him and other "savior figures" and non-Christian religions, since Jesus' uniqueness is not absolute but relational. In this sense, Jesus' revelation and salvation are also "complemented" by God's self-revelation and redemption manifested in other savior figures and non-Christian religions. In this context it is useful to remember that Jesus did not and could not reveal everything to his disciples and that it is the Holy Spirit that will lead them to "the complete truth" (John 16:12–13). There is nothing to prevent one from thinking that the Holy Spirit will lead the church to the complete truth through the dialogue with other religions in which he is actively present.

9) From what has been said about the Christian claim that Jesus is the unique and universal savior and the church as the sacrament of salvation it is clear that the complementarity between them and other savior figures and religions, though complementary, is, to use Dupuis's expression, "*asymmetrical.*"[23] This asymmetricality is required by the claim of the Christian faith that Jesus is the Logos made flesh and represents the climax or the decisive moment of God's dealings with humankind. What this asymmetricality intends to affirm is that according to the Christian faith, Jesus mediates God's gift salvation to humanity in an overt, explicit, and fully visible way, which is now continued in Christianity, whereas other savior figures and religions, insofar as they mediate God's salvation to their followers, do so through the power of the Logos and the Spirit. In this sense, Jesus may be said to be the "one mediator," and the other savior figures and non-Christian religions are participating mediators or "participated mediations."

10) Last, because of the saving presence of the Logos and the Holy Spirit in non-Christian religions, their sacred scriptures, prayers and rit-

uals, moral practices, ascetical and monastic traditions can be a source of inspiration and spiritual enrichment for Christians. Consequently, they may and should be made use of, at least by Christians who live in a religiously pluralistic context.

## THE FORMATION OF CHRISTIAN IDENTITY TODAY

In light of this theology of revelation, church, and religions, and to meet the challenges of religious diversity and pluralism, how should we view the process of forming Christian identity, especially in the young? Before answering this question, it is helpful to state briefly what may be regarded as the basic principles guiding the formation of Christian identity today.

1) Christian identity is both a dynamic process and an ever-evolving accumulated outcome of such a process. It is both personal and social. It answers the questions "Who am I?" and "Whose am I?"

2) The difficulties of the formation of Christian identity among American youth have been exacerbated not only by what has been called "Moralistic Therapeutic Deism" with all its cultural attendants but also by the growing phenomenon of religious diversity and the theological challenges as well as opportunities of religious pluralism. No discussion of religious identity in the United States can afford to ignore this new cultural and religious context.

3) Since Christian faith is both assent and trust, no formation of Christian identity can be complete without attending fully to this double dimension of intellectual acceptance and personal commitment.

4) Since faith is necessarily ecclesial and since Christianity is intrinsically communitarian, no Christian identity is complete without Christian belonging. This fact questions the validity of the disjunction between being "spiritual" and being "religious." Religious practice within a particular Christian community is essential to the shaping and deepening of Christian identity.

5) Within our religiously pluralistic context, it is necessary to develop a theology of Christ as the universal savior and of religions that offers a coherent justification for the compatibility between being a faithful Christian and being receptive to the doctrinal, liturgical, and moral traditions of other religions. In other words, today we must contemplate the possibility and even the desirability of including within

Christian identity and belonging multiple (dual) religious identity and belonging.

Presuming these five principles I will briefly consider in the remaining pages three key issues in the formation of Christian identity, namely, the role of particular (denominational) traditions, rhetorical strategies in religious education, and the conditions for fruitful multiple religious belonging.[24]

### *Christian Identity and Particular/Denominational Christian Traditions*

There has been in the post–Vatican II era (i.e., since 1965) a deliberate effort at healing the centuries-old division within Christianity to achieve the unity in his church that Christ prayed for. While acknowledging the scandalous nature of interchurch division and its deleterious effects on the formation of Christian identity itself, and hence, with wholehearted support for the ecumenical cause, it is important to note that it is neither feasible nor productive in religious education to aim at the formation of a generic brand of interdenominational Christian identity. In fact, it is only through a particular/denominational community of faith, with its specific beliefs, rituals, and ethical and spiritual practices that people, especially the young, gain access to and are socialized into the common Christian heritage.

Of course, in the formation of this specific Christian (i.e., Roman Catholic) identity, religious educators must familiarize those under their charge with what other Christian communities believe and practice and show them how to critically appropriate these diverse traditions to enrich their self-understanding and practices. Nevertheless, members of a particular religious community cannot do this effectively unless they are already well established in their own tradition. To put it differently, in ecumenical dialogue, one cannot "cross over" and "come back" unless one is already familiar with and dwells comfortably in the spiritual home from which one ventures forth into other Christian communities and from which one returns, strengthened and enriched in one's own religious identity.

This task of teaching American youth about their own religious traditions is all the more urgent if many of them, as Christian Smith has noted, are quite ignorant of or confused about what Christians are required to believe and practice, either because religious instruction is outlawed in public schools or because their other religious teachers lack clarity about and confidence in Christian teachings.

That said, it is important to recall that Christian identity is shaped not by doctrines alone. Perhaps more effective than indoctrination are public worship, private prayer, and work for social justice and peace. Indeed, the most effective catechesis is one that is built on the four pillars of Christian identity, namely, doctrine, liturgy, ethical praxis, and private prayer. For American youth in particular, who often enjoy material abundance and all kinds of freedom, nothing so shakes up and shapes their Christian identity as working for a prolonged period of time, in imitation of and discipleship to Christ (*imitatio et sequela Christi*), with and for the poorest of the poor, the politically oppressed, the victims of diseases, the migrants, and other suffering people in the world, and sharing their daily fears and joys.

## *Rhetorical Strategy in Religious Education: The "Indirect Approach"*

Among Roman Catholics, complaints have been voiced, sometimes stridently and vociferously, that Catholic identity has been jeopardized by a watered-down and liberal religious education. It has been suggested that the most effective means to restore and strengthen Catholic identity is faithful presentation of Catholic doctrines and fervent promotion of Catholic practices, preferably by means of a common catechism such as the *Catechism of the Catholic Church.* On the face of it, it is hard to see how anyone can disagree with this proposal in its general thrust. However, in my judgment, the problem is *not* that the Catholic faithful do not *know* what the official church teaches. Except in arcane matters such as trinitarian theology, rare indeed is the Catholic who is ignorant of church teachings on issues such as sexual morality (e.g., masturbation, premarital and extramarital intercourse, artificial contraception, and homosexuality), priestly celibacy, or the exclusion of women from hierarchical priesthood. The Magisterium has repeatedly proclaimed its teachings on these issues, *opportune et inopportune.*

The real problem in religious education lies then not in the ignorance of church teachings but in presenting the *reasons* that the official church uses to justify its teachings. To take two examples: presumably no Catholic is ignorant about the church's ban on artificial contraception and the ordination of women; the problem is that the reasons for the church's positions do not appear reasonable and convincing, to judge from polls, to many Catholics, even devout ones.

The religious educator must of course present the reasons fully, competently, sympathetically, clearly. But no amount of rhetoric, persuasion, pedagogy, repetition, or even threat can augment one bit the objective force and logic that these reasons possess in themselves. The teacher will rightfully appeal to faith and respect for the teaching church, but he or she cannot urge obedience to church authorities against the negative assessment of the logic of certain church teachings. One of the hallmarks of the Catholic Church is a profound respect for human reason and freedom as authentic ways to know God. Unless the student accepts and internalizes the reasons given in support of church teachings, and not just the teachings themselves; unless he or she perceives the *reasonableness* of the teachings (which is not the same as their purely *rational* grounds), Catholic identity, which these teachings and religious education intend to maintain and develop, remains very weak.

What is one to do when the reasons for church teachings fail to convince? Rather than repeating the same arguments or concocting more and more arguments in *direct* support of church teachings, I suggest what can be called the "indirect approach."[25] The indirect approach does not seek to prove the validity and truth of a particular teaching by examining its intrinsic evidence but by investigating and appealing to the ontological and existential conditions in the hearer that make the acceptance of the teaching possible. This approach is particularly helpful when objective proofs are too many and too complex for the average mind to be able to grasp them all in their individual specificities. Indeed, in my judgment, this indirect rather than direct approach is the common one by which people reasonably arrive at certitude in matters that profoundly affect their lives, such as ethics and religion.[26]

With regard to the question of Catholic identity, this approach is predicated on the conviction that personal and social identity are shaped and maintained not primarily by the specific differences that an individual or a society possesses over *against* others, which may be many but superficial, but by what might be called "deep structures," which may be few and shared with others. For example, my Vietnamese cultural identity is defined less by my particularities of birth, educational achievements, social status, and material acquisitions than by such long-lasting and pervasive factors such as language, gender, race, and the culture that I have in common with other Vietnamese people.

Analogously, what constitutes a person as a Catholic and defines his or her Catholic identity is not so much what differentiates him or her from a Protestant, Orthodox, or Anglican (e.g., acceptance of the Petrine office), but the fundamental and deep structures, even though these may be common to others.[27] Such deep structures may include but are by no means limited to doctrines. Religion, as anthropologists have pointed out, is a system of symbols that includes not only doctrines but rituals, institutions, art, and behaviors.[28] Thus, a Catholic's identity is shaped by doctrines but as much (if not more) by sacramental celebrations (though sacraments are shared in common with the Orthodox, the Anglicans, and most Protestants), by devotions to Mary and the saints (shared in common with the Orthodox), by episcopal structures (shared in common with the Orthodox and the Anglicans), and by artistic monuments such as architecture, the visual arts, and music (shared in common with people in many secular societies). These deep structures have been variously identified as sacramentality, mediation, communion, and the "analogical imagination."[29] My intention here is not to add other candidates to the list but to argue that to form Catholic identity in their students, religious educators should attend to these deep structures, especially when the reasons for official doctrines fail to carry weight with the audience. Indeed, unless these structures are shaped, cultivated, and nurtured with care, most of the reasons for the church's controversial teachings, especially those that contradict popular trends, are not readily understandable.

It is commonly admitted that in moral and religious matters, besides the knowledge derived from formal inference and logical deduction, there is a knowledge achieved through "connaturality," by "instinct," as it were. Though not opposed to the knowledge acquired through philosophical reasoning, this knowledge through connaturality is gained not so much from the technical accumulation of data and its logical ordering but from a personal, deep, and prolonged familiarity with the subject matter. This familiarity, which is often a product of technical expertise but far exceeds it, gives the individual an uncanny ability to see a pattern among disparate data, to intuit a *Gestalt* in disconnected parts, to anticipate the conclusion before the reasoning process is completed, to predict the outcome of an experiment, to tell true from false and right from wrong from the "feel" of the thing. In short, it is a kind of the sixth sense, the knowledge of what Blaise Pascal calls the "heart." This is the ability, for example, of the detective to figure out who is the culprit despite confusing clues, of the archaeologist to reconstruct bygone cities from bits and pieces of pottery, of the historian to interpret the meanings of events from conflicting records, of the artist to see beauty amidst what appears to be disharmony and ugliness, of the virtuous person to discern with ease what is good and evil on the basis of his or her experience.

This ability Cardinal Newman calls the "illative sense," that is, the ability of the practical reason (akin to Aristotle's *phronesis*) to arrive at certitude in practical matters, particularly in matters concerning Christianity, which is, according to Newman, addressed to both our intellect and imagination, "creating a certitude of its truth by arguments too various for direct enumeration, too personal and deep for words, too powerful and concurrent for refutation."[30]

Catholics, it may be argued, cultivate a special illative sense with which they grasp and assent to the Christian faith. It is characterized by the inclusiveness of both-and rather than either-or thinking, a positive appreciation of creaturely realities as mediation and sacrament of their divine creator, a high regard for the community as the locus of God's self-communication, and a basically optimistic attitude of hope for the redemption of everything. Prior to the explicit acceptance of each and every Christian belief and practice, there are these deep structures of Catholic identity that function as both the religious context and the epistemological warrant for these beliefs and practices. These structures do not provide specific justifications for a particular belief and practice *per se*, each of which needs to be justified on its own merits, but they offer the context in which these arguments, "too various for direct enumeration, too personal and deep for words," and perhaps, we must add, not strong enough to convince, can acquire a certain plausibility and *invite* a faithful acceptance. The religious educator cannot and should not expect immediate acquiescence on the part of the listeners to the church teachings presented, but he or she must explain how they can make sense within the whole complex of the fundamental options of Christianity and hope that the listeners will give, eventually, a sympathetic consideration to perplexing church teachings. As Catholic religious educators, they can do no more but also no less.

## Multiple Religious Belonging and Christian Identity

In the religiously pluralistic context that exists in the United States, and especially among the college-educated population, the reality of "multiple religious belonging" or "hyphenated religious identity" has become more frequent, as Diane Winston has reported.[31] Such a phenomenon is of course deeply ambiguous, and in many respects constitutes a threat to Christian identity as an ecclesial process.[32] At one level, multiple religious belonging may designate the "spiritual but not religious" outlook, which can be described as "unchurched" or "non-ecclesial" spirituality.[33] At another level, it may be an expression of the instrumentalist understanding of religion or New Age syncretism according to which religion is a smorgasbord of religious beliefs and practices from which religious seekers can pick and choose whatever "fulfills" their "needs" best.

While acknowledging such dangers and others, it must be admitted that dual religious belonging can be spiritually fruitful and is not incompatible with a robust Christian identity. Edifying examples of such dual belonging are not lacking, at least among Roman Catholics. One paradigmatic case is Raimundo Panikkar, a Spanish-Indian Catholic priest, who confessed: "I 'left' as a Christian, 'found myself' a Hindu, and I 'return' as a Buddhist, without having ceased to be a Christian."[34] However, it must be frankly admitted that multiple religious belonging is a deeply unsettling religious experience and is a prophetic vocation that should be assumed only after careful and prayerful discernment. From an analysis of several well-known cases of dual religious belonging, at least the following conditions would have to be present for it to be both spiritually fruitful and compatible with Christian identity.[35]

1) The quest for multiple religious belonging should not originate, at least principally, from some kind of uncertainty about Christian identity or spiritual crisis or even discontent with one's church, much less from ignorance of the Christian tradition. Of course, a degree of dissatisfaction with one's religious tradition is expected; such dissatisfaction impels one to seek theological and spiritual resources beyond one's own tradition. But, as has been said above about ecumenical dialogue, just as one should not "cross over" into and "come back" from another Christian denomination until one is firmly rooted in and formed by one's own denomination, so also in interreligious dialogue, one should not attempt to learn from and adopt the spiritual practices of other religions unless one is well schooled in the Christian tradition. At any rate, the motivation for multiple religious belonging must not be a kind of spiritual dilettantism with which one samples various religions and, out of a medley of beliefs and practices of one's liking, one constructs a sort of universal religion.[36]

2) For multiple religious belonging to be deep and long-lasting, a continual effort to engage in a serious and even scholarly study of the doctrines and practices of the other religions is required. Needless to say, this is an arduous task, since it often requires a command of quite difficult languages and superior intellectual acumen to grasp the philosophical and theological conceptual apparatus of these religions. Making hasty and facile syntheses of ideas and practices of different religions is a constant danger.

3) Beside study, there is the need of spiritual practice. To begin with, this includes the use of the prayers and the holy scriptures of other religions in one's spiritual life. More advanced techniques of meditation and asceticism will eventually be learned under the direction of a master. Ideally, living in a monastic community, at least for a period of time, and sharing its spiritual way of life, should be encouraged.

4) Finally, practitioners of multiple religious belonging should remember that as with Christian identity, multiple religious belonging is a dynamic process and an ever-evolving accumulated outcome of such a process. To a great extent it is much more complicated and demanding than the formation of Christian identity by itself. Neither syncretism nor synthesis is possible. Both syncretism and synthesis violate the unique identity of each religion. At best, as Aloysius Pieris has said, only a "symbiosis" can be aimed at, that is, a way of life in which followers of different religious traditions live and work and pray together, especially with and for the poor and the marginalized. In such a symbiosis Christians learn how to be better Christians from the followers of other religions, just as these people learn from Christians how to understand more fully and practice more faithfully the teachings of their own religious traditions.[37] One must be willing to live the unresolvable tension between the Christian faith and other religious traditions, without attempting at harmonizing them, at least on the theoretical level, until, in the memorable words of the French Benedictine Henri Le Saux (1910–73), also known as Swami Abhishikananda, "the dawn appears."[38]

To return now to our youth, especially our college students, who are searching for and even struggling with their religious identity: what light and guidance can these reflections on faith and tradition and on the formation of religious identity provide for their religious quest? Allow me to address them directly and personally, especially those youth who have been raised Catholic, with the hope that at least some of them will chance to read these pages:

1) Your searching for religious identity may very well be, and I think that it is, a gift of God. It is God's invitation to you to deepen your relationship with God. Faith is not something that can be possessed once and for all and kept safe in a lockbox like a treasure. Rather, it is both a gift and a task. It shines on you unmerited and unexpected like a lover's smile; like a healing balm, it quells your restless mind; and, like a fire, it warms your heart and soul. At the same time, like a powerful wind, it shakes your comfortable home and thrusts you outward and forward. Faith gives you *certitude*, not *certainty*, about the most fundamental things in life. Hence, a faith that does not question itself, that is not beset by occasional doubts, that does not do the difficult work of thinking about its own grounds, deprives itself of opportunities for growth into maturity. Your quest for religious identity should be seen in this light. It is part of the Holy Spirit's challenge to you to grow in your faith, and we adults should not be alarmed by your questioning and apparent loss of faith.

2) However, your quest should not be undertaken in isolation. Faith is primarily God's gift to a community, not to the individual as individual. It is given to you as a member of a community of faith, which we Christians call church. This community is shaped by a set of particular beliefs, rituals, prayers, and ethical practices, which we term the Tradition (with a capital *T*). In your search for religious identity, steep yourself as much as you can in this Tradition. Make an effort to learn the doctrines of your church, without which faith is reduced to a blind feeling. Take an active, conscious, and full part in the sacramental and liturgical celebrations in your parish or congregation, without which faith is reduced to an arid intellectual affair. Devote yourself to regular prayer, without which faith is cut off from its life-source. Follow the moral teachings of your church as much as you can, without which faith is a form of cheap grace.

3) Most probably, you will say: "That's precisely the problem. Many teachings and practices of my church do not make sense to me. That is why I feel I have to look elsewhere." You have a point there. The church is not preserved from errors and mistakes in everything it teaches. Guided by the Holy Spirit, the Catholic Church is preserved from errors only when it "defines" infallibly about faith and morals. So, the first thing to do is to find out what level of authority a particular teaching has. If after a serious, responsible, and prayerful search and reflection, perhaps with the help of someone whose wisdom and holi-

ness you trust, you find yourself unable to agree with a certain non-infallible teaching, you may certainly follow and act according your enlightened conscience. I do not think that you have to leave your church or reject your Christian identity on that account, nor should you let anyone force you to leave the church. As for what the church and its officials do, I would urge compassion for the church, which is after all made up of sinners, like you and me. Sometimes it is even mired in widespread scandals, as we have recently seen in the American Catholic Church. But the church is called to constant conversion and holiness. With your continued presence and support, the church may carry out the task of self-purification more effectively.

4) Unlike most of us older Catholics, you live amidst religious pluralism. Many of your friends belong to different religions, and their beliefs and practices appeal to you. Some of these may even seem better than those of your church. The Catholic Church acknowledges that God is present and active in these religions and urges respect for what is true and good in them. There is therefore no reason we should not learn from their beliefs and practices. But there is the danger of becoming a religious butterfly trying to sample everything that various religions offer. You must be deeply grounded in one tradition and competent in its practices before you can profitably learn from other religious traditions. The experiences of the pioneers in interreligious dialogue show us that interreligious sharing is an extremely difficult act, a God-given vocation to be undertaken with fear and trembling.

5) In sum, religious identity is a lifelong process, to be shaped by the beliefs, rituals, prayers, and ethical practices of your church and enriched by those of other religious traditions. Furthermore, it is not something you do by yourself. Rather, it is a project performed with the help and guidance of your parents, teachers, friends, and religious leaders. Indeed, by forming your religious identity you help others shape their own. And throughout this process you are accompanied by the Holy Spirit who inspires, encourages, corrects, and strengthens you.

# Section Five

Passing on the Faith to the Next
Generation of Muslims

# IDENTITY AND COMMUNITY IN A NEW GENERATION: THE MUSLIM COMMUNITY IN THE EARLY SEVENTH CENTURY AND TODAY

*Ghada Osman*

The history of Islam in the United States has been a multilayered and complex one. At least 10 percent of African slaves in antebellum America are estimated to have been of Muslim origin, although it appears that none of them survived slavery while maintaining their adherence to Islam. The second phase in the history of Islam in the United States occurred with the migration of Arabs from the Ottoman Empire in the post–Civil War period; while most of these Arabs were Christian, a minority was Muslim. Some immigrants from British India, southern Europe, and Ukraine were also Muslims. The early and middle decades of the twentieth century witnessed the migration of Muslims from Central Asia, the Middle East, and East Asia, in large part as a reaction to the Cold War and to the policies of communist and socialist governments. It also witnessed the arrival of Muslims who were coming to the United States temporarily, mainly as students, as well as the growth of conversion (sometimes termed reversion, in the African American case) to Islam among Americans.[1]

The situation of Islam in the United States is different in several ways from that of Judaism and Christianity. First of all, while Islam has existed in the United States for a long time, its visibility is relatively new, meaning that Muslims are still at the beginning of negotiating their group identity, particularly in terms of drawing the line between religion and culture. As John Esposito points out, "The majority of Americans have yet to realize that Muslims are 'us,' but many Muslims have not solved the problem of the relationship of their faith to national identity either: will they remain Muslims in America or become American Muslims?"[2] Or as explained by Gary David and Kenneth Ayouby, Muslims in the United States face the dichotomy between "becoming American vs. becoming Americanized."[3] Is it possible to embrace a hybrid American Muslim identity that is often seen as incompatible with being both fully American and fully Muslim?

Furthermore, Muslim immigrants, coming from their relatively homogeneous countries, are presented with the novel situation of a heterogeneous American Muslim community: "Islam in America is a mosaic of many ethnic, racial, and national groups. The majority are first- or second-generation immigrants or African-American converts."[4] Haddad further details that the community

> includes immigrants who chose to move to the United States for economic, political, and religious reasons from over sixty nations of various ethnic, racial, linguistic, tribal, and national identities. It also includes émigrés and refugees forced out of their homeland, who still retain allegiance to it and are reluctant to relinquish the intention of returning to it to help restore the order they left behind. It also includes a large number of converts, both African Americans and white, who through the act of conversion have opted out of the dominant American cultural identity, and a significant number of Muslims whose forebears immigrated between the 1870s and World War II and who are in varying degrees already integrated and assimilated. The majority of Muslims in America today, however, are foreign born, socialized and educated overseas, and come from nation states whose identity has been fashioned by European colonialism.[5]

Esposito continues:

> Their problems, like those of other religious minorities, center on assimilation or integration and the preservation and practice of religious faith in an American society informed by Judeo-Christian or secular values, the relationship of religious traditions to the demands of current realities, and gaining a place in American

politics and culture. The situation is complicated by the historical relationship between Islam and Christianity, especially between the West and Muslim societies, which includes everything from memories of the Crusades and European colonialism.[6]

Despite the plethora of backgrounds, most Muslims in the United States are nonwhite. Therefore, unlike religious Jews and Christians who may be marginalized by secular peers because of their religious practices, Muslims often have the double disadvantage of being both racial and religious minorities. Furthermore, because of the association of Islam with "foreignness," sometimes even Muslims of European origin, particularly women who wear the headscarf, are perceived as foreigners.

An additional challenge facing the Muslim community is that of language maintenance. While maintaining the parents' native tongue throughout the generations is a key issue for any immigrant, American Muslims face the challenge of wanting to maintain their culture through teaching their children their own language to preserve their heritage, and also wanting to maintain their religious adherence through teaching their children Arabic to at least read, if not understand, the Qur'an. For example, about a third of my Arabic classes each semester are composed of non-Arab Muslims wishing to read and understand the Qur'an. This dichotomy of language maintenance is a situation that is even shared by Arabic-speaking parents because of the diglossic nature of their language: they wish their children to know their Arabic dialect, as well as understand the significantly different classical Arabic of the Qur'an.

And of course, we cannot underestimate the significant changes brought about by 9/11 and its aftermath. Many Muslims who had taken for granted their identity as Americans now began to question the simplicity of such categorization. September 11 had particular psychological effects on those who had not previously emphasized their Muslimness, and who had not thought about it as a measure of their identity. Individuals with Arabic-sounding names were no longer lost in the sea of multiculturalism; my third-generation Arab American friend Linda Salem (as in the Oregon and Massachusetts cities), who all her life had been called Linda Salem, suddenly found herself being referred to as "Linda Saleem," "Linda Sallam," and a plethora of other creative misnomers.

Muslims in the United States have therefore had to negotiate their identity on several levels. Some (particularly those with fairer skin and non-Arabic names) have decided to assimilate fully into mainstream American society, others are walking the tightrope between being American and being Muslim, while still others see the two identities (especially in light of recent U.S. foreign-policy decisions) to be completely in conflict with each other. In other words, like any minority group, Muslims can be aggressive toward their host society, show a willingness to work within it, or simply isolate themselves from it. Garbi Schmidt points to "the move from a status as transient to one of settlement that this religious community has undergone during the last hundred years,"[7] tracing the status of the American immigrant Muslim as visitor, sojourner, citizen, and then American-born native.[8]

Converts to the religion, who do not even have the extensive luxury of negotiating their identities, but rather are forced to walk the tightrope between being American and being Muslim, add a level of complexity to the issue. Often wishing to emphasize the difference in their lives before and after conversion, they abandon many customs thought of as "American," customs they see as being in direct conflict with their beliefs and new way of life. In this way, converts create a niche for themselves as a minority American Muslim group within mainstream American society.

In trying to reconcile their various identities, practicing Muslims of all persuasions try to model their behavior on the early seventh-century Muslim community under the guidance of the Prophet Muhammad. It was in Mecca that the Prophet Muhammad was born and raised, and it was in that city that he received his first revelation and began preaching the message of Islam. Yet while comparisons made are often made in terms of dogma,[9] highlighting how the Meccan community worshipped or gave charity, for example, very little comparison is done in terms of context. While one has to exercise caution in discussing contexts that are geographically and chronologically disparate, the context here is crucial in comparing the two situations, with the social context of the community in Mecca being one of the most obvious points from which to draw parallels. Comparisons have been made between the Muslim community in the United States and those of Medina and Ethiopia,[10] but these comparisons are superficial at best. Medina, the city to which Muhammad and the Muslims migrated in 622 CE, came to have a Muslim majority and was ruled by the Prophet as a city-state. Ethiopia, to which a minority of Muslims migrated in 615–16 CE, served as a temporary home for a small portion of the Muslim community, whose leadership was still in Mecca. Neither of these situations is at all demographically similar to the one in the United States.

The comparison between the circumstances of the Muslim community in the United States with that of pre-Hegira Mecca, however, is more valid in several ways. In addition to being the example to which Muslims look today for inspiration, the early community also represents one of the few significant instances of the Muslim community having a minority status, with the Muslim community of the city numbering only in the several hundreds at the time of the Hegira. As a minority, the community was subject to the codes and laws of the non-Muslim majority. Despite having a religious (but not political) leader, it was a community still trying to negotiate its identity vis-à-vis the mainstream, walking the tightrope between asserting identity and attempting to maintain reasonably harmonious relations with the mainstream. It was also, as Karen Armstrong points out, a community born into a "society . . . in crisis. Many felt that their old religious ideas no longer spoke to them in their dramatically altered world and, like many today, they were experiencing a spiritual vacuum."[11]

A comparison between the Muslim minority community in seventh-century Mecca and the Muslim minority community in the United States today therefore brings to light some useful social elements that can serve as a helpful guide to American Muslim identity and behavior today. It is important to point out here that the relevant comparison is to the pre-Hegira Meccan community specifically, rather than the situation of the Muslims after the conquest of Mecca, since the former is the minority situation that is comparable to that of the American Muslim community. Despite some obvious differences between the two communities, an examination of the social circumstances of each reveals a deep similarity. At a time when Muslims in the United States are attempting to renegotiate the core of their identity and their place in society, a look back to the early community provides some thought-provoking motifs and lessons.

## SIGNIFICANT DIFFERENCES

Before we begin this comparison, we must bring to light the significant differences between the two contexts. In Mecca, the nascent community had a Prophet to whom it deferred in religious matters. The Prophet served as a religious leader, although he had no political role at the time. Religious adherence and practice in Mecca was still in a clearly formative period, with Meccan verses focusing on issues of faith rather than law. As Yahya Emerick points out, "The major teachings of Islam, as it existed in the Meccan Period (610–622 CE) consisted of three main areas: theological, ritual, and moral."[12] The Prophet was the law-giver of a continuously changing and expanding body of beliefs and practices.

However, it is also important to realize that Islam was in a formative period, where flexibility was an important caveat. As Watt explains, "The Muslim scholars, not possessing the modern Western concept of gradual development, considered Muhammad from the very first to have been explicitly aware of the full range of orthodox dogma."[13] As a result, they have not taken into account the transitional nature of many aspects of the message, and the need for that transitional status before permanent laws were given. For example, Muslims were instructed first not to approach prayer while intoxicated (4:43), before being told to abstain from drinking altogether (5:90, 2:219). After the end of revelation and particularly after the closing of the doors of *ijtihad* (the ban on reaching a legal decision through independent interpretation of the sources of law in the tenth century), such admission of graduation in religious belief and practice was considered sacrilegious.

Another important issue to note here is the nature of leadership in the two communities. In general, groups always "need a leader or a subgroup to impress its will and gain a hold on the minds of its members."[14] While in the early community the person who did this was Muhammad himself, in later communities it was also Muhammad who fulfilled this role and continues to do so. The absence of clergy for most Muslims means that there is no religious leader who would take on such a significant role. While Muslim scholar-leaders such as imams, muftis, qadis and 'alims hold some context-specific authority, there is no established institution with the recognized broad-sweeping authority of a minister or a rabbi. As a result, the community is continuously looking back to the Prophet as the one figure who can provide guidance in all matters. This is in marked contrast to both Judaism and Christianity, who hold certain founding figures in high regard but who also have contemporary individuals to whom they look for religious guidance. This means that in Islam, there is no intermediary between the individual and God, and also no intermediary between the individual believer and his or her history, with the apex of that history being the person of the Prophet Muhammad.

## SOCIAL ASPECTS

There are three significant points of comparison between the community of Mecca and that of the United States. These fall under the categories of the composition of the Muslim community, its relations with the majority, and its methods of coping with and promoting its identity as a minority. While some of these points relate to the position of any minority—especially religious—vis-à-vis the dominant majority, others are specific to these two particular cases.

## 1) THE COMPOSITION OF THE MUSLIM COMMUNITY

The socioeconomic status of a group is one of the most important factors affecting that group's standing in its society, and therefore its ability to negotiate its identity. Before the Prophet's migration to Medina and his subsequent role as both religious and political leader, the community in Mecca was one with limited social standing. With few notable exceptions, early Meccan converts tended to be from the clans of Hashim, al-Muttalib, Zuhrah, Taym, al-Harith b. Fihr, and Adi, which were weaker clans that had needed to take part in the pre-Islamic pact of Hilf al-Fudul in order to safeguard their position.[15] The prominent historian of early Islam, W. Montgomery Watt, divided the "early Muslims" into three groups:

1) Younger sons of the best families. . . . These were young men from the most influential families of the most influential clans, closely related to the men who actually wielded power in Mecca and who were foremost in opposing Muhammad.
2) Men, mostly young, from other families. . . . As we move down the scale to the weaker clans and to the weaker branches of the chief clans, we find among the Muslims men of greater influence within their clan or family.
3) Men without close ties to any clans. There was also a comparatively small number of men who were really outside the clan system, though nominally attached to some clan.[16]

Karen Armstrong elaborates that "many of [Muhammad's] first converts were among the disadvantaged people of Mecca: slaves and
women both recognized this religion offered them a message of
hope."[17] Likewise, Ibn Ishaq tells us that when the Prophet's close
companion Abu Bakr would recite the Qur'an, he would be moved to
tears, and "youth, slaves, and women used to stand by him when he
recited the Qur'an, astonished by his demeanor."[18]

Here we see a focus on three particular groups. The first of these is
the youth, the young men mentioned above—not surprisingly, since it
is often young people who are dissatisfied with the status quo and want
change. Likewise, in seventh-century Mecca, "Most of the early converts were younger men and women who were easily motivated to join
a new concept and idea that upset their parents."[19] The second group is
slaves; Islam prided itself on counting among its adherents slaves such
as Bilal, the Abyssinian slave that was the first caller to prayer, as well
as numerous others. We know that the Prophet's freedman Zayd was
among the first to convert to Islam.

And the third group, interestingly, is women. We find a number of
cases in the early community where women converted to Islam, but
their husbands did not. Islam's first convert was the Prophet's wife
Khadija. Among the families of the Prophet's uncles, "the wives of
both [the Prophet's uncles] 'Abbas and Hamzah had no patience for
their husbands' timidity, however; Umm Fadl and Salamah both became Muslims, as did [the Prophet's cousin] Ja'far's wife Asma, and
Muhammad's aunt Safiyah bt. Abd al-Muttalib. Umm Ayman, Muhammad's freedwoman, also joined the sect."[20]

These details about the Meccan community are of course very general. It is nevertheless interesting to compare them to the demographics
of the American Muslim community, which are similar in some ways.
Based on a 2002 poll, 23 percent of the American Muslim population
is aged eighteen to twenty-nine, and 51 percent is aged thirty to forty-
nine. In other words, a full 74 percent of the population is under the age
of fifty.[21] This is a result of immigration, but also of conversion. In a
1993–94 study focusing on American converts, Carol L. Anway noted
that in her sample of fifty-three women, 51 percent converted between
the ages of eighteen and twenty-four, 34 percent between the ages of
twenty-five and thirty, and 11 percent between the ages of thirty-three
and forty-four.[22] In the contemporary United States, Muslims come
from a wide range of socioeconomic backgrounds. Immigrants are a

mix of university students, blue-collar workers, and white-collar work-ers. In terms of income, 10 percent of the Muslim population make less than $15,000, 10 percent make between $15,000 and $24,999, 13 per-cent between $25,000 and $34,999, 17 percent between $35,000 and $49,999, 22 percent between $50,000 and $74,999, and 28 percent more than $75,000.[23] Converts, which official government figures esti-mate as between 17 percent and 30 percent of the total American Mus-lim population,[24] tend on average to have a lower average income. In general, like the early Muslim converts, they are people who are drawn to Islam in large part because of its strong social-justice agenda.

When it comes to the issue of women, we find that among the Mus-lim population of the United States, 59 percent of the population is male, and 41 percent is female.[25] In her study of female American con-verts, Carol L. Anway noted that over a third of the women (38 percent) converted while still single, and the remaining 62 percent converted while married to Muslim men. The single women were introduced to Islam through Muslim neighbors or college friends, travel to Muslim countries, or courses or books about Islam. Fifty-three percent of An-way's sample had a BA or higher secondary degree, with 35 percent holding a BA or BS, 12 percent an MA or MS, and 6 percent an MD or PhD. Seven of the women were working toward college degrees.[26]

## 2) Relations with the Majority

The Meccan society was generally monoreligious, with a few individu-als practicing religions other than the prevailing polytheistic one, whereas American society is officially pluralistic. Nevertheless, in comparing the relations of each community with its non-Muslim major-ity, we see a significant parallel between the early Muslim community and the American one today. As Armstrong points out, "Unlike the Prophets of Israel, Muhammad was not working towards the difficult monotheistic solution with the support of an established tradition which had its own momentum and insight and could provide ethical guidance that had been hammered out over centuries. Jesus and St. Paul were both embedded in Judaism and the first Christians came from the Jews and their supporters."[27] Rather, Muhammad was operating in an envi-ronment that did not recognize his religious agenda to be in any way connected to theirs, but rather saw it as a problematic and even danger-ous "other." Mecca was a significant trade and religious center in pre-

Islamic, polytheistic Arabia, and the Meccan oligarchy was fearful of the effect that Islam—with its beliefs of monotheism and economic and social justice—would have on the material prosperity of the city.

Likewise, American Islam, while sharing beliefs with the Christian majority, has always been viewed as an outsider religion. Like the American Jewish community before them, Muslims and their religion are seen to be inherently incompatible with the American mainstream.[28] Most Americans do not think of Islam as a religion that is similar to theirs, despite Islam's self-definition as the culmination of the Judeo-Christian prophecy. In fact, according to a recent (October 2004) poll, a full one-fourth of Americans have a negative view of Islam, a point that is elaborated upon below.[29]

Thus Islam, both in the early Meccan and contemporary American societies, has had an uneasy relationship with the mainstream. Both groups have been connected to their general societies through their members' occupations, their domiciles, and in some cases their family descent, but in following their religious beliefs, they also are separating themselves from that majority in terms of behaviors and practices. This tension of identity has had two results: a universal belief by each community that in its way of life was a clear solution for the malaise of the dominant majority, coupled with a fear by the group of its unprotected minority status in the face of that dominant majority.

## A Solution for the Society

Despite their uneasy relation to the majority, both the early Meccan and the contemporary American Muslim societies felt that they had specific answers to particular problems from which the majority society suffered. Seventh-century Mecca was known to be in a stage of "social malaise."[30] Muhammad "was living in an age that was just as cruel and violent as our own. His society was in crisis. Many felt that their old religious ideas no longer spoke to them in their dramatically altered world and, like many today, they were experiencing a spiritual vacuum."[31] Many in the society, including Muhammad himself, would withdraw to the hills to ponder life and its challenges. Muhammad was "something of a budding social critic, decrying the excesses and cruelty of everyday life in a place bereft of laws, let alone law enforcement."[32] In a society that was heavily focused on economic prosperity and trade, the difference between the haves and have-nots was severe. For example, in Mecca, it was "beneath the dignity of an upper-class citizen to sit with slaves and common folk."[33] Islam was specifically responding to the problems of its own society.

Likewise, our American society today—like others around the world—suffers from many social problems. We are living in a world of broken homes and families, divisions between rich and poor, violent crime, and poor education, to name just a few challenges. The Muslim community (like adherents of other religions) believes that its religion, with its emphases on the relationship between the individual and God, the family, and societal rather than individual rights, can halt and eventually put an end to these problems. In the words of one woman's response to Anway's survey: "You can't stray too far when the next prayer pulls you back."[34]

American Muslims also point to particular societal challenges that they feel their religion in particular addresses. For example, they cite problems resulting from uncontrolled alcohol consumption, such as alcoholism, drunk driving, etc. Likewise, the Meccans also suffered from this issue. For example, we are told that Abu Bakr "kept aloof from the nighttime reveries and drinking binges that took place around the Ka'bah."[35]

## The Fear of Minority Status

But of course because of their self-definition vis-à-vis the majority society, both groups live in tension with the majority. This tension was far more visible in Mecca than today in America since Muslim practices and beliefs then emerged as a reaction against the host country: Muslims in Mecca were the main threat to the rest of society, and as time went on, violence against them escalated. As Emerick points out, "Although Arabian society more or less accommodated every religious persuasion, this new faith taught that truth was absolute, and that there was no validity to beliefs that contradicted it."[36] In general, "Islam was beginning to touch on many areas of life: religious devotion, neighborly conduct, morals, manners, and even personal hygiene."[37] In other words, it posed a threat to the status quo. Once Muhammad went public with his mission, "No longer could he walk the streets and enjoy the hustle and bustle of his hometown."[38]

Islam in America exists among a plurality of other religions, with Muslims often coming to the United States seeking economic and/or professional opportunities, or fleeing oppression in their home countries. Due to recent political circumstances, however, the community has endured serious burdens. As early as 1990, then Vice President Dan Quayle enumerated Nazism, Communism, and Islamic fundamentalism as the three threats the Western world must address collectively. According to the American-Arab Anti-Discrimination Committee, Muslims across the country experienced, in the aftermath of September 11, a range of discrimination, from the loss of jobs to hate crimes that resulted in at least seven deaths. More than eighty thousand men from mostly Muslim countries were forced to register with the federal Department of Homeland Security, and deportation proceedings have begun for roughly thirteen thousand of them, even though none of these men have been charged with terrorism-related offenses.[39] Results of a poll carried out by America's largest Islamic civil-liberties group, the Council on American-Islamic Relations (CAIR), released on October 4, 2004, illustrate that one in four Americans holds anti-Muslim views. Survey results, based on one thousand telephone interviews conducted between June 23 and July 2, 2004, showed that over one-fourth of survey respondents agreed with stereotypes such as "Muslims teach their children to hate" and "Muslims value life less than other people." When asked what comes to mind when they hear "Muslim," 32 percent of respondents made negative comments (terrorism, war, killing), and only 2 percent had a positive response.[40]

Both the Meccan community and the American one suffer from negative press. In Mecca, "the propagandists of the Meccans and their cohorts among the Arabian tribes claimed that the Muslims were troublemakers."[41] Poets, that society's equivalent of the media, would write negative verses about Muhammad and his followers. And today, in its search for sensationalism, much negative press is given to Islam and Muslims.

3) METHODS OF COPING WITH AND PROMOTING
MINORITY IDENTITY

A minority—particularly one in the spotlight—uses several methods to cope with its reality. As Schmidt points out, "In Weberian terms it may be described as a movement from *gesellschaft* (solidarity with a society or a nation) to *gemeinschaft* (solidarity with a community)."[42] In order to feel that this second form of solidarity is as strong as the first, the minority needs to establish a set of rules that mark it as a coherent whole, and that help it to establish itself as part of the fabric of the majority society. This can be done through personal manifestations of identity formation, such as dress codes, as well as institutional measures, such as community gathering places and organizations.

## Maintaining Identity

The early Muslim community retained its identity in key ways. Most of the religious practices were codified during the Medinan period. During the Meccan period, the community was more geared to identification with the People of the Book (Christians and Jews). Muslims were encouraged to wear their hair and beards like the People of the Book.[43] They gathered to worship the One God, by reading or reciting what had been revealed of the Qur'an thus far.

As with any minority today, and particularly one without a clearly apparent contemporary leader, Muslims in the United States have varying views on what it means to be Muslim, and what are the exact duties and values that should be precisely observed. As Jane Smith points out:

> For many years, then, the response of many Muslim immigrants was to attempt to hide their religious and ethnic identities, to change their names to make them sound more American, and to refrain from participating in practices or adopting dress that would make them appear "different" from the average citizen. Gradually, as the Muslim immigrant community became much larger, much more diversified, much better educated, and much more articulate about its own self-understanding, attempts to blend into American society have given way to more sophisticated discussions about the importance of living in America but, at the same time, retaining a sense of one's own religious culture.[44]

Many Muslims in the United States see no contradiction in being American and Muslim; just as others are American Jews, American Christians, or American Buddhists, they are American Muslims. Their Muslimness is thus manifest in their beliefs, and is particularly visible in their practices. The second and third pillars of their faith, prayer five times a day and fasting from dawn to dusk during the month of Ramadan, are practices that are evident in a Muslim's public behavior; prayer times punctuate the work or school day, and abstention from eating and drinking draws attention to the Muslim practitioner. Abstaining from alcohol is another clear identity-marker, as is the wearing of the headscarf, a practice that is adopted with more frequency among the youth. Often women whose mothers would have never thought of adopting the scarf take on the scarf with enthusiasm, wishing to embrace a practice that they believe is religiously mandated, but also presents a clear sign of their identity to those around them. Those who do not practice the tenets of Islam but share the belief system will sometimes wear jewelry with "Allah" or a Qur'anic verse on it, similar to the cross and Star of David necklaces worn by Christians and Jews. Young men often take on practices that were carried out at the time of the Prophet even if they are not specifically "Islamic," such as growing a beard or wearing Arab-style gowns.

Identity establishment occurs in other, more subtle ways among the youth, particularly the second generation. For example, many second-generation American Muslims distance themselves from their ethnic backgrounds, claiming that their parents' countries of origin are not sufficiently Islamic. In this way they highlight their religious identity but subvert their ethnic background, relegating it to a position that actually places it in direct conflict with (and ultimately losing out to) that primary religious identity.

This focus on religious identity over ethnic background became particularly clear even in the immigrant first generation in the aftermath of 9/11. A six-year study released by Columbia University on October 3, 2004, shows that in the last three years, New York City's estimated six hundred thousand Muslims "have identified more deeply with their religious roots." The public began to think of them as Muslims first, so that "though New York City's Muslims are from many places—Guyana, Turkey, Pakistan, Morocco—they were united after September 11 by a common burden," the study found. "The increased public scrutiny and acts of bias they suffered caused many who had previously identified mostly with their countries of origin to unite under the larger cultural banner of Islam." As an anonymous South Asian Muslim interviewee explained, "I was made to think more of myself as a Muslim from the outside world."[45]

*Building Institutions and Structures to Create Physical and Mental Space*

But maintaining identity through personal cues is not enough. For a minority to feel its presence in a society, it needs concrete institutions and structures to create its own physical and mental space. Even as an initially clandestine, then a more visible but persecuted minority in Mecca, the first Muslim community sought refuge at a house owned by the Companion al-Arqam b. Abi al-Arqam of Quraysh (*dar* al-arqam). Situated at the hill of al-Safa, close to the Ka'ba, the house served as a sanctuary (*bayt*) for the budding Muslim community, where the members would meet to read and study the Qur'an, to worship and pray, and to connect as a community.[46]

While it has been estimated that the majority of immigrant Muslims are not affiliated with any Islamic organization,[47] there is a plethora of "Islamic" institutions that have been founded in the United States. Muslims have asserted their identity and existence through the establishment of mosques, schools, political and social advocacy groups, food stores, publications, Web sites, and higher learning. These establishments validate the Muslim experience by showing the community—and especially those of the younger generation who are apt to feel isolated and markedly different from their societal peers, particularly post–9/11—that their practices are part of a synchronous whole. If so many friends, neighbors, and community members can come together to practice the tenets of their religion, then surely so can little Muhammad and little Zaynab. As a result, by the late 1990s, there were over 1,200 mosques in the United States, with 227 of these in California.[48] There are around 165 full-time Islamic schools, two universities, 426 associations, and 89 Islamic publications (www.islam101.com). When Muslim students came to the United States in the 1950s and 1960s, there was a need for them to band together in affirmation of their religious convictions; and thus, in 1963, the Muslim Student Association was formed.[49] In public schools and at the university level, Muslim Student Associations are commonly found on campuses, and attract significant Muslim populations.

CONCLUSION

In his 1997 study of Muslims in Los Angeles, Kambiz GhaneaBassiri noted that:

> In general, the prevailing attitude of Muslims towards the United
> States is one of ambivalence. . . . This ambivalence is rooted in
> the age-old discussion of the extent to which individual freedoms
> should be limited in order to ensure the prosperity of the society

as a whole. A conversation with virtually any Muslim will show the omnipresence of alcohol, drug addiction, nudity on television and in movies . . . and the constant drive for wealth in the United States are all viewed as signs of an immoral society and a decaying nation. . . . On the other hand, immigrant Muslims have benefited from the opportunities found in the United States. They opted to immigrate to the United States to take advantage of the educational and economic opportunities available here.[50]

The ambivalence expressed by the author here succinctly encapsulates the feelings of immigrant and second-generation American Muslims. Amid their appreciation for freedom of speech, and the American values of honesty and hard work, lies their dislike of what they regard as the social disintegration of the family, the community, and the society as a whole. Such a tension is once again very similar to that of the Meccan Muslim community, which on the one hand was against the rampant materialism and social decline of the society, but on the other hand benefited strongly from the city's position as a trade and religious center, both with regard to economic prosperity as well as the opportunity to interact with groups from around the peninsula. It was, after all, thanks to Mecca's position that groups from Yathrib/Medina first came to visit, and it was thanks to this visit that Muhammad and his supporters were granted the opportunity to migrate from Mecca to Medina, escaping persecution and launching the establishment of the first Islamic city-state.

This juxtaposition of the positive and the negative aspects of American society is negotiated in different ways across the Muslim community. Some see the negatives as more rampant, some are only concerned with the positives, while others see the two as a natural balance that exists within any society. Some even try to reconcile the positives of American society with the positives of Islam. As a young American engineer put it, "American values are, by and large, very consistent with Islamic values, with a focus on family, faith, hard work, and an obligation to better self and society."[51] It is, after all, the definition of American society that in large part shapes one's view of it.

But this discussion, based on GhaneaBassiri's 1997 work, is now just a backdrop for a more salient post–9/11 debate. "The general comfort level felt by most Muslims was truly jarred by Sept. 11, and they became a threatening minority who would be defined mostly by their

religion," explained Peter J. Awn, a professor of Islamic religion at Columbia who helped coordinate the six-year Columbia University study
of New York City Muslims. September 11 "has caused serious soul-
searching by the community."[52] The passage of the Uniting and
Strengthening America by Providing Appropriate Tools Required to Intercept and Obstruct Terrorism (USA Patriot Act, 2001) gave the government the right to intercept wire, oral, and electronic transmissions
relating to terrorism, computer fraud, and abuse offenses (Sections 201
and 202); and the subsequent Patriot Act II (2003), among other things,
created a new category of "domestic security surveillance" that permits
electronic eavesdropping of entirely domestic activity under looser
standards than those governing ordinary criminal surveillance (Section
122), gives the government secret access to credit reports without consent and without judicial process (Section 201), and authorizes secret
arrests in immigration and other cases, such as material-witness warrants where the detained person is not criminally charged (Section 201).
As a result of this legislation, American Muslims are feeling that the
positives of their society have been severely undermined. Despite the
specific clauses cautioning against discrimination against Arab and
Muslim Americans, the groups nonetheless feel that the invasion of
their privacy is an invasion of the American freedoms that they had so
cherished. Living in fear, their identification as Muslims has become
more loaded, more thought-provoking. Their American Muslim hybrid
identity is now viewed as even more incongruous.

And again, Muslims' reactions differ. A small minority believes that
the laws are warranted, and that they target the illegal immigrant and
the potential terrorist, but not average Muslims living their daily lives.
A substantial percentage believes that the laws are a by-product of the
views of the present government, and that a change in government will
bring about a change of policy. And others have sunk into a state of
shocked hopelessness, convinced that they are the victims of a persecution that they fear may escalate to a new holocaust, with Muslims as
the obvious targets, presumed guilty until proven innocent. Only time
will tell which of these groups was the wisest in its outlook. But for
now, the American Muslim identity, shaped by its history, its social
outlook, and its political position, remains a constantly evolving dynamic presence, just like its Meccan predecessor before it.

# Making Safe Space for Questioning for Young American Muslims

*Amira Quraishi*

I chose to speak today of making safe space for young Muslims with questions because the two organizations I studied were frequently described as programs that specifically address a need to think critically about Islam in an American context. The mission statement of one of these organizations, the Muslim Youth Camp (MYC), explains that it

> brings Muslim families and individuals of diverse backgrounds together for a fun-filled week of Islamic living, learning and inspirational experiences in nature. By encouraging camaraderie, personal spiritual exploration and respect for diversity of Islamic practice, MYC seeks to be a strong catalyst in the creation of American Muslim identities.

The second organization, the American Muslims Intent on Learning and Activism (AMILA), was founded in the San Francisco Bay Area in 1992 by second-generation American Muslims in their early twenties. AMILA describes itself as "committed to spiritual enrichment, intellectual freedom, and community service."

I myself was involved with both of these organizations during my twenties, which makes objectivity in my research difficult; on the other hand, it gives me the advantage of observing the inner mechanics of the organizations over a considerable period of time. This invitation to speak about them at this conference has allowed me to step back, study them, and think about them in the larger American fabric of pluralism. It has been touching for me to hear once again the voices of so many young Muslims, who spoke to me with such an earnest desire to be heard. They spoke as if they were entrusting me with personal opinions and experiences not accepted in the larger Muslim American community. These young Muslims repeatedly stated they were drawn to these two organizations because they best reflected their American Muslim experience and vision. My research goal was to record as accurately as possible how participants between the ages of nineteen and thirty viewed these programs. In the case of the Muslim Youth Camp, my research included people who are now in their forties and fifties and have been involved with the camp since their twenties.

MYC and AMILA are two organizations with very different structures. However, respondents from both groups affirmed three common goals: 1) the need for a nonjudgmental environment in which to explore themselves and different ideas; 2) an environment that reflects an American Muslim culture; and 3) a need to contribute to the community in meaningful ways. One respondent explained that it was not enough just to volunteer to help at a mosque fundraising dinner. MYC gave her the opportunity to be a counselor, an experience that enriched her understanding of herself and also allowed her to have a positive and meaningful role in the lives of teenage American Muslim girls.

HISTORY, PROGRAM, STRUCTURE OF MYC

The Muslim Youth Camp started in 1962 with a handful of American Muslims. For one week every summer, they gathered to share their faith, to pray the five daily prayers in congregation, to learn about Islam, and to share their experiences as a new minority in America. Before local communities and mosques were established in America, the MYC was the only place where these Muslims could hear the call to prayer (*adhan*). The daily program has always included the five daily prayers in congregation, beginning with the pre-dawn prayer (*fajr*). The rest of the day is filled with sports, nature hikes, recreation and crafts, campfire, intergenerational charitable projects, classes on a chosen theme for the week, and group counseling sessions. The theme for MYC 2004 ("And do good works") allowed us to focus on a phrase that is frequently repeated in the Qur'an and related to belief in God.

Every activity at the camp is designed to reflect on a given theme. The camp environment continues to operate solely because of the work of a volunteer staff. This dedication to community and volunteerism is reflected in the MYC environment, which reinforces that each individual is a valuable and dynamic part of the whole community. Adults and youth alike take part in preparing meals, cleaning the grounds, charitable projects, etc. It is a reflection of the Islamic duty to God to take care of humanity and the earth.

In the early years, the camp attracted twenty to thirty people. Some were American converts to Islam. Many were immigrants from the Middle East and South Asia who had come to America for education and for a chance to pursue the American dream. All of them were in their mid-thirties or younger. Some were married with young children. As the children of this new minority grew older, MYC had to respond to the challenges and pressures facing them; they focused more on developing a dynamic curriculum and counseling program. The counseling program created a safe space for these Muslim youth to share, with the help of young American Muslim adults who overcame similar obstacles, their fears and frustrations. The MYC has always stressed that each individual is a valuable member of the community, and that the community is a diverse one. Individuals differ in their level of Islamic practice, their ethnic backgrounds, and even their ideologies. This diversity is as much a reality as the new American Muslim culture. This internal diversity, as it becomes part of a secular American society, gives rise to many questions. The MYC believes that these questions should be faced and discussed with respect and thoughtful criticism. Moreover, the MYC relies on the guidance in the Qur'an. They believe that it is a book for people who think, contemplate, and ponder.

The MYC curriculum is dedicated to demonstrating the diversity of thought within Islam. Different schools of thought, including minority schools (e.g., Shiite) are all recognized as authentic, but with different methodologies of interpretation. The emphasis is on getting Muslims to think for themselves, by educating themselves and asking questions. The dynamic format of the three daily forty-five-minute classes aims to draw out what the young people think, and encourages them to apply their own skills and strategies as they face complex issues that pertain to their lives and their futures. Through case studies and role-playing, they explore their own experiences, play out leadership roles, and engage in problem solving by working with others. In these ways, the

MYC doesn't try to teach the young people what to think but how to explore diversity of thought in a supportive and respectful environment.

All the respondents in this study commented that the subjects addressed at the MYC are issues that relate directly to the lives of young American Muslims. These issues, unfortunately, are not addressed in the mosques. Furthermore, the mosque style of teaching or preaching is not stimulating to young Americans. For example, one respondent noted that one might find an imam who tells people not to waste water; the MYC, however, approaches the same idea in the familiar terms of "Reduce, Reuse, Recycle," and presented environmental sensitivity as a religious obligation, giving participants the opportunity to discuss and ask how this value applies to their lives. Other important topics mentioned by respondents that are discussed at the MYC (and not at the average mosque) included controversial issues such as adoption, women performing wedding ceremonies, and the etiquette of giving advice to a peer. In one class, campers were given a complex scenario that encouraged them to think about multifaceted aspects to life. Campers were instructed to discuss how a local community is to utilize its funds. Individuals were given roles to play (e.g., immigrants, American-born Muslims, people with ideological differences, people with different interests and agendas, such as demands for services, education, social activities). As the drama played out, campers had fun acting out other personas, using accents, drawing upon what they have observed in their own communities. When put in a role-playing situation, these teenagers enjoy debate and argument; it is thrilling to see them vibrantly engaged and actually expressing their opinions. The teenagers often comment that the class was simply fun, but the twentysomething counselors who help facilitate these role-plays understand the deeper purpose of the exercise. The students realize later that through these exercises they can better analyze the real world that they encounter, whether in their local community or on a college campus. Case studies put current issues into cultural, social, and political contexts, demonstrating that someone's statement about Islam may not simply be "incorrect" or based on selective sources, but also may be entirely driven by one's socioeconomic, political, or cultural circumstances. Campers gain a breadth of understanding for competing interests in a community because they are forced to put on another's shoes, and to interact with them.

Classes such as these are designed for each age group, including postgraduate adults. Since the 1970s, the majority of campers have been between the ages of nine and seventeen, and many are the children and grandchildren of the first MYC campers. The past twenty-five years of MYC has supported approximately two hundred campers each year. There is typically a drop in attendance of campers between the ages of seventeen and twenty-one (the college years) and an increase again in the twentysomething age group, when many individuals return to MYC as counselors and staff. Many staff and counselors who returned to MYC in their twenties noted that, in their college years, they needed time to separate from their parents' direction and explore their own choices as young adults. In addition to the simple practicalities of life such as preparing for a career and holding down summer jobs, they were "finding themselves," which, for them at that time, did not include MYC. Others, who did not return to MYC after their high school years, said that what they got out of MYC was mainly having fun and meeting friends. Many of these MYC campers who did not attend in their twenties nonetheless returned in their thirties with their own children.

The twentysomething generation mentioned several different reasons for their participation in MYC. Many are attracted to the leadership opportunities, such as counseling or coaching sports at camp. Some mentioned the importance of feeling valued for their personal initiative and creativity, something that they do not find when volunteering at a local mosque. Some respondents, who attended the MYC as youth, commented that when they interacted with older Muslim role-models such as their counselors and teachers, they learned the value of giving back to their community. As campers, they were surprised to learn that their counselors were actually lawyers, medical students, or engineers who had donated a week's vacation to MYC. That stuck with them. One first-time counselor noted the impact that her MYC counselor had on her career choice. Meeting a Muslim who was a history major opened her eyes to the importance of the humanities; she is now getting a degree in education. Others mentioned that the relatively long history of MYC is a strong appeal. Strong family bonds are formed between campers and generations of families over the years; the history is visible in the continued participation of every age group. They realized that they always have a home at MYC and that they never outgrow it. Some counselors are the grandchildren of MYC campers from the 1960s and 1970s. One respondent expressed her specific desire to contribute the same support that she had received from her MYC counselors when she was young. As a youth, she recognized that her counselor understood her experience of being raised Muslim in America, something her immigrant parents had trouble understanding. Many respondents mentioned the valuable insight they gained into themselves as a result of their leadership roles at MYC. "I learned about my own character and how others perceive me," one first-time counselor said. "I didn't know that I had leadership skills until someone at the end of camp told me I demonstrated them." Overall, respondents mentioned a feeling of connectedness because MYC is a project run by their peers. It places them in a larger family network that values the insights of every generation.

In addition to the leadership opportunities at MYC, respondents stressed that the nonjudgmental atmosphere was particularly attractive. One respondent noted that MYC doesn't push an ideological agenda; if there were any agenda it would be, she remarked, "to stress that everyone should get along." The method for "getting along" is through asking unconventional questions, putting oneself in another's shoes by role-playing, examining oneself and how others perceive them, and living with Muslims who have different backgrounds. Many noted that this MYC culture was something distinctively American, something that is not readily seen in most local Muslim communities. They perceived MYC as an independent organization that doesn't have an agenda like other groups that have the same governing board forever and perpetuate culturally specific views of Islam, many of which exclude other Muslims. "MYC is a group of people of different cultural backgrounds tied together by two things: being Muslim and American." Another camper said "MYC has a really unique American Muslim culture." Many noted that this environment allowed for a healthier interaction between males and females, one that was neither too segregated nor too integrated and allowed for everyone to feel comfortable. This environment also provides more opportunities for women to serve in leadership capacities. One respondent compared the "down-to-earth setting" at MYC with other Muslim programs: "Usually big gatherings of Muslims are restrictive, intensive learning. MYC is laid-back and enjoyable." Another respondent described the atmosphere this way: "It gives everyone an opportunity to express who they are as a person rather than be around their parents. Everyone opens up."

## AMILA

The second organization I studied was AMILA (American Muslims Intent on Learning and Activism), an acronym for the Arabic word 'amila, to work. The Muslim American twentysomethings who started this organization in 1992 represent a culturally mixed group. They are the children of American converts to Islam, immigrants from South Asia, the Middle East, Turkey, Afghanistan, Iran, and Africa. Many of them are biracial. These twentysomethings grew up in a culturally diverse Muslim community, characterized by mutual respect and appreciation for the diversity of Muslim cultures amongst them. Their parents shared a common faith and Muslim identity; most of them also shared the immigrant experience. These circumstances demonstrated to this second generation that a Muslim identity was compatible with a wide range of cultural identities and that an American Muslim identity was not impossible, but rather just new. This realization drove their desire to shape what the new American Muslim identity would become. AMILA's mission states that "We are at the forefront of forging an American Muslim identity, one that, *inshallah* [God willing], will strengthen the faith of individuals, foster respect for our beliefs, and contribute in a compassionate and meaningful way to the community around us."

The hopes articulated in this mission statement reflect the challenges these young Muslims experienced growing up in America. First, the Muslim community's failure to recognize an *American* Muslim culture as a legitimate Muslim cultural identity frustrated them. As a result, many of them suffered a religious identity crisis that challenged the strength of their faith in God and Islam. AMILA responded to these circumstances by openly recognizing that these young Muslims were born into the unprecedented situation of being American and Muslim. AMILA asserted that they, like their parents, should not have to choose between their cultural identity and their religious identity. While still very much a part of their local Muslim communities, AMILA sought as an organization to distinguish itself from the existing Muslim community by fully recognizing and embracing their American-ness and by affirming the value of a vibrant American Muslim experience.

Second, AMILA founders recognized that America is the only country they ever called home. American society, however, is largely ignorant about Islam and its history, cultures, and contributions. While growing up, they experienced a mixture of both prejudice and sincere interest from non-Muslim Americans. AMILA saw the potential for American-raised Muslims to educate the non-Muslim American community about Islam from their unique perspective. Thus, AMILA generated projects like media outreach and the AMILA Speaker's Bureau, which worked with schoolteachers to arrange visits to classes studying Islam. The experience of growing up Muslim in America sparked many questions about Islam unfamiliar to the immigrant Muslims in their local communities. AMILA, therefore, sought a deeper understanding of Islamic beliefs, history, law, culture, and spirituality, and arranged intensive educational retreats with college-level requirements.

Third, AMILA aimed to express their religious values through action that served the American community. While many local Muslim communities focused largely on international issues and ritual, AMILA formed its new Muslim American identity, aimed "to contribute to the growth of humanity in America and to be influenced by those aspects of American customs and culture which do not contradict Islam." These pioneers described themselves as "freely practicing Muslims engaging in American ideals of democracy, education, social welfare, participating in American society, and motivated by their belief in God and in Islam as in agreement with American ideals of good works, social welfare, social justice, democracy, freedom of thought and religion." AMILA wanted to act on these values by addressing wider issues than just those pertaining to the Muslim community and Muslim countries. Furthermore, with the growth of the immigrant population and the increase in ethnic divisions within the American Muslim community, AMILA saw itself as uniquely positioned to bridge growing gaps between these smaller, ethnically defined Muslim communities.

Fourth, AMILA founders witnessed the challenges faced by their parents, who struggled to establish institutions for Muslims in America amidst cultural and ideological differences. Having grown up with American standards of higher education and innovation, AMILA founders worked hard to create a constitution and by-laws that would ensure the organization's smooth operation. Several respondents of this study, former AMILA officers, attributed the smooth transition of leadership to these clear directives. AMILA's governing body is a "Steering Committee" with equal members who, to pursue any course of action, must agree by consensus. AMILA members credit this structure for encouraging a sense of equality and mutual appreciation within the group. In this way, the resolution of a problem demands that everyone be satisfied and act in the spirit of true cooperation. One former AMILA officer noted that this structure enabled increased participation by women. In many Muslim communities, a woman holding a position of leadership (e.g., president of an organization) would be challenged by those who believe there are no Islamic grounds for it. The AMILA steering committee structure ensured that the legitimacy of a woman holding a position on the steering committee was not easily challenged by other Muslims. AMILA did not have any male or female leaders or presidents; all steering committee members worked and acted together as a group. Therefore, a woman could not be called "the leader," and her position could not be challenged on a religious basis. In addition to the constitution and by-laws, AMILA stressed its obligation to operate with high standards of organization, punctuality, and following through on its promises. Several members noted that it was precisely the lack of these qualities in other Muslim organizations that made them lose confidence in them. Consequently, members wanted AMILA to demonstrate a religious obligation to these values.

The early study groups helped realize the values of organization and punctuality by focusing on self-improvement as an aspect of Islamic religious learning. The study groups focused not only on religious learning but also relied on peer support to remedy personal shortcomings. The saying of the prophet Mohammed, that a Muslim is a mirror to another Muslim, reinforced the young AMILA community's obligations to each other. For example, in one study-group assignment, members identified each others' weaknesses and strengths in an effort to improve their characters. A person with a flaw such as chronic tardiness demonstrated a degree of disrespect to those waiting for him. And if Muslims act as mirrors to each other, they will in turn not respect the person who is tardy. Study group members kindly and supportively helped each other strive toward personal improvement, focusing on correcting their weaknesses and reinforcing their strengths.

In its twelve years of existence, AMILA has never had a physical building as its center of operation. Many members noted this as an advantage. The AMILA members host events at their homes in towns and neighborhoods around the San Francisco Bay Area. They noted that this contributes to a feeling of community since everyone is a host and no one is a guest. In addition, the events draw only those who are like-minded or interested in AMILA's philosophy. A local mosque, whose membership draws on individuals in close proximity to it, may as a result draw many individuals with a wide range of conflicting attitudes. AMILA members, in contrast, attend events primarily because they agree with the purpose of the event, and are often willing to travel long distances.

To allow for maximum participation, AMILA events are varied and frequent. Weekly study groups, like the one mentioned previously, demand open space for questioning and in-depth learning of Islam. Subjects highlighted in these classes include "the Science of the Qur'an," its revelation and compilation, methods for interpreting and understanding, and a study of the Prophet Muhammad's life alongside a chronological study of the revelation of the Qur'an. Annual AMILA events have become very popular even outside the AMILA community, sometimes attracting participants from around the country. The Islamic Art Fairs promote cultural and philanthropic dimensions of the American Muslim experience and support American Muslim artists and their work. "Eid for Everyone" is a gift drive that takes place every Ramadan and provides hundreds of gifts for underprivileged Muslim children in the Bay Area. The Spiritual Retreat is also held every Ramadan. It is a weekend dedicated to focusing on daily and additional nighttime prayers in congregation (*salat*), congregational praise and remembrance of God (*dhikr*), quiet reflection, and intimate discussions about faith. AMILA conducts other charity projects and collaborates with organizations providing social services such as domestic-violence intervention, improved healthcare access, financial services to the poor, and educational forums.

The monthly General Meetings are usually the best introduction to AMILA's purpose and culture. They always include a social potluck meal and a presentation or discussion. Discussion of ideas is of great importance to the culture of AMILA. For example, one recent General Meeting focused on the question "Should Muslims participate in American Holidays (e.g., Halloween, Christmas, Thanksgiving, the Fourth of July)?" Participants broke up into small groups and listened to research on the origins of the holidays, as well as the meanings of symbols associated with the holidays. Then they discussed the following questions:

Are there moral values or precepts implied by "participation" in this holiday's activities? Do the religious origins or significance of the holiday conflict with Islamic beliefs?

Are any of the holiday's activities clearly forbidden in Islam?

How does nonparticipation in this holiday affect a child, teen, or adult?

What do you think this holiday symbolizes today to people who celebrate it?

Does commercialization of the holiday affect your participation?

If you've celebrated this holiday, what did it mean to you personally?

Do you think this holiday plays an important role in helping us appreciate the beauty of God's creation: the seasons of the year?

Should a Muslim's acceptance or rejection of this holiday be active or passive?

In this setting, participants are not pressured to conform to one opinion. Rather, emphasis is put on educating oneself and acknowledging personal differences. In this way, AMILA approaches any subject with much more depth and openness than is often found in the local mosques.

Another meeting addressed the difficult issue of finding a spouse. There are multiple ways in America to meet one's life-partner. Various Muslim cultures have different ways of finding a spouse, and most AMILA members are caught between their parents' methods and American methods. Young American Muslims' ideas about marriage are often different from their parents' views. This AMILA meeting explored these conflicts in a group of married and single participants. Some of the issues raised were self-exploration, reasons for marrying, the role of parents and extended family in choosing a spouse, wedding planning, future life, the role of marriage in your religious life, the role of both spouses' professions in marriage, compatibility in managing the family budget, social activities and recreation, ideas about raising children, the wife's changing her name, managing household duties, and the importance of the marriage contract. AMILA has made available online a sample marriage contract developed by American Muslim lawyers. This contract is significant because many Muslims (especially women) do not know their rights in marriage. In addition, some elements of the Islamic marriage contract, e.g., the obligatory gift to the bride (*mahar*), do not easily transfer to the American court system. And finally, this online contract is significant because, in many divorce cases, Islamic marriage contracts are not upheld in American courts because of their peculiar legal language. Other General Meetings featured the following topics and speakers:

Filmmaker and Speaker: Naem Mohaihimin, "Presentation of his documentary on the persecution of Ahmadi Muslims by Muslims in Bangladesh"

Speaker: Maad Abu Ghazaleh, Democratic Candidate for Congress,
  California District 12

"Muslims And The 2004 Elections"

Speaker: Traci Tokhi, www.lovingparenting.org

"Exploring the Spirit of Parenting"

AMILA 11th Anniversary Meeting!

"The Tastes & Sounds Of Ramadan"

Speaker: Matthai Chakko Kuruvila, Reporter, *San Jose Mercury-
  News*: "Islam In The Media: A Reporter's View"

Activity: A Collaborative Mural Painting in Downtown San Francisco and Picnic With the Japanese American Community

As you can see, AMILA general meetings attempt to have innovative
programming and to address current issues that reflect the concerns of
young Muslim Americans.

As part of the early structuring of the AMILA constitution and by-
laws, founders designed an invocation (*du'a*) to start every AMILA
gathering. The invocation calls on several of the ninety-nine Qur'anic
names for God:

**In the name of God, the Most Merciful, the Most Beneficent.**
We thank You for blessing us with our families, friends, safety,
and sustenance. We thank You for giving us the ability to worship
you through learning and acting upon Your teachings. We begin
this meeting in Your name.

**In the name of God, the All-Embracing.**
We pray that You help us increase our *taqwa, iman, sabr*, humility, knowledge, and kindness so that we may grow spiritually
close to You and to each other.

**In the name of God, the Wise and the Ever-Patient.**
Increase us in knowledge of ourselves so that we may know You.
Increase our wisdom and patience by respecting each other's
ideas, opinions, and beliefs, even if these are different from what
we are used to.

**In the name of God, the Extender, the Compassionate.**
Help us extend our hearts to You and to each other. Help us to
worship You and humble ourselves by using kind words and for-
giving spirits.

**In the name of God, the All-Knowing.**
Please help us in using our intellect, faith, and wisdom to increase our knowledge of Islam, the Qur'an, and the way of the Prophet. Purify our souls and make us worthy of receiving knowledge so that we may comprehend and live in the true spirit of the religion.

**In the name of God, the Sustainer.**
Help us to make the best use of our time and talents. Help us to worship You and be conscious of You in our pursuit of personal and professional goals. Help us translate our worldly affairs and rituals into worship for You. All praise is due to You and to You is the end of all journeys. We ask for Your forgiveness, always. *Amen (Ameen)*.

In addition to these projects, AMILA maintains a discussion listserv (amilanet) that reaches people around the globe as well as an excellent Web site (amila.org). The Web site features articles of interest for and by members, allowing everyone to see what young Muslim Americans are thinking about. In one article, the author, Shahed Amanullah, confronts a sort of "schizophrenia" that many Muslims experience regarding their responses to terrorism. "Many Muslims," he writes, "are strangely schizophrenic; on one hand they condemn the portrayal of Islam in the media as a violent religion, but at the same time they engage in inflammatory violent rhetoric against real or perceived enemies." These voices belong to Muslims raised in America, and as adults need to be heard and recognized by Muslims and non-Muslims alike. Their concerns come from their Islamic ideals as well as their American ideals.

AMILA's success has encouraged the development of similar organizations throughout the United States and Canada. Many young Muslims have found AMILA attractive not only because it reflects their perspectives, but because it has been so successful. Nevertheless, some former AMILA steering committee members have noted certain areas for improvement. Because the steering committee is so large and AMILA's projects so numerous, they believe most of the burden of the projects falls on them and not on the general members. Often general members benefit from the activities without contributing their time and energy. As a result there is a high burn-out rate among steering committee members, who typically hold two or three one- or two-year positions and then remove themselves completely from the administration of the organization. Another member pointed out an advantage to this trend: the short terms in office ensure a smooth transition of leadership because many committee members, though the same from term to term, assume different assignments. Therefore, the vision and cultural environment remains consistent. One member observed that as AMILA-goers have aged, married, and started families, much of the focus has been divided between family and child-friendly activities rather than on young-adult activities and discussions. Nonetheless, AMILA has survived its first twelve years and has over time attracted new members while maintaining its structure and vision. One AMILA founder, who had long since moved away from the San Francisco Bay Area, remarked, "When I go back to visit, I can walk into an AMILA meeting today and it looks and feels like AMILA, but I don't know anyone there!"

## CONCLUSION

I have found that AMILA and MYC are programs born out of needs to synthesize American and Muslim ideals and to resolve cultural conflicts residing within individuals. They are born out of people's need to reaffirm their place both in the Muslim world and in American society at large. Both organizations emphasize the importance of examining this need by encouraging critical thinking, while seeking information and welcoming diversity of thought. Whereas many Muslims feel their Muslim organizations promote only one perspective, the goal of AMILA and MYC, at the end of the day, is to help Muslims think intelligently about issues, and question their sources of information. Naturally there will be differences among these individuals, but the cultures of equality and mutual respect generated by these organizations is founded on a belief in God as the ultimate Judge and on a realization that every person is on a journey to understand themselves and God. These organizations sustain the hope that human beings can get along better when they understand that there are legitimate reasons for differences of opinion, reasons that are much more complex than the labels of "conservative" or "liberal" suggest.

# SECOND-GENERATION MUSLIM IMMIGRANTS IN DETROIT MOSQUES: THE SECOND GENERATION'S SEARCH FOR THEIR PLACE AND IDENTITY IN THE AMERICAN MOSQUE

*Ihsan Bagby*

Muslim immigrants started arriving in America in large numbers after the 1965 liberalization of immigration law. They achieved economic success, raised families, and established mosques as a commitment to retaining their faith and passing on that faith to their children.[1] Now, after four decades, the children of these immigrants are maturing—a significant portion of them are in high school and college and some are starting their own families. Using data and interviews from a study of Detroit mosques,[2] this paper looks at second-generation mosque-goers and addresses three issues: 1) the second generation's sense of belonging to the mosque; 2) their identity; and 3) their approach to understanding Islam. The overriding question in these three issues is the assimilation of the second generation—whether the second generation will leave the mosque and abandon their religious and ethnic identity. This paper does not attempt to answer this question directly, but focuses instead on one set of second-generation Muslims. Indirectly, however, this study offers reflections and some insight on the issue of assimilation.[3]

Assimilation theory, whether "straight-line,"[4] "bumpy,"[5] or nuanced,[6] predicts that the second generation of Muslim immigrants will inevitably assimilate into American culture and move away from "traditional" Islam, especially as that generation moves up the economic ladder. Assimilation constitutes the great fear of many mosque leaders and Muslim parents. According to this theory, the assimilation of new immigrant groups into the dominant American culture is progressive and irreversible.[7] Straight-line assimilation theory views assimilation as a generational process wherein each generation seeks its own accommodation to the larger society. In particular, the second generation accelerates the process of turning away from the stigmatized ethnic culture of their parents. Subsequent generations might retain a "symbolic" ethnicity,[8] but it is only a shell with little substance.

Another refinement is to view assimilation as a process of stages. In his authoritative work, Gordon[9] depicted the assimilation process in seven stages, which can be reduced to two essential stages: acculturation, whereby the immigrant group adopts the values and cultural practices of the core culture; and structural assimilation, which is characterized by membership and participation of the immigrant group in the societal network and groups and institutions of the dominant society.[10] Acculturation or cultural assimilation, according to Gordon, includes two distinct components: intrinsic and extrinsic cultural traits. Intrinsic traits include religious beliefs and practices, essential ethnic values, a historical language, and a sense of a common past. Extrinsic traits include dress, manner, English usage, and so on. Gordon hypothesized that extrinsic cultural traits would be the first to be acculturated,[11] but that if structural assimilation took place then assimilation of intrinsic traits would follow.[12]

More recent studies of Asian Americans point to the conclusion that the assimilation paradigm, which was based largely on the experience of European immigrants in the early part of the twentieth century, does not fit the experience of Asian Americans who immigrated along with other non-Europeans, non-whites, and often non-Christians, in the later part of the twentieth century.[13] These studies indicate that second-generation Asian Americans are retaining their ethnic identity, while integrating into the socioeconomic fabric of American society. Moreover Asian American religious organizations, including the mosque, are viewed as playing an important role in maintaining group identity and cohesion even as they provide important values for success in American society.[14]

The overall conclusion of this paper is that second-generation Muslims, like their Asian American counterparts, do not seem to be following the assimilation model; that is, they are not abandoning the ways and identity of their parents. At the same time, the second generation is not simply passively inheriting their parents' culture and religion. Instead, they are redefining and reconstructing their parents' culture and religion into something that better matches their own sense of authenticity and appropriateness. Thus, acculturation is taking place, but it is not a simple process of discarding immigrant traits and adopting American ones.

The observations for this study are drawn from the Detroit Mosque Study, conducted in 2003–4 under the sponsorship of the Institute for Social Policy and Understanding. The study included interviews with mosque leaders in all of the thirty-three mosques in Greater Detroit, questionnaires distributed in twelve mosques to attendees during Friday prayers and other mosque events (only eight mosques had sufficient responses),[15] and focus-group interviews with mosque youth. In addition, follow-up focus group sessions were conducted for this paper with the youth in a suburban South Asian mosque and two Muslim Student Associations. The study collected 1,298 completed questionnaires from mosque participants, and of this number exactly one-third of the responders were second-generation Muslims. For this paper I have included in the category of second generation those Muslims who were not born in America but arrived here when they were twelve or younger; this group is often called the 1.5 generation.

**Mosque Participants in the Detroit Mosque Study**

| | |
|---|---|
| Second-generation | 33% |
| Immigrant | 54% |
| African American | 13% |

The ages of the second generation are almost evenly divided between those under twenty and those over twenty.

**Age Breakdown of Second Generation**

| *Age* | *Percentage* |
|---|---|
| 13–20 | 52 |
| 21–39 | 44 |
| 40 + | 4* |

In all subsequent charts, the 40 + age group, being extremely small, was joined with the 13–39 age group.

DETROIT MOSQUES AND YOUTH ACTIVITIES

Detroit mosques are organized mainly along ethnic lines—much more so than the average American mosque.

**Mosque Grouped According to Dominate Ethnic Group***

|  | *Detroit* | *Actual Number* | *National* |
|---|---|---|---|
| South Asian | 33% | 11 | 28% |
| Arab | 30% | 10 | 15% |
| African American | 18% | 6 | 27% |
| Other | 12% | 4 | 14% |
| Mixed Arab/South Asian | 6% | 2 | 16% |

*Dominate groups are calculated by: 35%–39% of participants in one group and all other groups less than 20%; 40%–49% of one group and all others less than 30%; 50%–59% of one group and all others less than 40%; any group over 55%. Mixed groups calculated by two groups with at least 30% of participants each.

While only 7 percent of U.S. mosques have only one ethnic group that attends the mosque, 24 percent of Detroit mosques are attended by a single ethnic group. Detroit, as a big city with a large immigrant population, has more ethnic-enclave mosques than the rest of America. As might be expected, most of the ethnic-enclave mosques are located in an urban area. Of the fifteen urban immigrant mosques, fourteen are located in ethnic enclaves: the Arabs (Iraqis, Lebanese, Palestinians, and Yemenis) of Dearborn, and the Bangladeshis, Yemenis, and Bosnians of the Hamtramck area. Of the twelve suburban immigrant mosques, none is located in an ethnic enclave, although a residential pattern of Muslims living in the neighborhood of the mosque exists for the majority of suburban mosques.

Although largely ethnically based, almost half of immigrant mosques in Detroit use English and another language in the Friday congregational services, which indicates an effort to transcend purely ethnic boundaries and reach out to second-generation worshippers. One-third of the mosques use no English in their Friday services, perhaps the best indicator that these mosques emphasize ethnicity and attempt to retain the feel of their home-country mosques. Four of the five mosques that use only English are located in the suburbs; all of the mosques that do not use English at all are located in urban ethnic enclaves.

**Languages Used in the Friday Congregational Services of Immigrant Mosques**

| *Language used* | *Actual number of immigrant mosques* | *Percentage of mosques* |
|---|---|---|
| English only | 5 | 18.5 |
| English and another language | 13 | 48.2 |
| Other language only | 9 | 33.3 |

Immigrant mosques in Detroit, although ethnically based, can be divided into mosques that emphasize ethnicity and a more traditional view of the mosque, and those that deemphasize ethnicity and are more open to viewing the American mosque as unique. Some mosque leaders expressed, in interviews, their desire to serve their ethnic group and to recreate their home-country mosque in America. Other leaders indicated, and some quite forcefully, that they did not want their mosque to be perceived as an ethnic mosque and that they realized that the American mosque was necessarily different from the mosque in the Muslim world.

All Detroit mosques are concerned about their youth. This concern is motivated largely by the realization that in the absence of an Islamic society, their youth will be assimilated into the dominant society unless the mosque actively tries to pass on the legacy of Islam to their children. Among Detroit mosque participants, youth programming was listed next to Islamic education as the second most important mosque priority.[16]

The success of Detroit mosques in involving the second generation in the mosque is uneven. As one youth stated in response to a question about how well mosques have done in passing on the legacy of Islam to the youth: "They definitely are not a failure, but they're not a success either." However, the overall presence of second-generation youth in Detroit mosques is significant and noticeable. Mosques have adapted different strategies toward their youth. More traditional mosques, often attended by recently arrived immigrants, emphasize the traditional role of the mosque as a place of gathering for prayer and learning, including the youth of the community. Other, less traditional mosques focus on a variety of programming including youth groups and activities.

**Youth Activities**
**Percentage of mosques that have these activities**

|  | Regular | Occasional |
|---|---|---|
| Weekend school | 72 | |
| Full-time Islamic school | 27 | |
| Youth programs | 50 | 25 |
| Qur'an memorization | 47 | 12 |
| Sports/fitness activities | 37.5 | 12.5 |
| All five daily prayers held | 71 | |

Some inner-city and suburban mosques are located in areas with substantial Muslim populations, and the daily prayers offer a chance for large numbers of Muslims, both young and old, to congregate for prayer as well as socialization and play. Even some highly ethnic mosques with little youth programming are nonetheless filled with youth, especially around evening prayer—when the youth pray and then remain after prayer to socialize around the mosque.

Education is the prime focus of all youth activities in mosques. Education explains why second-generation Muslims express in their interviews a well-informed understanding of their faith. Most mosques (72 percent), no matter the location or orientation, invest in weekend schools that average about 144 students. Some of the more traditional ethnic mosques focus on after-school programs on the age-old custom, especially in South Asia, of teaching youngsters to memorize the Qur'an. These mosques have large, well-attended programs that typically meet three nights out of a week. A remarkable indication of mosque concerns for youth is the fact that nine out of thirty-three Detroit mosques (27 percent) have full time Islamic schools: four are elementary, three go through middle school and two have grades up to twelfth grade. On average 211 students attend each school. Other mosques focus on youth groups and other extracurricular programs such as sports and camps.

These mosque activities for youth, however, are aimed at youth up to middle-school age. Most mosques seem filled with younger youth, but the young adults in their twenties do not have the same noticeable presence. In only a few mosques are there activities and groups for high-school-age youth. And no mosque has programming that targets the 21–30 age group.

The eight mosques that were the focus of the mosque participant survey are representative of Detroit mosques in terms of ethnicity (two South Asian, two Arab, and one mixed) and location (three suburban and two urban), but none is a traditional, ethnically focused mosque. The results of this study, therefore, are more indicative of the mosque that is trying to move away from the traditional, ethnic mosque.

The youth in the eight mosques display a substantial level of acculturation to at least the extrinsic aspects of American culture. Youth activities are conducted in English, even though most of the youth apparently can speak their parents' language. Casual conversations are spoken in vernacular English, typically about movies, sports, and other entertainment. Although two of the mosques are located in urban areas, the youth seem to be part of the upwardly mobile middle class. They express their desire to succeed in education and careers, and all the college-age youth seem to be in college. The dress of the youth is American but clearly on the more conservative side. Females do not wear ethnic dress as many of their mothers do, but they do cover their body and wear scarves inside the mosque. Some females apparently do not wear the scarf outside the mosque; for example, at a major high-school graduation party held at a mosque, the female honoree wore a scarf, but in proudly displayed pictures of her accomplishments in high school, she did not wear a scarf. Youth activities are usually divided by gender, but when they are conducted together, females and males are seated separately.

## BELONGING AND MOSQUE PARTICIPATION

In the Detroit mosque survey, slightly more than two-thirds of the second-generation Muslims responded that they have a sense of belonging to their mosque. Almost one-fourth (23 percent) said that they "somewhat" have a sense of belonging, and 5 percent said that they had no sense of belonging. These figures are a clear indication that second-generation mosque-goers are not alienated from their mosques; they are attending mosques and overall they feel good about their mosques. The bad news, however, is that the second generation, in particular second-generation males, scores lower than any other population of the mosque.

All second-generation participants in the focus groups responded that they have a sense of belonging, and in almost all cases, the main reason given was their feeling of being part of a mosque community—a community where you make friends, hang out, play, and learn. Three members of the suburban South Asian mosque commented:

A lot of us live close to there [the mosque] and you can go there for your daily prayers. And if you do that on a regular basis it just becomes part of your daily life. And you're going to make a lot of friends there. And your friends, if you want to see them you're going to go there. It becomes an established institution in your life.

Our masjid is not just a prayer area—everything goes on there. Weddings go on there, parties, people go there to play sports, a basketball court's there, every Friday guys get together and go over there. It gives them a better outlet to go there instead of going some other place to get involved in *haram* [prohibited action]. It's a school too; we have *halaqah* [study] groups. A lot goes on there.

Family togetherness—that's what builds a community and that's what you totally see around here; its that togetherness. If you go to a *shavi* [wedding] I mean you're going to find all your friends there.

In this suburban mosque, most families live nearby. For the daily sunset and evening prayer, approximately two hundred people gather daily, a significant portion being youth. The mosque also has a gym that is constantly in use before and after the prayers, with young people playing volleyball and basketball. The mosque has become a community center with prayer as the main purpose for gathering.

Another oft-cited reason for feeling a sense of belonging is the welcoming and open atmosphere of a mosque and its youth group. The second generation clearly feels accepted and not looked down upon or judged. One Arab college-age youth expressed her initial hesitation about joining a Shiite mosque's youth group:

Before I came to [the youth group] I was—oh my God, like these people are going to be holy rollers. They're going to be judgmental and I am going to be uncomfortable. . . . I think [this youth group] does a pretty good job in alleviating that stuff.

At another mosque a youth remarked, "I feel welcome here. Feels like family here. The people, if they don't see me, they ask, where have I been."

Others said that the mosque is special because that was where important elements of their Islamic identity were formed.

Growing up, you have a lot of questions. The place where you find the answers has a special meaning. So a lot of questions about what should I be doing, what do I value, who am I were answered at that masjid—Sunday school, *halaqahs* [study groups], with my friends. So the place is really special.

Although the majority of second-generation mosque-goers feel a sense of belonging, they score the lowest in comparison to immigrants and African Americans.

**Sense of Belonging**

|  | Second Generation | Immigrants | African Americans |
|---|---|---|---|
| Yes | 68.3% | 76.3% | 78.0% |
| No | 4.8% | 3.0% | 2.1% |
| Somewhat | 23.0% | 17.3% | 12.8% |
| Don't know | 3.9% | 3.4% | 7.1% |
| Number in each | 357 | 566 | 140 |

$N = 1064$ Chi-Sq $= .015$ tau-b is not significant

While 68 percent of the second generation said that they feel a sense of belonging, 76 percent of immigrants and 78 percent of African Americans feel a sense of belonging. Almost one-fourth (23 percent) of the second generation stated that they only somewhat felt that they belonged, compared to 17 percent and 13 percent for immigrants and African Americans.

Among the second generation, the 21–39-year-old age group scores significantly lower that the other groups—64 percent of this age have a sense of belonging, but 26 percent say they have somewhat a sense of belonging, and 8 percent say they do not have a sense of belonging. The age group of 13–20-year-olds scores higher: 72 percent say yes to belonging and 21 percent say somewhat. Of the small percentage (13 percent) of second-generation respondents over forty, 92 percent of them said they have a sense of belonging.

**Sense of Belonging of Second-Generation Age Groups**

|  | 13–20 | 21–39 | All others |
|---|---|---|---|
| Yes | 71.6% | 64.0% | 75.7% |
| No | 2.5% | 8.0% | 3.7% |
| Somewhat | 21.1% | 25.3% | 16.5% |
| Don't know | 4.9% | 2.7% | 4.1% |
| Number in each | 204 | 150 | 727 |

$N = 1081$ Chi-Sq $= .006$ tau-b is significant at .036

The younger age group of 15–21-year-olds scores higher in sense of belonging, probably because so much of the programming at the mosques including youth groups, weekend schools, and sports is geared toward them. There are few organized activities organized especially for the 21–39-year-old age group. For those in college, a local chapter of the Muslim Student Association (MSA) becomes the principal means of organized activity. The youth group in the Shiite mosque does include a significant number of college-age students, which might partly be because Detroit MSAs seem to be dominated by Sunnis. After college and marriage, most of the second generation indicate that they are too busy for extensive mosque involvement, and so they socialize instead with their married friends, usually of the same ethnic background.

In analyzing the sense of belonging by age groups, without reference to whether they belong to the second generation, the 40-and-above age group has the strongest sense of belonging.

**Sense of Belonging and Age Groups of All Mosque Participants**

|                | *13–20* | *21–39* | *40+* |
|----------------|---------|---------|-------|
| Yes            | 70.3%   | 66.9%   | 85.7% |
| No             | 4.0%    | 5.4%    | 2.1%  |
| Somewhat       | 20.8%   | 23.5%   | 10.4% |
| Don't know     | 5.0%    | 4.1%    | 1.8%  |
| Number in each | 202     | 459     | 336   |

$N = 997$ Chi-Sq = .000 tau-b is significant at .000

The older mosque participants, those who are most likely married with children and more settled, feel the greatest sense of belonging, while the 21–39-year-olds who are either in college or establishing their family and career feel the least connected.

Second-generation males scored the lowest in the sense of belonging. In fact, the clear conclusion is that the low score of belonging among the second generation is due to the low score of males. Why do second-generation males score significantly lower than the females? Because they are given more freedom by their parents, males possibly feel more pressure to acculturate to American popular culture and, as a result, experience a greater disconnect between mosque and American culture.

**Sense of Belonging and Second Generation Grouped by Gender and Age**

|                | *Male* *13–20* | *Male* *21+* | *Female* *13–20* | *Female* *21+* |
|----------------|----------------|--------------|------------------|----------------|
| Yes            | 65.1%          | 59.6%        | 76.1%            | 70.0%          |
| No             | 4.7%           | 11.2%        | .9%              | 3.3%           |
| Somewhat       | 26.7%          | 25.8%        | 17.1%            | 25.0%          |
| Don't know     | 3.5%           | 3.4%         | 6.0%             | 1.7%           |
| Number in each | 86             | 89           | 117              | 60             |

$N = 352$ Chi-Sq = .028 tau-b is not significant

Although our interviewees all felt a sense of belonging, they also talked about problems they have with belonging. They also spoke about those youth who do not come to the mosque. In the suburban South Asian mosque, the interviewees felt that the vast majority of the Muslim youth in their area are involved in mosque activities—up to 80 percent, according to some. Social networks of friends, family, and relatives, and the fact that the mosque serves as a hangout and a place to meet friends, might best explain the observation that most youth are involved in the mosque. Interviewees mentioned that a sure sign of a drift away from the mosque and Islam is a youth's preference for non-Muslim friends. Another sign of a desire to leave the Muslim social network is enrollment in a faraway college where there are few connections with Detroit Muslims. Apparently, however, these second-generation Muslims are not all that isolated from their American environment since almost all talked about their non-Muslim friends. In one focus group, participants were asked about their five closest friends: half of the participants indicated that two to three of their closest friends were non-Muslims.

Interviewees mentioned some of the factors that decrease a sense of belonging. Some adults created problems by being too critical of the second generation for not fitting into the expected norms of the older generation. This problem was mentioned even by the youth in the suburban South Asian mosque, which is much more accommodating to youth than other mosques.

> Aunties [adult women] can really get down on us [girls] sometimes. We're not dressed quite right; we're not acting quite right. It's a hassle sometimes.

Related to this issue is the oft-heard complaint of the second generation that the mosque is sometimes too restrictive. Second-generation boys at the suburban South Asian mosque had to argue to win the right to organize basketball games on Friday night; they lost their attempt, however, to have a pool table in the mosque. Restrictions are even greater at more traditional mosques, which apparently causes greater alienation.

MSA students mentioned that probably only 10 percent of the Muslim youth in the area attend another more conservative immigrant mosque. That particular mosque and others were criticized for being unwelcoming.

> Some youth don't go [to that mosque] because they feel shame. They don't want to go and hear why they haven't come.

> Some youth feel that older people are looking down on you. Masjids need to be less judgmental. My brother went to a masjid . . . and he said that he didn't feel that he belonged in that masjid. People were staring at him—judging him. He was just wearing jeans and a jersey. He said he didn't want to go back there—he felt out of place.

Muslim youth who are less sure of their Islam might feel reluctant to attend a mosque if they think they are going to be criticized or made to feel like an outsider.

Many MSA second-generation females expressed resentment and a lack of a sense of belonging toward those traditional mosques that do not offer accommodation for women. Growing up in one of these mosques, girls thought it was natural for women not to go to mosques. When, however, they became more exposed to other mosques, they developed an animosity for their home mosque. In the suburban South Asian mosque, second-generation females were the most boisterous part of the drive to allow women to sit in the main prayer area as opposed to the area partitioned off for females. In the focus-group interviews with the women of the mosque, first-generation immigrant women expressed their satisfaction with the fact that they had at least a place and role in the mosque, as compared to no place or role in mosques in their home country. Second-generation females on the other hand were less comfortable with the circumscribed role of women in the mosque and were intent on seeking a greater role for women. Even though the second-generation women (along with other women) had to struggle to win a greater role in the mosque, all of them expressed a sense of belonging to the mosque—perhaps because they won.

Another reason for a decreased sense of belonging among interviewees is the feeling that the views and suggestions of the youth are ignored by the older mosque leadership. A youth of the South Asian mosque explained his lessened sense of belonging this way:

> The leaders of the mosque are filled with men who are fifty years and older and they hold a certain ownership of the masjid and they don't want to change; they don't want to do new things.

> When we suggest things or want new activities, we're shut out.
> For instance we suggested an open house [for the mosque] but no
> one would listen until 9/11.

In a similar vein, a college-age student commented, "We're too old for
kids' stuff, and we're too young for organizational involvement. People
are just not interested in our views."

The second generation in the eight mosques under study demonstrated a healthy sense of belonging to their mosques, largely due apparently to the fact that these mosques serve as a nexus for activities
and are welcoming and nonjudgmental toward youth. However, even in
mosques with strong second-generation involvement, the second generation has a lingering sense of disconnect with mosque leaders who are
more conservative and ethnic in their view of the mosque and who do
not sufficiently listen to the second generation or involve them in
decision-making or leadership roles.

## IDENTITY ISSUES AMONG THE SECOND GENERATION

Second-generation Muslims juggle but embrace three identities—
religious, ethnic, and national (American identity). For women, there is
a fourth identity—gender. Overwhelmingly, participants in the focus
groups prioritized their identities as being first and foremost Muslim.
Responses were divided on whether their ethnic identity or their American identity was more important to them. Some women placed their
gender identity next in importance to their religious identity, viewing
themselves primarily as Muslim and then as female. Although their
identities were prioritized, these second-generation youth clearly embraced all these identities with varying degrees of pride. They constructed their different identities so that they'd be compatible. Only one
interviewee voiced a rejection of his ethnic and American identity in
favor of an Islamic identity. However, other participants expressed their
disapproval of this approach as extreme.

With an unequivocal voice these mosque-going second-generation
youth expressed their view that Islamic identity comes before all else.
Two youths of South Asian origin commented:

> I'm Muslim, that's the first thing. And then it would probably be
> like American, then Pakistani. But, I don't consider a lot of those
> things important. Muslim is what I am and that's the main thing.

Nationality doesn't really represent us. I'd rather say that religion is the dominating factor in all of our lives. Whether you're Christian, you're Jewish—it's religion that makes you the person that you are. Not that you're Taiwanese, not that you're any of those type of cultures—it's just that your religion should be the most important thing.

The second generation has clearly embraced the Islamic teaching that accentuates the unity of all Muslims and downplays the importance of ethnicity. A regular topic of mosque sermons and talks focuses on the oft-quoted Qur'anic verse, "God made you into peoples and tribes so that you might know [and learn from] one another. Indeed the most honorable in the sight of God are those who are the most mindful of God" (49:13).

In this ideology, the committed Muslim gives little value to ethnicity. Thus mosques and student groups are not supposed to be organized along ethnic lines. Although the reality does not always match the ideology of Muslim unity, the Christian example of separate church congregations—one Anglo and one Asian or Hispanic, using the same church building or separate ethnically based campus student-fellowship groups—does not exist among Muslims. Separate Muslim student groups or separate ethnically based congregations using the same mosque would be a clear contradiction of Islamic teaching and therefore unacceptable.

Although most mosques are predominantly made up of one ethnic group and therefore youth groups come from one ethnic group, there are citywide educational programs, special events and camps that bring many of the second generation together across ethnic lines. College campus Muslim student groups are another vehicle for contact across ethnicities. As a result, many of the second-generation mosque-goers are familiar with other youth in other immigrant mosques. The ethnic divide between South Asians and Arabs does not seem to be especially great. However, there exists virtually no contact between second-generation Muslims and African American Muslim youth, and little contact between the Sunni and Shiite second generation.

Although accepting of their ethnic heritage, second-generation youth are adamant about distinguishing between what is religion and what is ethnicity, culture, or custom. An almost universal point of view among second-generation youth is that they want to separate what is religious—and therefore based on the holy texts of Qur'an and Sunnah—from what is cultural, which their parents have brought with them from back home. Although Islam teaches children to honor and obey their parents, ultimate obedience is given only to God; therefore, a Muslim can legitimately challenge the validity of a parental practice or belief that is not explicitly sanctified by the Qur'an and Sunnah. This ideological opening allows the second generation to detach religious authority from inherited culture, and gives the second generation legitimacy in opposing many customs of their parents as being only a form of ethnic culture and not Islamic. With this wedge, the second generation can argue for substituting ethnic customs with customs that from their point of view are more authentically Islamic. They can also argue that certain ethnic customs are not religiously mandated and therefore should be considered optional. Thus, American customs which are not contradictory of Islam can be adopted. A recently married South Asian respondent observed:

> My parents pretty much taught me most everything I know. . . . I think I'm a little bit more different [than my parents], because they put their culture into their religion a lot. So, I kind of disagree with them a lot of times when they do things like that. I mean, like my dad, there's a *shirwani*—like an Indian, Pakistani type of outfit—he's like, this is an Islamic dress. He says this is what you have to wear—like that.

A college-age woman said:

> I try to separate culture from religion. My dad on the other hand is very cultural. He's Iraqi and holds to his cultural beliefs. For instance a girl should not be as active as a male.

The second generation thus argues for acculturation of certain extrinsic as well as intrinsic elements of their ethnic culture, using Islam as an authority. They argue that certain styles of dress, food (for example, pizza as the main dish at a mosque function), and even midnight basketball are open areas in the religion; that a greater role for women in society or a greater role for young people in picking their mates are rights given by Islam and, therefore, parents should not use the authority of ethnic culture to proscribe them.

Many youth indicated that their parents had come to accept that some customs were cultural. One college-age youth remembered:

My dad [a Palestinian] once told my older sister that he would die before he allowed her to marry an Egyptian. But my dad became more religious and now he's opened up to having me marry a man who's not Palestinian. It's all because he became more Islamic.

A college-age South Asian youth remarked:

I came to realize that a lot of culture is mixed with religion, but my parents have changed also. An example is weddings—there's a lot of un-Islamic customs. Here [America] weddings are different. They [parents] now see the same point of view.

Parents and mosque leaders seem willing to trade some ethnic customs—what they might consider to be extrinsic traits—for a more idealized form of Islam in which more intrinsic values and customs are retained. They give the second generation room to adopt the clothes, food, sports, etc., of American culture but retain the moral restrictions against fornication, alcohol, and drugs, and stress the Islamic values of discipline, hard work, and studiousness. Parents undoubtedly recognize that these religious values are ingredients for educational and economic success—upward mobility.

An element that seems to accentuate their religious identity is the sense among the second generation that they have personally chosen Islam and not simply inherited it.

Over here [in America] we're a minority. Over there [in Pakistan] everyone's part of a majority. Therefore, your race and your religion are pointed out to you more over here and you're different. When we grew up—it's always—we're different. Different—why are we different? Who are we? You get asked, who are you? You get those questions more.

A lot of people I know—our generation, have inherited it [Islam]. We've all inherited it. And, once they've inherited it—they love it, they love being a part of it, they love being a part of Muslim culture. But, there are also the other breed of people who, inheriting it, sat down, thought about, and chose to really make it theirs. And when those people did that, then it really brought about a certain change in their life, change in their habits, and it probably kept them from assimilating to the same extent as Americans do.

Islam is their choice as their primary identity, over and above ethnic or American identity. In this regard, the second generation is somewhat like converts who have invested in a commitment to a new faith—and in this case the investment and commitment is even dearer because the faith is not readily sanctioned in society.

For these mosque-going youth, ethnic identity is de-emphasized in preference for a religious identity; ethnic identity, however, is not rejected. Second-generation youth participating in the focus groups were divided as to whether they placed their ethnic identity over their American identity. Those who favored their ethnic identity over their American identity had two arguments: one was a response to the perceived prejudice in American society, and the other was based on a perceived need for an alternative culture as an antidote to the harmful aspects of American culture.

One South Asian man in his mid-twenties remarked:

> You're Muslim no matter what nationality you are. . . . But there's nothing wrong in being proud of where you're from, whether that be America or anyplace. Now, to choose between the two [being American or Pakistani], for me, is very difficult. My wife is truly Pakistani and she sees me as American. When I go to Pakistan, I'm an American. But, when I'm here, I'm not viewed as an American. . . . At the end of the day, my skin color is still brown. . . . As much American as we like to think we are, I think we can't be one hundred percent accepted by the average white American in society.

This second-generation Pakistani is perceived in Pakistan and even by his Pakistani-raised wife as being American because he has become acculturated to many aspects of American culture. But at the same time he feels that American society does not accept him fully as an American. Ethnic identity is preferred over American identity because of the perceived discrimination of whites and the unlikelihood of being fully accepted in American society. Researchers have noted the same phenomenon among second-generation Asian Americans who are fully acculturated into America but still desire to retain a strong ethnic identity, largely due to discrimination they have experienced.[17] They hypothesize that ethnic identity among non-European immigrants will remain as long as prejudice against nonwhites exists.

The focus-group interviews of second-generation Muslims support the argument that structural prejudice bolsters ethnic and religious identity. In the face of social rejection, it is natural to seek self-confirmation among people who share a similar background.

Two second-generation college-age immigrants expressed another reason for retaining their ethnic identity.

> I want my children to have some cultural background. I don't want my children to think of themselves as only American. It's best to preserve some culture to keep them away from *haram* [unlawful behavior].

> Religious identity is important, but I like Syrian qualities. It's important to have culture. It's an important part of who you are.

These same youths expressed the view that culture had to be distinguished from Islam and had acknowledged that they are perceived as American when they visit their parents' home country; nevertheless, they still see a role for ethnic culture to fill in the cultural gaps of Islamic practice. Ethnic culture supports Islamic identity and allows Muslims to avoid adopting American culture, especially those aspects of American culture that contradict Islam. Therefore, American identity, not religious identity, is lessened in the face of ethnic prejudice.

The persistence of ethnic identity is also seen in one focus group of fifteen people who unanimously agreed that they would be willing to marry outside their ethnic group; however, almost all of them also indicated that they would most likely marry within their ethnic group. The wish of parents and concern for cultural and linguistic compatibility were the main reasons given. Many others in the focus groups, although loudly proclaiming their desire to detach immigrant culture from Islam, still acknowledged an attachment to their ethnic background. One newlywed male, after pinpointing all the non-Islamic aspects of Pakistani weddings, admitted that he was married according to all those customs, and, in deference to the wishes of his parents and Pakistani-raised wife, he would most probably marry off his children according to those same customs.

The other half of second-generation youth preferred their American identity over their ethnic identity. One college-age woman stated:

> I feel more American Muslim than Libyan Muslim. When I went overseas I knew I was American. Just one time trying to use an Arab toilet and that's it.

Another college-age South Asian man reflected on the evolution of his identity:

> I now feel more American than Pakistani. My parents sheltered me more when I was young and I felt more Pakistani. When I moved out [to college] and was more exposed to the general society and to other people, I came to feel more American. Over time I became more accepting, but I don't see it as dichotomous.

The discussion of this issue ignited friendly but fierce debate in two focus groups. In response to the South Asian who said he felt more Pakistani because his brown skin prohibited him from being accepted by white America, one person retorted that "you can be brown and American. Look at African Americans who built this country. . . . They are Americans, even if they are not accepted." In giving primacy to American identity over their ethnic identity, these youth were willing to look beyond the prejudice of certain white Americans and stake their claim to an American identity that did not require white acceptance.

The interplay between ethnic and American identities has two storylines, as described in focus-group discussions. One storyline, which is described directly above, is one of youth who grow up in an ethnic "bubble," but then, as they move away from their parents' home environment, their identity broadens and the sense of being American dominates. Another storyline is that of youngsters who grow up away from their ethnic group and from Muslims who live in an American bubble, and their first identity is more strongly American. As they left their parents' home environment, they developed a stronger ethnic identity. This last model is described as the typical model for second-generation middle-class Asians. The reason these Asians seek a stronger ethnic identity is the social prejudice that turns them away from embracing fully an American identity.

It seems likely, nevertheless, that the ethnic identity of second-generation Muslims will weaken as they mature and seek their place in American society, a process that will likely bring about greater acculturation. These second-generation Muslims have invested their sense of a unique self in Islam, and therefore ethnic identity, although accepted, is less relevant as a vehicle for identity formation. Religious identity replaces ethnic identity.

## ISLAMIC APPROACH OF THE SECOND GENERATION

In order to produce a rough estimate of moderation and conservatism among mosque-goers, Detroit mosque participants were asked a question about how they interpret and understand Islam. The question was:

Which statement comes closest to your understanding of how Qur'an and Sunnah should be practiced: the Qur'an and Sunnah

1) must be carefully followed as understood by one particular *madhhab*,
2) must be carefully followed as understood by the *salafi* school of thought,
3) must be carefully followed in accordance to the opinions of the great scholars of the past,
4) should be followed in a flexible fashion, in light of modern circumstances and the opinions of modern scholars, and
5) should be accepted but not necessarily practiced.

In the first choice, *madhhab* refers to one of the classical legal schools of thought. A person who follows one of the classical schools would most likely be more traditional in understanding and practice of Islam.

The second choice, "the *salafi* school of thought," at least in its recent historical manifestation, tends to be very conservative and literal in its interpretation of Islam. The *salafi* school of thought holds, for example, the position that all Islamic issues should be referred back to the sources of Islam—Qur'an and Sunnah—and to the opinions of the early scholars (the *salaf*), as opposed to adherence to any particular classical school.

The third option of following "the opinions of the great scholars," means that the individual is not bound to any one *madhhab* or classical school, but still looks to the great scholars of the classical period for answers. Islamic interpretations based on this perspective can vary greatly and include liberal as well as conservative viewpoints, but most likely the interpretation would tend to be slightly more conservative.

The choice of following in a "flexible fashion" represents a greater willingness in interpreting the texts to take into consideration modern circumstances, the purposes of the Qur'an and Sunnah, and opinions of modern Muslim scholars. This point of view will be called the "contextual" approach. Some respondents mentioned that they would have liked to have checked both this choice and the third choice (look to great scholars of the past), because in practice, they do both. However, by having respondents choose only one response category, the question forces them to indicate their primary inclination.

The last response category encompasses the position that although the Qur'an and Sunnah should be accepted, their injunctions should no longer be considered obligatory. This position is comparable to those religious adherents who view their religious texts as being historical and not necessarily the word of God.

The responses for all mosque participants were as follows:

**Islamic Approach of Detroit Mosque Participants**
**Percentage of participants who hold this interpretation**

| | |
|---|---|
| Contextual approach | 37.8 |
| Follow *madhhab*/classical school | 27.9 |
| Follow great scholars of past | 25.5 |
| *Salafi* approach | 7.9 |
| No need to practice | 9 |

$N = 764$

The responses for second-generation and other mosque participants are as follows (the last response category of "no need to practice" was excluded because it was too small):

**Islamic Approach and Breakdown of Mosque Participants**

| | Second Generation | Immigrants | African Americans |
|---|---|---|---|
| Contextual | 29.1% | 41.8% | 41.6% |
| Great Scholars | 35.2% | 21.7% | 24.8% |
| *Madhhab* | 29.1% | 29.2% | 23.8% |
| *Salafi* | 6.6% | 7.2% | 9.9% |
| Number per category | 213 | 318 | 101 |

$N = 632$ Chi-Sq $= .01$ and tau-b is not significant

These figures indicate that overall the second generation does not differ greatly from the other segments of Detroit mosques in terms of Islamic approach. This should not be too surprising, since the religious beliefs of youth do not usually deviate greatly from their parents.

However, it is surprising that overall the second generation is slightly more conservative than the other groups. The second generation scores lower than immigrants and African Americans in preferring the more flexible contextualist approach—29 percent for the second generation as compared to 42 percent for immigrants and African Americans. As for the more conservative approach of following the great scholars of the past, more of the second generation adopt this approach than the other groups—35 percent of the second generation as compared to 22 percent and 25 percent of immigrants and African Americans respectively. The second generation and other mosque participants score the same in the other two approaches, the more traditional approach of following one of the classical legal schools (*madhhab*) and the more literalist *salafi* approach.

A slightly different picture emerges when the second generation is divided by age group.

**Islamic Approach and Second-Generation Age Groups**

|  | *13–20* | *21 +* | *All others* |
|---|---|---|---|
| Contextual | 22.4% | 37.9% | 42.1% |
| Great Scholars | 34.5% | 36.8% | 22.3% |
| *Madhhab* | 34.5% | 22.1% | 27.7% |
| *Salafi* | 8.6% | 3.2% | 7.9% |
| Number per category | 116 | 95 | 430 |

$N = 641$ Chi-Sq $= .000$ and tau-b is significant at .015

It turns out that the conservatism of the second generation is largely due to the younger age group (13–20) of the second generation and not the older age group of 21 years old and above. The 13–20-year-olds score the lowest (22 percent) in preferring the contextual approach; they score the highest (34.5 percent) in adopting the more traditional *madhhab* approach. The older members of the second generation are much closer to other Muslims in adopting the contextual approach (38 percent), but, significantly, they score higher than the other groups in preferring the more conservative approach of following the great scholars (37 percent). They also score lower in following the *madhhab* approach and the literalist *salafi* approach.

One college-age youth explained the perceived conservatism of some second-generation youth:

Youth might be more conservative because identity is more important to them. Muslim identity is more important and therefore they are more likely to hold to a rigid idea. Youth are looking for legitimacy. What is more legitimate is more accepted. The more modern approach and the more cultural approach seem more suspect.

A high-school-age youth expressed a similar idea.

> In America, as we've grown up, we need to find an identity and
> hold on to something. And since we are the people who tend to
> identify themselves as Muslim youth, we have chosen Islam.
> That's probably why they're more practicing, more rigorous in
> their application. . . . They grew up in a society where they really
> understood that [the early generation of Muslim scholars] know
> what they're talking about—they're worth listening to. And so, we
> generally think of them [the early scholars] as the right canon to
> refer to and to think about. And although I, personally, in my prac-
> tice tend to think a lot about modern circumstances, when deciding
> where I draw different lines, I still would probably on that piece
> of paper write down that I refer to the scholars of the past and my
> particular *madhhab*. Because, I think that I've been brought up to
> think that that is the correct way, the safest way to go.

In struggling to shape an Islamic identity, the younger generation
believes that authenticity is all-important. In committing to Islam, especially in an often hostile environment, the young second generation has
more often opted for the more straightforward, less nuanced, conservative approach of following the great scholars of the past or following a
classical *madhhab*.

The drive for authenticity is also linked to the second generation's
desire to distinguish their parents' inherited culture from the teachings
of Islam. By focusing on religion they are able to distance themselves
from their immigrant culture and to create a distinct understanding and
identity that is more distinctly their own. In so doing, their efforts can
lead to a greater conservatism.

The evolution of Islamic understanding among the older second generation is described by a college-age youth:

> Traditionally Pakistanis are considered to be quite strict in the
> Hanafi *madhhab*, and immigrant Pakistanis have continued down
> this path. Due to this, my exposure or consideration of other
> methodologies of the fundamentals of how we practice our reli-
> gion was based on the Hanafi view only. Not only did I not know
> other opinions, it was only toward the end of high school that I
> came to understand even the existence of some particular schools
> of thought, i.e., the Salafiya. That being said, as I moved on to

college I came across a wide variety of different people following different beliefs. . . . As I moved away from my "strict" Hanafi path, I also simultaneously moved away from a "Pakistani Islam," which is based around that strict following of Hanafi Law. Thus I came to a more pluralistic and holistic understanding of the glory of multiple accepted opinions in Islamic Law.

From this narrative, the following of the more traditional *madhhab* by the younger second generation (13–20 years old) can be explained as simply their acceptance and adoption of the more traditional Islam of their parents. In college the second-generation youth are exposed to new ideas—some even more conservative and some less so—and this experience widens and deepens their understandings of Islam, and allows them to moderate some of their earlier views. As part of this process, many of the second generation adopt the more flexible contextual approach.

The second generation's slight lean toward conservatism is reflected in their slightly lower support for Muslim involvement in the American political process. Although there is solid endorsement for political involvement, the second generation scores lower than first-generation immigrants but higher than African Americans: 70 percent of second-generation Muslims "strongly agree" that Muslims should be involved in politics, as compared to 86 percent of immigrants and 65 percent of African American Muslims. More than one-fourth (21 percent) of African American Muslims disagree with political involvement, indicating that a significant minority of African Americans are disenchanted with American politics. Only 6 percent of the second generation disagrees with political involvement; therefore, the vast majority favors involvement. Overall, however, they are less enthusiastic than their immigrant parents.

**Political Involvement and Breakdown of Mosque Participants**

|  | Second Generation | Immigrants | African Americans |
|---|---|---|---|
| Strongly agree | 70.3% | 86.2% | 64.8% |
| Somewhat agree | 23.4% | 9.3% | 14.4% |
| Disagree (strongly/somewhat) | 6.2% | 4.5% | 20.8% |
| Number per category | 337 | 535 | 125 |

$N = 997$ Chi-Sq = .000 and tau-b is significant at .000

The younger age group (13–20 years old) in the second generation also shows the same pattern of greater conservatism than the older group (21 + years old) in supporting political involvement, but the differences are not as significant as the differences with Islamic approaches. More than two-thirds (68 percent) of the 13–20 age group strongly agree with political involvement, compared to almost three-fourths (74 percent) of the group of 21 years old and above.

**Political Involvement and the Second Generation**

|  | *13–20* | *21 +* | *All others* |
|---|---|---|---|
| Strongly agree | 67.9% | 74.1% | 81.9% |
| Somewhat agree | 25.1% | 21.1% | 10.3% |
| Disagree (strongly/somewhat) | 7.0% | 4.8% | 7.8% |
| Number per category | 187 | 147 | 680 |

$N = 1014$ Chi-Sq $= .000$ and tau-b is significant at .000

The lower scores of the younger second generation (13–20 years old) in political involvement might simply reflect a lack of appreciation of political involvement that is reflected in American youth culture as a whole. One college-age youth echoed this sentiment:

> I registered to vote recently. I didn't register earlier because I really didn't think it made a difference. I'm older now and I want to take a stance on issues. I'm more mature and I understand how I can influence things.

The second generation also might be more affected by the more rejectionist message of noninvolvement. In each of the focus groups, there was at least one youth who indicated doubts whether voting was permitted in Islam. One MSA group acknowledged that "there is an element that says that political involvement is *haram*" [unlawful]. Some youths commented that *salafi* and other groups espouse a rejectionist message against all things American. These youth observed that the rejectionist message was prominent among the second generation, especially college students, in the Detroit area in the early 1990s but had waned by the late 1990s, and then markedly declined after 9/11.

CONCLUSION

1. Second-generation mosque-goers in Detroit are not showing signs of abandoning the mosque or their religious and ethnic identity, as evi-

denced by their visible presence in mosques, their relatively high sense of belonging to the mosque, and their preference for an Islamic approach, which in some regards is more conservative than that of their parents. Although retaining their Islamic identity, the second generation is acculturated to American culture in terms of extrinsic traits such as dress, food, and language, but has not discarded the intrinsic values and morals of Islam. The second generation has acculturated but not assimilated—integrated but not assimilated.

Comments by the second generation indicate that structural prejudice against Islam and Muslims is a motivating factor in retaining their Islamic identity. The perceived inability to be accepted as being fully American is an incentive to invest in an Islamic identity rather than in an American identity. Moreover, the attacks on Islam and Muslims after the 9/11 tragedy have given many of the second generation, who are acculturated to America and fluent in English, a role and higher status as defenders of Islam.

2. The second generation is critical of much of the ethnic culture of the mosque and their parents, but their criticism has led them to seek a more authentic Islamic culture rather than adopt wholesale American culture. For second-generation mosque-goers, religious identity is more important than ethnic and American identity. However, in defining authentic Islamic culture, the second generation is able, on the one hand, to delegitimize many extrinsic practices of ethnic culture such as dress, food, and language as being extraneous to true religion, and, on the other, to legitimize certain religious values and practices that are also honored in American culture, such as a greater role for women, greater latitude for children in choosing their marriage partners, and the acceptance of people who are outspoken and independent-minded. By so doing, the second generation has achieved an autonomous identity that is distinct from their parents' ethnic culture but not in conflict with much of the values and practices of their parents' culture. Many mosques and parents are more than willing to accept this tradeoff: giving up extrinsic "ethnic" practices and values for the second generation's adherence to the intrinsic religious practices and values of Islam.

Seeking an "authentic" Islamic identity puts a premium on being true and faithful to the religion. There is, therefore, a tendency for the second generation to look askance at "contextual" or "modern" understandings of Islam. In some sense the second generation is religiously more conservative than their parents. However, their conservatism translates not into an embrace of traditionalism but rather the creation of a synthesis of modern sensibilities and classical Islamic values. For example, many second-generation females might be more careful in covering their heads than their mothers, but they reject the notion that their only role is motherhood.

3. The embrace of an "authentic" Islamic identity has not led second-generation mosque-goers to reject either their ethnic or their American identities. While recognizing the challenges and difficulties of bringing these identities into harmony, the second generation does not start with the premise that any one of the identities has to be discarded. This acceptance of their various identities is what allows the second generation to maintain a largely nonconflictual relationship with the more "ethnic" Islam of the mosque and the American core culture of school and job. Thus, the second generation remains in the mosque and retains their educational and career aspirations to succeed in American society. Second-generation mosque-goers are committed to being both Islamically oriented and upwardly mobile.

4. The second generation's sense of belonging to the mosque seems to be linked to certain factors: (a) a community mosque that affords the second generation (males and females) opportunities to gather regularly for prayers and learning as well as for socialization and play; (b) a nonjudgmental attitude within the mosque, which allows the second generation to participate without accusing stares or comments; an accommodating attitude toward the views and needs of the second generation; and (c) programming that addresses the concerns and questions of the second generation.

5. The second generation is still relatively young. As the second generation becomes more settled into careers and family life, the final shape of second-generation attitudes and practices will become more apparent. The Detroit study showed that Muslims over forty years old have the highest sense of belonging and the most flexible approach in understanding Islam. Will the same be true of the second generation when they are forty? Will the second-generation mosque-goers remain in the mosque and retain their Islamic identity? And finally, what about the third generation? Just as the resolution of the long-term question of the assimilation of the children of Muslim immigrants remains to be seen, so also is the shape of Islam in America yet to be determined.

# Section Six

## Two Evaluations of the Research

# THE LEISURE OF WORSHIP AND THE WORSHIP OF LEISURE

*Jack Miles*

*Man asks of religion, "What is it for?"*
*Religion asks of man, "What are you for?"*

—Keiji Nishitani

The dialogues that take place among organized religions matter less than the dialogue, such as it may be, that each religion has with the institutions and attitudes of international secularism. Within the life of any organized religion, those most exposed to secular institutions and most imbued with secular attitudes are likely to be young adults, some of whom will be making their way from the more or less religious homes of their youth into the larger culture in which they will make lives and homes of their own. Therein lies the originality and relevance of an encounter drawing together bona fide representatives of major organized religions not, for once, to talk about their own theological similarities and differences, their own historic quarrels and reconciliations, but about their common encounter with this larger culture. The larger culture is represented here twice: first, in absentia by the young themselves, once and perhaps future members of religious congregations; and second, in operation, by academic research looking on religious attitudes among the young, religiously affiliated or not, with secular detachment. Yet in both the students and the studied, the contemporary puzzle or paradox of double allegiance, secular and religious at once, is variously on display.

What initially sparked this gathering was the anecdotal but widespread observation that in the United States young people between the ages of eighteen and thirty tend to drift away from the religions of their family heritage. The question that this observation immediately provokes is simply: why?

Economic conditions surely are a part of the answer and indeed have generally been taken as the larger part of the answer, at least for the middle class. For that class of Americans, the experience of "going away to college" has been thought a salutary separation away from childhood itself, a coming of age, a major forward step in individuation that would properly include a stock-taking with regard to religion no less than to other aspects of prior personality formation. But because American education has been growing longer and more costly, this interruption between childhood and achieved adulthood has been growing longer as well. American marriage has been taking place later, and parenthood has come later as a result. In an earlier era when college education, marriage, and first parenthood were all accomplished by age twenty-five, the early adulthood hiatus frequently enough ended with a religious wedding ceremony that was simultaneously a kind of spiritual homecoming. Now the seven years have grown to twelve or fourteen or more. And the longer the hiatus lasts, the more likely it is to become permanent.

And yet whatever the merit in this kind of socioeconomic explanation, the broad philosophical and political considerations that in the seventeenth century played so large a part in what historian Herbert Butterfield called "the Great Secularization" are surely with us still. American religious history continues the European story and bears in rarely recognized ways on the religious condition of the age group under consideration. Polling information about the actual attitudes of young Americans vis-à-vis religion gives us invaluable material for the writing of the very latest chapter in the story. Yet for me, I confess, the most fascinating aspect of this latest chapter is the question: Who, if anyone identifiable, gains when religion loses? The question of what is happening to religion strikes me as inseparable in our day from that of what is happening to secularism. Both are troubled, and it may well be that neither is troubled only or principally by the other.

If religion and secularism divided the ideological terrain between them in such a way that a gain for one was inherently a loss for the other,[1] then the question with regard to eighteen-to-thirty-year-olds could be put quantitatively in terms of leisure hours and leisure dollars. Does this pivotal demographic group withdraw time and money from church, synagogue, or mosque in order to spend it on anything analogous? There have been revolutionary moments in other times and places when an organized and identifiable cultural winner stood standing in inverse relationship to religion as loser. The French Revolution, with its national cult of Reason and its Voltairean cry of *Écrasez l'infame* against the church, was such a moment. The Italian *Risorgimento,* waging literal war against the Papal State, was another; if Camillo Cavour was your man in the 1860s, Pio Nono was not. The Russian Revolution, inspired by the most evangelically atheistic political ideology ever to take power, was yet another, as was the Cultural Revolution in Communist China, with its Mao cap set so fiercely against Confucianism. Down the list, and the list can easily be lengthened, there has typically been something to join—something more often than not nationalist—as well as something to quit. But in the twenty-first-century United States, does religious disaffiliation lead to any identifiable new affiliation? And if not, if there is—in organizational terms—no entrance corresponding to this exit, is there at least a reasonably comprehensive, coherently, and socially available default ideology? And if there is neither a clear organizational nor a clear ideological alternative, then how can religion's loss coherently be regarded as secularism's gain?

I began these remarks by stating that the encounter of any organized religion with the institutions and attitudes of international secularism was more important than its encounter with another organized religion. I believe that that observation still has merit, but my thesis is that in the United States the encounter of religion with secularism has been overtaken by the encounter of both with American consumerism. Consumerism is as subversive of, and yet as compatible with, secularism as it is with religion. It is consumerism, then, rather than secularism as traditionally understood that gains when organized religion loses.

This picture, as we shall see in due course, can become rather bleak, but for the purposes of the present inquiry, at least, there is a bright side to it as well. For all the erosion that American consumerist culture brings about in religious commitment, it does facilitate at least the first stages in interreligious dialogue. Listening to the addresses given during this conference and, perhaps even more, to the discussion following the addresses, one cannot fail to notice that the same common culture that may separately undermine the appeal or the credibility of different religious traditions also gives them a common idiom in which to address a common challenge.

A common idiom does not, of course, guarantee a common effort. A great scholar of comparative religion once observed of interreligious dialogue that each side typically compares its own noble ideals with the other side's shabby performance, never its own shabby performance with the other side's noble ideals. I would add that the cleverest polemicists do not stop there but go on to pervert even the other side's cherished virtues into disguised vices. Yet in the American context, where everyone learns quite early just how to be a smart shopper, canny tactics tend quickly to be recognized as such and foiled when they deserve to be foiled in the interest of an enlarged self-interest.

A story making the rounds just now bears amusingly on this. It seems that a certain balloonist was blown off course and didn't know where he was. He lowered his altitude until he spotted a fellow in a boat below and then shouted out:

"Excuse me, but can you help me? I promised a friend I would meet him an hour ago, but I don't know where I am."

The boatman consulted his portable GPS and replied, "You're in a hot air balloon approximately 30 feet above a ground elevation of 2,346 feet above sea level. You are at 31 degrees, 14.97 minutes north latitude and 100 degrees, 49.09 minutes west longitude."

At this, the balloonist rolled his eyes said, "You must be a Democrat."

"I am," replied the other, "but how did you know?"

"Well," came the answer, "everything you told me is technically correct, I presume, but I have no idea what to do with it. I still have no idea where I am. Frankly, you've not been much help to me at all."

At this, the boatman smiled and said, "You must be a Republican."

"I am," replied the balloonist, "but how did you know?"

"Well," replied the boatman, "you don't know where you are or where you're going. You've risen to where you are due to a large quantity of hot air. You made a promise that you have no idea how to keep, and you expect me to solve your problem. You're in exactly the same position you were in before we met, yet somehow now it's my fault."

This joke strikes me as apt for interreligious dialogue because it can so easily be run backwards, as follows:

A balloonist was blown off course and didn't know where he was. He lowered his altitude until he spotted a fellow in a boat below and then shouted out:

"Excuse me, but can you help me? I promised a friend I would meet him an hour ago, but I don't know where I am."

"Let's see," replied the other, "you don't know where you are or where you're going. You've risen to where you are due to a large quantity of hot air. You made a promise that you have no idea how to keep, and you expect me to solve your problem. You must be a Republican."

"I am," replied the balloonist, "and it would be just my luck that you're a Democrat, but can you help me anyway?"

"With pleasure, my friend," replied the boatman, consulting his portable GPS. "You're in a hot air balloon approximately 30 feet above a ground elevation of 2,346 feet above sea level. You are at 31 degrees, 14.97 minutes north latitude and 100 degrees, 49.09 minutes west longitude. And have a *wonderful* day!"

Both interreligious dialogue and the more fateful encounter between religion and secularism depend on the participants' capacity to read their own stories backwards as well as forwards—from the inside looking out but also from the outside looking in.

And much is gained as well when, bracketing the question of whether religion or secularism deserves to fail or succeed, all parties turn their attention to the practical measures by which each makes its way forward. Some years ago, I was surprised to learn that a certain PhD candidate did not read the Sunday *New York Times Book Review*.

"But your field is English literature!" I objected.

"Yes," she replied, "but my period is Nineteenth Century."

I was speechless for the moment. Only later did I manage to fit an argument to my objection, and it was that the historical understanding of literature is a two-way street. My friend expected, and rightly so, that contemporary writers would learn from the writers of her chosen period. But critics who, like her, live and work, mentally, among the creative writers of the past will understand them better by considering the writers of the present. We learn what our own writers are like by learning what their forebears were like, but we recognize the seeds that the forebears were planting by observing what has flowered in the off-spring. It is this living, reciprocal exchange that gives life to the entire undertaking.

Among all contemporary social phenomena, religion has the longest history and the strongest proclivity to bring its past forcefully into its present. Those who study this phenomenon but never darken the door of a church, synagogue, or mosque are at least in some danger of being like the PhD candidate in English who never reads the *New York Times Book Review*.

In a similar way, art museums, carefully preserving works centuries or even millennia old, have one meaning in a world where contemporary art still matters and another in a world where it does not. Those who run the museums gain an enriched understanding of their proper work when they occasionally visit the galleries where contemporary work is bought and the studios and ateliers where it is made. At the Getty, where I work, nothing so heartens me as the annual Getty Underground show. The Getty is built along a mountain ridge, and below the plaza level where one enters the Museum are four lower levels built into the mountainside. For eleven months of the year, the rarely visited lowest corridor, called L4, is a weird and silent concrete tunnel, its high ceiling draped with mysterious conduits and cables. But for one month, its gray walls come to life as Getty employees display their own artwork, and one discovers that one's colleagues—often at the lower as well as the higher reaches of the organizational chart—are, so to speak, churchgoers as well as students of religion. The special strength of those gathered for this conference is a strength of this sort.

But having now mentioned the Getty, let me relive a moment in its life that first captured, for me, what I have come to regard as distinctive about the twin encounters of secularism and religion with American consumerism. The time was the autumn of 1999. The Getty Museum in its dazzling new mountaintop location had been open for two years. The flood of first-time visitors had abated. Ahead lay a bright future as a normal, if highly visible, cultural attraction. Speaking on the occasion I wish to recall was Deborah Gribbon, the former director who was then associate director of the museum. Debbie is an unfailingly gracious woman one of whose many talents is a gift for concise and sudden candor. On this occasion, what she said was: "The Getty Museum is just one among many competitors for the leisure time of Los Angeles."

What could be more obvious, you might ask, or more unobjection-able? And yet a tremor passed through the room. In attendance, as I recall, were a number of younger employees whose dedication to the preservation and diffusion of artistic beauty approached the religious, or so it seemed to me, and who seemed faintly scandalized to hear their leader speaking of the Getty's mission so crassly as a mere leisure-time activity competing for local market share with other such activities.

No one took issue with her, however, because in the first place there was something obviously true about what she had said and because in the second place adequate language scarcely exists in which to raise an objection that would seem even to those making it to be like complain-ing about the weather. And yet a deep intuition exists all the same that the objection that would so like to find adequate expression is far more serious than just complaining about the weather.

In a rather mournful article published in the October 3, 2004, *New York Times Magazine,* James Traub made a valiant effort to step into this linguistic breach. In this article, Traub confessed himself troubled that the art museums of New York are no longer the hubs of reverence that they once were. They still look the same on the outside, these "massifs of limestone and marble, with their regal borders of open space amid our dense forest of skyscrapers," but inside something is going on that Traub cannot help but find unbecoming. His case in point, at the New-York Historical Society, was an Alexander Hamilton exhibi-tion that he describes, in part, as follows:

> The second, and principal, room was a long gallery with docu-ments and artifacts lining one wall and more giant video screens filling the others. The first screen, bafflingly, featured a contem-porary image of the White House, which gave way to the words "Rule of Law" and then to one of Hamilton's fine sentiments on the subject. Others illustrated or evoked or somethinged "The Free Press" (newspapers flying through presses), "Defense" (fighter jets) and so on. Here was an exhibition of America's most brilliant polemicist apparently mounted for the functionally illiterate.[2]

Traub does not wish to be and truly is not a snob. He gives ample ac-knowledgment to the treasure alongside the tinsel in this exhibit. Unlike some of today's art critics, he welcomes didactic signage. And yet something sends the same tremor through him that I felt that day at the Getty.

When the Historical Society mounted its Hamilton exhibition, it plastered a blocklong facsimile of a ten-dollar bill (the one with Hamilton on it) along the Central Park side of its venerable beaux-arts home. Traub writes:

> That was all unthinkably garish and self-aggrandizing for an institution accustomed to a high-minded diffidence toward the public. But it was just this decline of an old diffidence and the rise in its place of an aggressive market-orientation that were the kernels of this institutional drama.

I submit that the institutional drama evoked in this article is structurally akin to the one in which organized religion finds itself. The difference between the secular and the formally religious is real, and it still matters, but within American culture another struggle is under way between commitment and unchecked commodification.

This is the conflict that is captured in the cliché question "Is nothing sacred?" That question tends to be asked, often cynically or facetiously, as some revered source of meaning and value other than the conventionally religious turns out to be caught up, after all, in the Great American Hustle. The usual timing of the question suggests that the sacred, in our culture, is virtually defined as that which, one way or another, escapes the logic of the market. The question, of course, is whether anything ever does manage that escape.

Traub makes a grand claim for the art museums of Manhattan near the end of his article when he writes, "New York has both a Catholic and an Episcopal cathedral, but they don't impinge on the city's consciousness the way these secular cathedrals do." Personally, I suspect that St. Patrick's Cathedral may impinge on the working-class Roman Catholic consciousness of Bronx, Brooklyn, and Queens rather more than the New-York Historical Society or even the Metropolitan Museum does. But to the nation and the world, Manhattan undeniably matters more than the Bronx, Brooklyn, and Queens do. If art museums impinge as cathedrals upon the consciousness of opinion-makers like James Traub in America's largest and culturally most influential city, then perhaps, after all, there is something analogously religious to which a defector from traditional religion might still defect. But then again, Traub's thesis is that Manhattan's museums are decreasingly available—he stops just short of using the word *worthy*—of accepting such defectors. "Museums may continue to thrive as civic places and as sites for leisure activities," he sighs, "but not as secular cathedrals."

What I called, just now, the question of commitment vs. commodification is the question, finally, of whether a great institution offers a product or commands an allegiance. The rule in business is that the customer is always right. But can that authentically be the rule in art or education or government or, finally, religion? Are we not depressed when politicians offer the voters what they think the voters already want rather than telling the voters what they think the country needs? A now retired editorial writer at the *Los Angeles Times* used to tell a joke about a politician of which I remember only the punch line, delivered always in a more-or-less Strom Thurmond accent: "Ah kin lead yew anywheah. Jes' tell me wheah yew wawnt to gaow!"

The generic American religiosity that Christian Smith, summarizing the findings of his research, characterizes as Moralistic Therapeutic Deism is fairly characterized, I submit, as customer-is-always-right religiosity. The young survey respondents analyzed in the National Study of Youth and Religion see themselves as potential customers for the therapy that religion offers; and whether they avail themselves of it or not depends on how effective they happen to find it. They are customers of morality as well, we learn, at least to the extent—evidently considerable—to which they assign themselves authority in specifying what the deity is understood to require in terms of moral behavior. And their awareness of religious diversity, whatever its other-than-consumerist dimensions, surely bespeaks a customer's awareness that there are many stalls in the religious bazaar.

Smith is at his best crystallizing the earnestly but inarticulately expressed responses assembled by the NYSR. If I were to challenge his work anywhere, it would be at his claim that his respondents' reasons for their religious worldview are "quite unlike those of the historical religious traditions with which most Americans claim to identify."[3] If I am right to hear these responses as market-shaped, then their roots would reach back to the era when the American religious market came into existence.

And when was that? The marketization of American religious freedom dates back to the individualization of American religion after the ratification of the American Constitution. Nancy Ammerman writes:

> The Reformation had introduced Europeans to some modest notion of religious pluralism as the monopoly of the Roman Catholic church was broken. There were new dissenting sects, but most

of the new Protestant movements in Europe responded by setting up their own exclusive domains—Lutherans in Germany and Scandanavia, Anglicans in England, Reformed (Calvinist) Protestants in Switzerland and the Netherlands. Only the "radical" reformers (Mennonites, Baptists, and Brethren, for instance) argued for complete separation from state power. Only these separatists ventured complete reliance on voluntary membership, on spiritual rather than earthly persuasion. And in the United States, those radical impulses won the day. Other traditions have often complained that they have been "Protestantized" as they have accommodated to American culture. Whatever else that has meant, they are right in the sense that they have been pushed to adopt a basic commitment to live peacefully alongside religious others.[4]

I would offer a partial dissent from this picture of how American pluralism, which I see as the religious market by another name, came into existence. Rather than the triumph of radical Protestantism, the American Constitution represented, I believe, the high tide of Enlightenment thinking in the United States. The Founders had much to say about religion, but little or none of it, as I read them, breathes the atmosphere of Mennonite or Baptist piety. The Founders did indeed take a large step beyond the Treaty of Westphalia in guaranteeing that the federal government of the United States would establish no religion within the borders of the federation. However, they stopped well short of requiring the same disestablishment of religion in the thirteen constituent states taken separately. To the states was reserved the right, which some of them exercised for a good while after ratification, to impose, for example, a religious test for public office. Essentially, the Constitution as originally ratified reserved to the American states the same religious powers that were reserved to the signatories to the Treaty of Westphalia in Europe. And in that sense, it was statist rather than individualist Protestantism that played the larger role in the formation of American religious polity.

New England Puritanism and Virginia Anglicanism, the same two religious parties that had battled each other to a draw as Roundheads and Cavaliers in Britain, knew that neither could impose its will on the other on these shores either. Looming in the background was the far larger continental conflict between Roman Catholicism and all forms of Protestantism that had also ended in a standoff after the horrors of the

Thirty Years War. Westphalia stood for neither party's concession in principle but rather for the exhausted admission of both that neither could dictate to all Christendom. Our Founding Fathers decided to skip the religious war stage and proceed immediately to the exhausted admission.

And yet Ammerman is right in that individualist Protestantism did win out in the long run anyway and indeed as a direct result of the polity that Enlightenment political thought over a substratum of statist Protestantism had put in place. The prestige of the Constitution's settlement of the notoriously difficult religious question was such that, moving beyond law, it became a pervasive civic culture in the United States. As this happened, the more statist Anglican and Congregational forms of Protestantism, now progressively stripped of the states that had been their vehicles, lost much of their ascendancy, while dissident forms of Protestantism like Methodism and Baptism that had never enjoyed state sponsorship gained at their expense, particularly on the American frontier. Thereafter, the stage was set for other competitors, similarly without state sponsorship, to arise and thrive.

The Second Great Awakening, running from the 1790s through the 1830s, was thus not just a romantic, emotional, and pietist reaction against the rationalist, analytical, and deist or humanist political establishment. As that, it paralleled closely enough developments in Europe where in 1799 Friedrich Schleiermacher captured the public mood perfectly with his famous "On Religion: Speeches to Its Cultured Despisers." There certainly were elements of what has been called "Romantic Religion" in the United States, perhaps most especially in Transcendentalist circles in New England. But further West, in rough-and-tumble Jacksonian America, the time of the Second Great Awakening was the birth-moment of the great American market in religion. Then began the bewildering proliferation of new forms of religion that remains so distinctive of American Protestantism and that has gone so far beyond anything European Protestantism has witnessed then or now. In the United States, to a degree unparalleled anywhere in the world, even in Great Britain, religious consumers dissatisfied with what the existing producers were offering could and did go into business for themselves; and the pattern established then has continued right down to the present.

The market dominance established in religion has been rich in consequence for the whole of American life. For if market success can be made the only validation that ultimately matters even in so august and tradition-bound a domain as religion, then the marketization of the entire culture is essentially accomplished. Thus, the early marketization of religion portended the marketization over time of everything in American life, including notably anything that, like an art museum, might claim to function as religion for those children of the Enlightenment who would prefer to practice no religion. Is nothing sacred? Once religion is profaned by its transformation into a religion market, what other institution can hope to hold out?

One may grant that something like this has been the outcome without asserting, whiggishly, that the outcome has been a triumph. Peter C. Phan, among all the participants in this conference, is the most forthright in withholding his applause and the most astute in recognizing that such a triumph can only be a defeat for any religion whose understanding of itself is stated in terms of intrinsic rather than extrinsic or instrumental goods. Phan notes, however, that the same rampant and omnivorous marketization that bids fair to devour organized religions may threaten mere individuals all the more, and therein he sees an opportunity. The challenge, as he sees it, for traditional religion lies in devising ways, different in every case, to turn the personal crisis of an individual young man or woman experiencing dehumanization in the American marketplace into a "teaching moment" for the rediscovery of religion as an alternate conception of self and society to the one the market imposes.[5]

Though this is a large pedagogical challenge, Phan seems to me to have correctly identified the point where organized religion not only can mount a counteroffensive against marketization but has, in fact, done so in the signal instances presented at this very conference. The phenomenon of Taizé—aesthetically fascinating to me for the way that an essentially Protestant spirit has redeployed the forms and usages of Catholic monasticism—speaks most strongly to the young for a reason that has nothing to do with consciously recognized Protestant or Catholic usages. As Brother John explained to the conference, the young who visit Taizé in such numbers are touched by its liturgical and communitarian practices precisely because these are not undertaken *for them*. The word *experience* is a favorite these days in the promotional literature for posh spas. But Taizé is not a spa. The experience available there is not a product delivered up to a clientele for a price but a brief participation in a practice, a way of life, engaged in 365 days a year by the hundred resident monks. The monks intend to practice the sanctified life that they have chosen whether or not any young pilgrim shows up to take part in it or not. It is thus for the paradoxical reason that the young, though warmly welcomed, are not catered to at Taizé and are not its *raison d'être* that mediates for them a brief, blessed escape from the commercialization that elsewhere feels so inescapable.

One heard something strikingly similar in Rabbi Roly Matalon's explanation of why "BJ"—Congregation Bnai Jeshurun on Manhattan's Upper West Side—is winning young adult adherents when other synagogues are losing them. BJ does not exist to enable religious Jews to meet others like themselves, Rabbi Roly insisted. Networking is not its point. Neither is Jewish education for Jewish children or the propagation of a new generation in American Jewry. Neither is social service the point, whether to the BJ community or to the larger Manhattan community. All this happens around the edges of the community, but its core is worship; and for those who brought the community into existence, or brought it back into existence, worship will continue so long as a minyan shows up to carry it forward.

Worship at BJ is aesthetically synthetic in ways that bear intriguing comparison with Taizé. As at Taizé, worship at BJ is both scriptural and sacramental, both rational and mystical, both structured and improvisational, both traditional and innovative, both calming and cathartic, and so forth. But the taproot of their similarity is that each proceeds by testimony touched with mystery rather than by argumentation, much less by seductive salesmanship. Their market success arises from their refusal to engage in marketing.

And I note that it was just this refusal to engage in marketing that made the "implacably rooted" museums that James Traub remembers from his childhood—"archaic places, with an archaic regard for chronology, compendiousness, categorical crispness"—sacred in a way that today's museums are not. Those museums did not come to you. You went to them.

This consideration may properly return us to Nancy Ammerman's reminder that Protestantism has gone first where all American religion is eventually forced to go. On first acquaintance with them, American Protestant ministers do seem to immigrant clergy from other religious traditions rather like bright-eyed and bushy-tailed American salesmen. But recall that the Americans as a people have seemed to visitors from abroad like an entire nation of bright-eyed and bushy-tailed salesmen.

Read Charles Dickens on his American travels. For that matter, read the ever abashed and exquisitely sensitive Henry James. If the Jewish clergy has gone Protestant with less resistance than other immigrant clergy, it may be merely because the Jewish community as a whole has gone American more quickly and thoroughly than other immigrant subcultures have done.

I have been intrigued to read parts of a work in progress by Ross Miller advancing the claim that little of the overbearing rabbinic establishment as it existed in Russia and Eastern Europe crossed the Atlantic with the great wave of Jewish immigration from that part of the world. Miller argues that American Jewry, less channeled and checked by clerical supervision, has the more exuberantly made American civic institutions and civic usages its own.

Alexis de Tocqueville saw voluntary association, not least in its religious form, as distinctive of American society and an essential corrective to its otherwise all-corrosive individualism. But precisely because the Protestant clergy seemed somehow the normative or "official" clergy in the United States, theirs would be the model of clerical behavior that an aggressively Americanizing community would spontaneously adopt as its own. This being the case, the corrective that BJ represents within American Jewry applies to American Protestantism as well, even as the corrective of Taizé applies to American Jewry. One notes with interest that Rabbi Roly is Argentine, while Brother Roger, the late founder of Taizé, was Swiss. Though nothing is more global than marketization, the triumph of the market may have gone further, earlier in the United States than it did anywhere else—to the point that correction could only come from abroad.

Pluralism is both the polite and the political word—recall that *polite* and *political* come from the same Greek root—for a reality whose ruder name is market. The adjustment of immigrant groups to American religious culture is, as regards pluralism, an ordeal of civility, to borrow the title phrase of a penetrating book by John Murray Cuddihy. It is learning to say, as John Kerry did in one of the 2004 presidential debates, "I *happen* to be Catholic." Kerry did not mean to reduce his religious commitment to a matter of happenstance. He was merely playing by Protestant rules. And American culture has benefited incalculably from having those rules in place. But under its ruder name, the American religious market remains a far more taxing ordeal.

Surviving the ordeal begins with trusting that, sooner or later, even the coolest customer wants to be told something other than that he is always right. And there may be good counsel as well in recalling that well short of any such Kierkegaardian moment, raw market considerations are not always determinative. Something more psychological than economic—something like a market society's romance with numbers—is often at play as well and may be more easily tamed. We have acquired in the United States the habit of acting as if more is better even when, deep down, we believe otherwise. Thus, the desire of the Getty to attract substantial audiences to its exhibitions does not arise from fear that it will go bankrupt if the gate drops. The Getty is generously enough endowed to hold itself above such considerations. Even the more strapped New-York Historical Society, Traub asserts, "didn't need a blockbuster to stave off ruin." Many cultural institutions—above all, in the present context, many struggling religious congregations—do indeed live or die by their attendance and must fear even desperately when older congregants are not replaced by younger. But there remains a risk that more will be thought to be better even when more is not a matter of life and death.

I repeat that I do not minimize in the slightest the real day-to-day and week-to-week difficulty that attends the life of any voluntary organization at this moment in the history of the United States. Ours is a country that has almost certainly passed its peak as an economic power. The pie that was once expanding rapidly is shrinking because of world labor competition and the related world scarcity of essential resources. The ominous escalation in oil prices is quite probably the first of many such escalations. The "jobless recovery," rather than an aberration, may be a new paradigm by which the stock market and the employment rate will no longer rise or fall together. Americans, always inclined to be hustlers, are hustling faster because they know that little or nothing will be done for those who do not make the grade. They don't have to look back; they know that something is gaining on them. And by most empirical measures, they have less leisure time than do the citizens of other developed countries.

But this brings me to what will be my final point.

The triumph of the market has lately morphed into the triumph of entertainment. For "The customer is always right," we may now increasingly substitute "The audience is always right," and the audience is increasingly an audience of one. That is, collective entertainment is yielding steadily to technologically privatized entertainment. I recently read with grim interest an article in the August 2004 issue of *Wired* magazine entitled "The Lost Boys." The lost boys of the title are lost not just to high culture, not just to political responsibility, not just to religious commitment but even to broadcast television and to films in theatrical distribution. The 18-to-34 demographic group that advertising researchers call (a bit ominously if you ask me) "the Millennials" amuse themselves on the Internet, watch cable television by preference, and only then make a little room in their schedules for a sampling of network television. Videogames, moreover, are gaining steadily on network television, and from there the drop is steep to such old-fashioned diversions as films in theaters. As for what subject matter attracts the Millennials as they build their entertainment cocoons, the top four spots go to pornography at 71 percent, music at 53 percent, auctions at 51 percent, and sports at 48 percent. Depressingly, only 30 percent spend any media time even on their own careers.

This is surely a picture of American culture at its least appealing. "The moronic inferno," Saul Bellow called it in his greatest novel, *Humboldt's Gift.* What is a struggling pastor or rabbi or imam to think hearing such numbers? My own mind flees to a Shakespeare sonnet (65):

> Since brass nor stone nor earth nor boundless sea
> But sad mortality o'ersways their powers,
> How with this rage shall beauty hold a plea
> Whose action is no stronger than a flower?

Commodification was bad enough. The privatization of entertainment reduces everything and everybody not merely to a product but to an amusement, and woe to those who are not ready for prime time. In his landmark book *Entertaining Ourselves to Death,* the late Neil Postman made much of the phrase on the evening news, "And now this." A news report of plague, famine, pestilence, or war—or just now a fateful election—yields in those three words to, for example, an evocation of heartwarming camaraderie at McDonald's. What's the harm in the alternation?

Just this: nobody has to buy a Big Mac. You can take that kind of food or leave it. But when take-it-or-leave-it offerings become the paradigm for the entire news hour and, in effect, for the whole world, everything becomes optional. You can take the entire show or leave it too. And now, if you don't like all the channels, you can load your video game or take in an online orgy. It's all up to you because, by common but powerful consent, it's all offered for your amusement and for no other reason. You are the audience, and the audience is always right.

Where is the thread that leads out of the moronic inferno? I suggest that we find it in examples like that of Taizé, BJ, and Muslim Youth Camp, particularly when the campers rise at dawn to hear the Qur'an chanted in the chill of first light. The studied indifference of young people in the survey research reported on in this conference toward religion and even toward the questions being asked about religion comports very well with the data reported in *Wired* about the difficulty that anyone selling anything in our society has at this time reaching "the lost boys." But behind all those "whatevers," there lies, according to one of the advertising researchers, a great thirst for "authenticity." And perhaps the biggest surprise: "There's a huge lure to obscurity. That's one of the keys—giving people something to discover, which is the antithesis of the way most advertising works." Religious institutions, even making the most active use of showbiz techniques, cannot possibly compete in that game. But mystery is their own game, and perhaps they need to return to it.

As for that hunger or thirst for authenticity, let me suggest that it arises as the cry of the oppressed from the maw of the same omnivorous commodification in which our young people find themselves. Relentlessly prepped, tested, evaluated, sorted, and ranked, they are forced to such a considerable extent to think of themselves as commodities—and to fear that the market may not want what they have on offer—that an escape into another kind of relationship and another way of life, however dimly grasped, surely must have its appeal. Organized religion cannot effectively offer this escape if it goes too far in commodifying itself. Paradoxically, however, if it asks more, then even if it attracts fewer, it may succeed in watering an oasis in the desert of consumerism.

# TEACH YOUR CHILDREN WELL: CLOSING OBSERVATIONS ON CONSTRUCTING RELIGIOUS IDENTITY IN THE NEXT GENERATION

*Diane Winston*

> *Only take heed, and keep your soul diligently, lest you forget the things which your eyes have seen, and lest they depart from your heart all the days of your life; make them known to your children and your children's children—how on the day you stood before your Lord at Horeb. The Lord said to me, "Gather the people to me, that I may let them hear my words, so that they may learn to fear me all the days that they live upon the earth, and that they may teach their children so.*

Deuteronomy 4:9–11

From their origins, the Abrahamic faiths have placed a high premium on transmitting religious identity from one generation to the next. Yet each of the traditions has developed its own methods for religious training. That's why an opportunity for educators from different faith traditions and professional disciplines to come together holds special promise. Unexpected similarities may bring comfort, just as unanticipated differences can spur revelatory insights.

The October 2004 conference, "Faith, Fear and Indifference: Constructing Religious Identity in the Next Generation," and the subsequent collection of essays based on this gathering confirm this hoped-for outcome. Scholars, theologians and clergy, practitioners and theoreticians, parents and educators, Jews, Christians, and Muslims spanned customary divides in search of common ends. Surmounting differences in what they do and how they do it—as well as how and what they believe—conference participants reasoned together about handing down their deepest values and cherished beliefs to today's youth.

While the task is not unique to this generation, the charge has become more complicated in recent years. Old-time religion perennially battles the lure of the new, the glitzy, and the feel-good here-and-now. Today's perils, however, exist on a different scale. Contemporary consumer capitalism, hyper-individualism, and the ubiquitous entertainment culture feed restlessness and relativism, which is further fueled by increased mobility, technological advances, cultural pluralism, and changes in family life and the structure of work.

As the papers in this volume indicate, conference presenters have wrestled with these challenges both head-on and obliquely. As the concluding respondent, it falls to me to critique those efforts and point to paths not taken. As a historian, I view contemporary challenges within the larger framework of religious continuity. As a journalist, I ask the question, "So what?" What's the bottom line and why should we care? And for my starting point, I offer three snapshots from my own tradition, Judaism.

1) Before going to Sukkot services this year, I gave Isabelle, my five-year-old daughter, some background on the holiday. "We build and decorate a little hut and then eat dinner there." "Why Mommy?" "Because we want to thank God for being so good to us." She considers this briefly before announcing on our way out the door that "I don't want to be Jewish, I want to be Christmas."

Once we arrive at the synagogue, the youngest children are assigned to groups led by teenage girls, and Isabelle trots off for a holiday treasure hunt. Afterwards they paint fruit and make garlands to decorate the sukkah. The rabbi draws them near to talk more about the holiday and when it's time to go, Isabelle protests. She wants to know when we'll be building our own sukkah.

2) Sara Chandler is a twentysomething student at Jewish Theological Seminary's Davidson School of Education in New York City.[1] Asked how she chose her vocation, Sara said she was looking for an experience similar to her summers at Camp Eisner in Great Barrington, Massachusetts. "I really the missed the down-to-earth community of Jews who loved to sit and sing and celebrate Shabbat," she told a reporter.

Finding a *havurah* (a small group for study and fellowship) at school, she said, "was like water to me." The importance Sara herself assigns to her five years as a counselor at a Jewish summer camp echoes the findings of a new study by sociologists Amy L. Sales and Leonard Saxe that Jewish camps are a prime socializing experience and that the counselors, more so than campers, were the main beneficiaries.[2]

3) Ikar, a new *shul* in Los Angeles, calls itself "progressive traditional." Most congregants are in their early thirties to mid-forties, and at Rosh Hashanah—the Jewish New Year—hundreds of them are present to celebrate the holiday. Their davening, or physical immersion in prayer, has them swaying left and right, moving up and down on the balls of their feet. Tambourines and conga drums accompany the group chanting and when the rabbi holds the Torah aloft for the traditional procession around the sanctuary, many worshippers dance behind.

Interspersed with the singing and praying, founding members offer testimonials in which they describe Ikar as a spiritual oasis after years of wandering in a religious desert. They speak of Ikar as a community valuing Jewish learning, spiritual seeking, and social justice. Some compare its vibrancy to their memories of Jewish summer camp; others say it is the antithesis of the cold and lifeless synagogues of their childhood. Ikar, they say, is where they want to raise their own children.

These snapshots illustrate a child, a young adult, and older adults engaged by religion. At each age, there is a balance between intellect and emotion that allows participants to experience the encounter as accessible, authentic, and animating. Together they exemplify what I define as the gold standard for organized religion (and a model for enabling and promoting its continuity): an encounter that participants experience as authentic (rooted in a particular historical tradition, which can be expressed through language, ritual, art, and music), accessible (welcoming worshippers at different stages of their religious journey), and animating (providing an experience of reflection, revitalization, and renewal). My overview of the proceedings will focus on how presenters addressed different aspects of this dynamic.

## RELIGION VERSUS SPIRITUALITY: WHAT THE DATA SHOWS

The conference's first forum reported on the current religious and spiritual state of American youth. Both the UCLA survey "College Student

Beliefs and Values" (CSBV) and UNC sociologist Christian Smith's "National Study of Youth and Religion" (NSYR) revealed the thin shell that houses many young Americans' understanding of religion. In the widespread, functional faith that Smith calls "Moralistic Therapeutic Deism," adherents believe in being moral ("being kind, nice, pleasant, courteous, responsible") and expect—perhaps as a result of this behavior—to receive therapeutic benefits ("feeling happy, good, safe, at peace"). A creator God exists over all but "is not particularly personally involved in one's life dealings—especially dealings in which one would prefer not to have God involved."[3]

Smith and his research team found respondents wanted to be "good" and by the terms of their operative faith, they were—even in a world where formidable amoral forces, including materialism, consumerism, hyper-individualism, held sway. Moralistic Therapeutic Deism does not challenge the existing social, cultural, and political order, nor does it expect its adherents to do so. Rather it implies that if one is kind and nice, everything else will fall into place. Smith rejects traditional secularization theory, and its argument that religion must wither away in the chill atmosphere of secular society. Even though religion remains a social value in Moralistic Therapeutic Deism, Smith explains, it has undergone an "internal secularization" which threatens "the project of sustaining the integrity of the substance of faith and practice of historical religious traditions."[4]

A complementary perspective is offered by the CSBV survey, presented by Jennifer Lindholm. UCLA researchers, less prescriptive than Smith, found college students very interested in spirituality (overwhelmingly experienced through nature and music) but also participating in traditional religious activities (praying and attending services). Among students surveyed both as freshman and as juniors, researchers found over time an increase in the personal importance accorded to spirituality (e.g. "integrating spirituality into my life") and a decrease in service attendance.[5] Although they did not analyze the same markers as Smith did, the UCLA study substantiates a similar regard among young people for the functionalist and therapeutic aspects of religion. Lindholm's presentation addressed "how spiritual and religious practices affect students' academic and personal development" and "how students viewed themselves in terms of spirituality and related qualities such as compassion, honesty, optimism, and humility." The team's findings confirmed several of Smith's hypotheses.[6]

Ihsan Bagby's preliminary study of Muslim youth diverged from the other teams' investigations of Christian and Jewish young people. Muslim youth appear to have a deeper knowledge of their tradition. They are less likely to prefer "spirituality" to organized religion. In fact, young Muslims proactively redefine and revise their parents' religious identity to better suit their own sense of spiritual authenticity. For many, the mosque is an attractive destination, a gathering place for social and cultural, as well as religious, activities. The difference between this group and the other two may derive from the fact that the more corrosive aspects of American religion—what Chris Smith saw as an emphasis on functionality, an attenuated concept of tolerance, and an attachment to therapeutic spirituality—are not yet present in younger and more close-knit Muslim communities.

Underlying the presentations—and explicitly addressed by Smith—was the sense that many American youth lack the vocabulary to imagine God or to value institutional expressions of faith. Contemporary youth want to be good and feel spiritual, and they may even want to be part of a community. But they lack the words—and thus the ideas—which would enable them to envision a deeper, richer, and more complex conception of their relationship to God or their membership in a faith community. Smith argues that what is "arguably unfair and disrespectful to youth is to fail as communities of faith to provide youth with the clear and substantive belief content, defining identity boundaries, and moral expectations which they then can bounce around, digest, question, struggle over and eventually personally embrace revise or reject."[7]

## RELIGION ON THE GROUND: THE ETHNOGRAPHERS' EXPERIENCE

The ethnographic panel—Tobin Belzer, Richard W. Flory, Nadia Roumani, and Brie Loskota—supported Smith's contention by demonstrating its obverse: successful religious programming for youth and young people offered community and spirituality in the context of a clearly defined faith tradition. Such programs—be they Jewish, Christian, or Muslim—responded to youths' felt needs for empowerment, leadership opportunities, responsibility, and accountability, as well as authenticity and accessibility. Rather than feel limited by the particularities of their traditions, interviewees said it provided firm ground on which to stand. In other words, a lack of specificity does not facilitate pluralism and understanding for people of other faiths. Individuals who know who they are and what they believe are able to honestly encounter differences and explore areas of mutuality.

Likewise, the testimony of successful religious entrepreneurs—Brother John, Rabbi J. Rolando Matalon and Amira Quraishi—further confirms, in Hollywood's formulation, that if you build it they will come. All three describe religious projects deeply rooted in particularistic traditions and offering opportunities—through music, liturgy, activities, and prayer—to slip quotidian bonds. These speakers demonstrate that it is possible to develop a strong religious identity among youth if it is predicated on hard work, deep commitment, and teaching the rudiments of one's particular faith. Head and heart must be addressed together; teaching a religious vocabulary is as vital as eliciting experience through a tradition's prayers, rituals, liturgies, or aesthetics. The goal is not to recreate Taizé, Bnai Jeshurun or Muslim Youth Camp, but to understand the components of their success and draw on these lessons to build up local communities.

Brother John describes one of the Taizé community's aims as "providing time to become." This also can be to time to daven, to reflect, or just to slow down. At Taizé, the simple regimen of chores and worship facilitates the process. Prayer occurs three times each day. While some adjustments have made worship more accessible (for example, chanting short refrains in Latin and then in other languages), the services are a classic monastic blend of long stretches of meditative chanting and silence. By comparison, Americans churches, synagogues, and mosques must make do with much more restricted access to young people. As a consequence, it is much more difficult to provide "time to become" in that context. How and where to start is a very real dilemma. Within my own Jewish tradition, where would one place the starting line? Attending Shabbat services? Friday night or Saturday morning? It's a stretch to imagine going to both. What about prayer? Do you need to know Hebrew? Is reading transliterated Hebrew "better" than saying the prayers in English? Should you sway back and forth? What if you're moved more by folk songs than by Eastern European melodies?

Taizé's accomplishment—a transformative ministry that has reached thousands of youth over three-plus decades—is daunting. It's an experiment in living faith that is not easily replicated. However, some religious groups have developed creative interventions that provide occasions for religious education, experience, and community on a more modest scale.

- In 2002–2003, almost one thousand Mormon teenagers braved snow, subzero temperatures and the predawn dark to attend a daily six o'clock Bible study. Seminary, a program for ninth through twelfth graders, is sponsored by the Church of Jesus Christ of Latter-day Saints. Students must maintain an 80 percent attendance rate at daily classes through all four years of high school. Why do it? Teens say they like that the classes help them to draw on Scripture for assistance with daily problems, learn about their tradition, and develop a relationship with Jesus Christ.[8]
- Some Muslim elementary school students are electing to observe Ramadan, a month-long fast from dawn to sundown. Islamic law exempts children from the ritual, but some as young as seven have decided to try. In the Washington, D.C., suburbs, where there is a significant Muslim population, several public schools have set aside classrooms where Muslim children can study and play together during lunchtime. Many children use the time to talk about what their faith means to them and why they want to observe the fast.[9]
- Sixteen-year-old Johnny Nelson, a member of the youth group at Chaska Valley Evangelical Free Church in Minnesota, has waged a singlehanded campaign to build a state-of-the-art skateboard park to bring teens to church. Recently, Nelson found a local businessman who wanted to support a faith-based teen center and the two decided to coordinate their efforts. The result is JSAW Extreme, "Jesus Snow, Asphalt and Water." The twenty-thousand-square-foot facility will use extreme sports to reach out to unchurched young people.[10]

The third example may be more problematic than the first two as it rasies the question of where to draw the line between creative evangelism and cultural accommodation. Some observers have wondered if the Evangelical community's growing use of popular culture for teen outreach sacrifices authenticity for the sake of accessibility. Does *Revolve*, the *Cosmopolitan*-esque New Testament for teenage girls, bring Scripture alive or dumb it down? Can Impact Explode, a ministry that uses youth music and sports, turn young hearts to Jesus or does it simply provide a place to hang out? Unfortunately, neither presenters nor audience members probed the efficacy of pop-culture-based outreach in constructing religious identity in the next generation.

Whereas sociologists offered current data on youth's religious identity and ethnographers and religious leaders discussed what worked on the ground, a third group of presenters theorized on mediating between the two. They asked and tried to answer how might congregations and religious communities become more authentic, accessible, and animating. For sociologist Nancy Ammerman, one possibility is storytelling. Author Eli Wiesel has said, "God created human beings because he loves stories," and Ammerman, who recently completed an in-depth study of American congregational life,[11] emphasizes the importance of stories as key vehicles for experiencing and transmitting faith within religious communities.

> This is what congregations do as they gather for worship. In hymns, scripture, sermon, sacrament, prayer, chant, bowing, kneeling, lighting candles and incense, wearing vestments, displaying art—the words and signs and symbols tell the story of the gods and the creation and the direction of history. As people listen and move and see and smell, they are asked to encounter a reality beyond themselves.[12]

Catholic theologian Peter Phan further elaborates on the significance of storytelling by conceptually re-visioning the theological tools that explain who we are and our relationship with God. According to Phan, that work is accomplished by four pillars of Christian identity: doctrine, liturgy, ethical praxis, and private prayer. Each is a vehicle for storytelling. Doctrine is the explicit, pedagogical presentation of who the community is and what it believes. Liturgy is the community's affirmation of its relationship to God. Ethical praxis is the embodiment of the community's story through individual actions, and private prayer is the individual's retelling the story to God. Although Phan interprets these pillars in a Catholic context, Rabbi Matalon expresses a similar understanding in his description of how Bnai Jeshurun helps worshippers approach and understand the divine. Matalon employs the terms study, observance, service, and prayer, but the parallels are strong. Both provide road maps to guide seekers in understanding and growing in the faith.

If the four pillars provide a religious vocabulary, "deep structures," according to Phan, mediate a religious imagination that draws on and transcends that vocabulary. Phan envisions these deep structures as doctrine, devotions, the episcopacy, and the arts.[13] Within a Catholic context, these offer ways to experience the mystery, the authority, and the creativity that spark religious identity and belief. These deep structures, which can be translated into other religious systems, provide the passion underlying faith and the understanding for why Jews dance behind the Torah and Catholics kneel before the cross, why Muslims prostrate themselves in prayer and Evangelicals pore over Scripture.

Without exception, all the presenters assume deep attachment to their particular faiths. However, as we consider strategies for change, I wonder why none of the speakers offer warrants for preserving and continuing those traditions. Everyone takes for granted that religion— and specifically religions of the Abrahamic tradition—are important and worth saving. But why? Looking at these faiths from a truly external perspective, say through the eyes of an alienated teenager, one sees hatred, violence, senseless killing, and religiously based terrorism, not just now but down through the ages. What then are we passing on and why? Those who care about religious continuity need to make explicit why their particular faith is worth saving. Here, differences become meaningful. Wanting to save a soul from hell is very different than arguing for Jewish continuity. Likewise, seeking an experience of the transcendent is not necessarily the same thing as following God's commandments. Significant ideas separate us, yet our differences remain unarticulated in most of our discussions.

This leads to the "so what" question that constitutes the bottom line. Why go to church, synagogue, or mosque? Why be in a relationship with a demanding God? Why belong to a persecuted community? Why be obedient to peculiar doctrines, rituals, and traditions? So what and why?

The answer to the question spills into everything we do, indicting us when our actions fall short of our intentions. I see this constantly in my tradition—parents who choose a synagogue based on the convenience of the Hebrew-school schedule (lest it conflict with soccer, baseball, or ballet practice); interfaith homes where parents think of religious difference as decorating opportunities. I don't think we have begun to confront the challenge of intermarriage. We know that the statistics for Jews intermarrying is close to 50 percent, but it is difficult to get comparable numbers of Protestants, Catholics, and Muslims. Many interfaith households think it is possible to be Jewish and Christian, Muslim and Christian, Jewish and Muslim—and unless you believe it, too, this assumption needs to be confronted by religious communities and religious educators.

In closing, I want to address the role of the media as another channel for strategizing change. Sociologist Peter Berger once described America as a nation of Indians governed by Swedes, referring to the fact that India is among the most religious nations in the world and Sweden among the least. I would argue that today we're governed by Indians but mediated by Swedes. The media—broadly construed as news, entertainment, advertising, literature, film and television—is a vast field for disseminating ideas, values, and deep structures. Much of today's media assumes a secular perspective on culture and society. Whether this is accidental or intentional is, for this discussion, beside the point. More important is the pervasiveness of our mediated environment. We move in media as fish swim through water; we take it for granted. How do you begin the day? Reading the paper, watching TV, listening to the radio? After breakfast do you surf the net? Turn on your car stereo? Thumb through a weekly magazine? At work, do you troll the internet? Listen to your iPod? IM with your Blackberry?

We are continually interacting with mediated information, symbols, and signs. And much of what we take in and take for granted assumes that reality is naturalistic (rather than supernatural), materialistic (as opposed to spiritual) and presentist (it is all there is). Thus, the conditions of naturalism, materialism, and presentism habituate us to a world that is indifferent, if not hostile, to religious sensibilities.

In my professional life, I try to help journalists become more intentional about reporting on the faith dimension in stories they cover. In 1999 both the Pew Charitable Trusts and the Lilly Endowment funded studies of religion in the media, and researchers found that although the citations of religion were up, they were often empty markers. Journalists report the experience but miss the meaning. In other words, mentions of religion don't include how it affects individual or collective decisions and activities. Working first as a grant officer at Pew and now as an educator at USC, I want to give media coverage of religion, spirituality, morals, and ethics more content and heft. How do we write about the faith that animates politicians, rock stars, suicide bombers, and everyday saints? Because covering that is one way to spark religious imagination and to develop a religious vocabulary. It's also central to many people's real lives and of deep interest to readers.

There's a story in the Talmud that says when we stand before our maker we'll be asked many questions about our ethical activities, and at the very last God will turn to us and say, "Did you keep your eye out for the Messiah?" This underscores the Jewish belief that redemption is just around the corner and we must be always be ready for it. It also reminds us that we must live with hope. Hope is what has animated this conference—the hope that we can learn across religious divides and share strategies for change. Even more important, it's a hope that we can give our children intimations of the divine, appreciations for their community, and a sense of wonder for creation and the mystery of unconditional love.

# *Notes*

Introduction: Youth and the Continuity of Religious Traditions
*James L. Heft, S.M.*

1. The Lilly Endowment has been especially helpful to this entire project.

2. The Alliance of Confessing Evangelical Christians expressed in a striking way in 1996 their opposition to pandering to youth to attract them back to religious practices: "The loss of God's centrality in the life of today's church is common and lamentable. It is this loss that allows us to transform worship into entertainment, gospel preaching into marketing, believing into technique, being good into feeling good about ourselves, and faithfulness into being successful" (cited in William Placher, "Believe it or Not," *Christian Century*, September 20, 2003, 20–21).

3. Augustine (354–430), not known for his upbeat assessment of life in this world, once explained in similar tones many centuries after Plato why his congregation should not think the present times were so bad: "Is there any affliction now endured by people that was not endured by our ancestors before us? What sufferings of ours even bear comparison with what we know of their sufferings? And yet you hear people complaining about this present day and age because things were so much better in former times. I wonder what would happen if they could be taken back to the days of their ancestors—would we not still hear them complaining? You may think past ages were good, but it is only because you are not living in them. Just think what those past ages were like! Is there one of us who does not shudder to hear or read of them? Far from justifying complaints about our own time, they teach us how much we have to be thankful for" (Sermon Caillau-Saint-Yves 2, 92, PLS, 2, 441–42). This same quotation is referred to in the first chapter of this volume, again to gain historical perspective.

4. "Self Reliance," in *Selected Writings of Ralph Waldo Emerson*, ed. William H. Gilman (New York: The New American Library, 1965), 257–80.

5. The "spiritual but not religious" phenomenon admits many interpretations. For a basically positive assessment, see Leigh Eric Schmidt, *Restless*

*Souls: The Making of American Spirituality* (San Francisco: HarperSanFrancisco, 2005). For a more critical but still sympathetic appraisal, see Vincent Miller, *Consuming Religion* (New York: Continuum, 2003).

6. Jeannette Batz, "The Many Words of Walter Ong," *St. Louis University Alumni Magazine* (sometime before 1990). My comments on Plato and Ong draw freely from my article, "The Purpose of Christian Education," in *The Catechist* 22, no. 8 (April–May 1989): 27–28.

7. James Coleman, *The Adolescent Society: The Social Life of the Teenager and Its Impact on Society* (New York: Free Press of Glencoe, 1961).

8. In particular, W. V. D'Antonio and others, *Laity: American and Catholic* (Kansas City, MO: Sheed & Ward, 1996); W. V. D'Antonio and others, *American Catholics: Gender, Generation and Commitment* (Walnut Creek, CA: AltaMira Press, 2001); J. D. Davidson and others, *The Search for Common Ground: What Unites and Divides American Catholics* (Huntington, IN: Our Sunday Visitor, 1997); J. D. Davidson, *Catholicism in Motion: The Church in American Society* (Liguori, MO: Liguori/Triumph, 2005); and D. Hoge and others, *Young Adult Catholics: Religion in the Culture of Choice* (Notre Dame, IN: Notre Dame Press, 2001).

9. I am drawing freely here from James Davidson and James Heft's article, "The Mission of the Catholic High Schools and Today's Millennials: Three Suggestions," *Catholic Education: A Journal of Inquiry and Practice* 6, no. 4 (June 2003): 410–22.

10. See William Portier, "Here Come the Evangelical Catholics," *Communio: International Catholic Review* (Spring 2004): 35–66.

11. One is reminded of a somewhat flippant but nonetheless pertinent article by Jonathan Rauch ("Let it Be," *Atlantic Monthly*, May 2003, 34). Rauch writes approvingly about the growth of "apatheism," that is, "a disinclination to care all that much about one's own religion, and an even stronger disinclination to care about other people's religion." He considers this a "major civilizational advance."

12. Smith's findings are echoed by Alan Wolfe's book, *One Nation After All* (New York: Viking, 1998), which reports that the *summum bonum* of the American middle class is tolerance, which may be expressed as the eleventh commandment, "Thou shalt not judge!" (see pp. 29–30).

13. A more exact translation might be "being in God." In ancient times, the use of the term designated the *pythia*, a woman who got drunk or high on drugs and entered into a type of mania from which she uttered oracles. The mania was considered a type of divine possession.

14. Future research by Astin will focus on learning from professors why so few of them are willing to address the issues of spirituality in their classes.

15. One is reminded of Catholic philosopher Alisdair MacIntyre's worry that our universities have already surrendered to market forces: "Do we really want them [our present and future alumni] to become what, on the best evidence that we have, recent graduates of the best research universities have tended to become: narrowly focused professionals, immensely and even obsessionally hard working, disturbingly competitive and intent on success as it is measured within their own specialized professional sphere, often genuinely excellent at what they do; who read little worthwhile that is not relevant to their work; who, as the idiom insightfully puts it, 'make time,' sometimes

with difficulty, for their family lives; and whose relaxation tends to consist of short strenuous bouts of competitive athletic activity and sometimes of therapeutic indulgence in the kind of religion that is well designed not to disrupt their working lives?" From "Catholic Universities: Dangers, Hopes, Choices," in *Higher Learning and Catholic Traditions*, ed. Robert E. Sullivan, 15 (South Bend, IN: Notre Dame Press, 2001).

LOOKING FOR GOD: RELIGIOUS INDIFFERENCE IN PERSPECTIVE
*Melchor Sánchez de Toca*

I express a debt of gratitude to Richard Rouse for his assistance in preparing this essay, which was first presented at the international conference "Faith, Fear and Indifference: Constructing Religious Identity in the Next Generation," University of Southern California, Los Angeles, October 10–11, 2004.

1. "O Father, Where Art Thou?" *Time*, June 16, 2003.

2. Cardinal Paul Poupard and Pontificium Consilium de Cultura, *Where Is Your God? Responding to the Challenge of Unbelief and Religious Indifference Today* (Chicago: LTP, 2004).

3. P. Poupard, ed., *La foi et l'athéisme dans le monde* (Paris: Desclée,1988); Spanish translation published as *Fe y ateísmo en el mundo* (Madrid: BAC, 1990).

4. Some of the following passages are taken verbatim from *Where Is Your God?*, which contains a more extensive exposition of the research, deeper analysis of the causes, and broader range of proposals in response.

5. The expression "new religious movements" is not to be confused with "new ecclesial movements." The former is used to refer to "alternative religions" unless the context indicates otherwise.

6. Paolo Brogli, "Tolleranti e poco praticanti, ma religiosi" (Tolerant and infrequently practicing, but religious people [the Romans]) in *Corriere della Sera*, September 22, 2004.

7. Ibid.

8. Pontifical Councils for Culture and Interreligious Dialogue, *Jesus Christ, the Bearer of the Water of Life* (Vatican City, 2003).

9. Saint Augustine, Sermon Caillau-Saint-Yves 2, 92, *PLS*, 2, 441–42.

10. A. Rouco Varela, "La increencia y la secularización entre los jóvenes: la respuesta de las Jornadas Mundiales de la Juventud," *Religioni e sette* 26 (2004): 55–58.

11. F. Dostoyevski, *The Idiot*, pt. 3, ch. 5; cf. John Paul II, *Letter to Artists*, 16n.

JOURNEYS OF FAITH: MEETING THE CHALLENGES IN
TWENTY-FIRST-CENTURY AMERICA
*Nancy Ammerman*

1. These figures have been compiled from the General Social Survey, combining surveys from 1993 to 2002 and looking just at those who were eighteen to thirty years old in their survey year. National Opinion Research Center at the University of Chicago, *GSSDIRS General Social Survey: 1972–*

*2000 Cumulative Codebook* (2002), http://www.icpsr.umich.edu:8080/GSS/homepage.htm (accessed September 13, 2004).

2. I have elaborated on the challenges of modernity for religious life elsewhere. See Nancy Ammerman, "Conservative Jews within the Landscape of American Religion," in *Jews in the Center: Conservative Synagogues and Their Members*, ed. J. Wertheimer (New Brunswick, NJ: Rutgers University Press, 2000). Portions of the present essay draw on material first published there, as well as from my 1997 Presidential Address to the Association for the Sociology of Religion. See Nancy T. Ammerman, "Organized Religion in a Voluntaristic Society," *Sociology of Religion* 58, no. 3 (1997): 203–15.

3. Peter Berger's early writing was formative in making the link between diversity and loss of plausibility. See his *The Sacred Canopy* (Garden City, NY: Anchor Doubleday, 1969); and his "From the Crisis of Religion to the Crisis of Secularity," in *Religion and America*, ed. M. Douglas and S. Tipton (Boston: Beacon, 1982). This link he has subsequently come to doubt. See "The Desecularization of the World: A Global Overview," in *The Desecularization of the World: Resurgent Religion and World Politics*, ed. Peter L. Berger (Grand Rapids, MI: Eerdmans, 1999).

4. Among the theorists who have linked modernity and individuality, see Rose Laub Coser, *In Defense of Modernity: Role Complexity and Individual Autonomy* (Stanford, CA: Stanford University Press, 1991); Anthony Giddens, *Modernity and Self-Identity: Self and Society in the Late Modern Age* (Stanford, CA: Stanford University Press, 1991); and Georg Simmel, "Group Expansion and the Development of Individuality," in *Georg Simmel on Individuality and Social Forms*, ed. D. N. Levine (Chicago: University of Chicago Press, 1971).

5. For those who have argued that modern religion is characterized by individualism, see especially Robert N. Bellah, "Religious Evolution," in *Beyond Belief* (Boston: Beacon, 1963); Phillip E. Hammond, *Religion and Personal Autonomy: The Third Disestablishment in America* (Columbia: University of South Carolina Press, 1992); and Talcott Parsons, "Religion and Modern Industrial Society," in *Religion, Culture, and Society*, ed. L. Schneider (New York: Wiley, 1964).

6. Wade Clark Roof, *A Generation of Seekers* (San Francisco: HarperSanFrancisco, 1993).

7. See especially chapter 3 in Dean R. Hoge, Benton Johnson, and Donald A. Luidens, *Vanishing Boundaries: The Religion of Mainline Protestant Baby Boomers* (Louisville, KY: Westminster / John Knox, 1994).

8. Reported in Wade Clark Roof and William McKinney, *American Mainline Religion* (New Brunswick, NJ: Rutgers University Press, 1987).

9. Penny Long Marler and David A. Roozen, "From Church Tradition to Consumer Choice: The Gallup Surveys of the Unchurched American," in *Church and Denominational Growth*, ed. D. A. Roozen and C. K. Hadaway (Nashville, TN: Abingdon, 1993).

10. This summary of American religious history is drawn from chapter 8 of Nancy Tatom Ammerman, *Pillars of Faith: American Congregations and Their Partners* (Berkeley and Los Angeles: University of California Press, 2005).

11. Jon Butler, *Awash in a Sea of Faith* (Cambridge: Harvard University Press, 1990).

12. Sidney E. Mead, *The Lively Experiment* (New York: Harper & Row, 1963), 106.

13. Nathan G. Hatch, *The Democratization of American Christianity* (New Haven, CT: Yale University Press, 1989), 64.

14. Demerath has compared the United States to fourteen other societies where the mix of religion and politics has sometimes been violent. He concludes that religious liberty is not what distinguishes the United States, but that disestablishment (the unlinking of state power from religious privilege) is a key to our relatively less violent history. N. J. Demerath III, *Crossing the Gods: World Religions and Worldly Politics* (New Brunswick, NJ: Rutgers University Press, 2001).

15. The Protestant influence can also be seen in the typical organizational form new immigrants have adopted, what Warner calls "de facto congregationalism." See R. Stephen Warner, "Work in Progress toward a New Paradigm for the Sociological Study of Religion in the United States," *American Journal of Sociology* 98, no. 5 (1993): 1044–93.

16. See Max Weber, *The Theory of Social and Economic Organization*, trans. A. M. Henderson and T. Parsons (New York: Free Press, 1947) for this classic treatment of the contrasts between the traditional and the modern world. On the late-nineteenth-century shift to enlightened, rational, and professionalized bases of authority in American culture (in contrast to the existing Protestant establishment), see Christian Smith, ed., *The Secular Revolution: Power, Interests, and Conflict in the Secularization of American Public Life* (Berkeley and Los Angeles: University of California Press, 2003).

17. Bronislaw Malinowski, *Magic, Science, and Religion* (New York: Free Press, 1948) makes this most clear, but it is the underlying premise of the historical accounts given by Freud about the human psyche, and by Marx about human history. See Sigmund Freud, *The Future of an Illusion*, trans. J. Strachey (New York: Norton, 1961), and Karl Marx, "Contribution to a Critique of Hegel's Philosophy of Right," in *Karl Marx: Early Writings*, ed. T. B. Bottomore (New York: McGraw-Hill, 1963).

18. Dean M. Kelley, *Why Conservative Churches Are Growing* (San Francisco: Harper & Row, 1977).

19. Peter L. Berger, "From the Crisis of Religion to the Crisis of Secularity," in *Religion and America*, ed. M. Douglas and S. Tipton (Boston: Beacon, 1982), 20.

20. Smith offers a contrary view: cultural diversity creates just the right sort of context in which an adversarial religion can maintain its own identity by consistently highlighting what it is not. See Christian Smith and others, *American Evangelicalism: Embattled and Thriving* (Chicago: University of Chicago Press, 1998).

21. I have elaborated this delineation of the "postmodern" alternative to modern "either/or" thinking elsewhere and draw from those articles in the account that follows. See "Organized Religion in a Voluntaristic Society" and "Conservative Jews within the Landscape of American Religion."

22. Smith argues that the actual contrast between "rational" science and "irrational" religion was never so dramatic as the antagonists claimed. See Christian Smith, *The Secular Revolution: Power, Interests, and Conflict in the Secularization of American Public Life* (Berkeley and Los Angeles: University of California Press, 2003).

23. Peggy Levitt, *Transnational Villagers* (Berkeley and Los Angeles: University of California Press, 2001).

24. Ammerman, *Pillars of Faith*.

25. This metaphor is borrowed from Walter Brueggemann, "The Legitimacy of a Sectarian Hermeneutic: 2 Kings 18–19," in *Education for Citizenship and Discipleship*, ed. M. C. Boys (New York: Pilgrim, 1989).

26. R. Stephen Warner, *New Wine in Old Wineskins* (Berkeley and Los Angeles: University of California Press, 1988).

27. Thomas Bender, *Community and Social Change in America* (New Brunswick, NJ: Rutgers University Press, 1978) provides an excellent historical argument for the "both/and" character of modern community. It is both alien and impersonal and laced with dense webs of affiliation.

28. This section on congregational community-building draws on material from chapter 8 of my *Pillars of Faith*.

29. R. Stephen Warner and Judith G. Wittner, *Gatherings in Diaspora: Religious Communities and the New Immigration* (Philadelphia: Temple University Press, 1998).

30. R. Stephen Warner, "Growing Up Hindu in America: A Surprising Success Story" (Chicago: Youth and Religion Project, University of Illinois at Chicago, 2002).

31. R. Stephen Warner, "Changes in the Civic Role of Religion," in *Diversity and Its Discontents: Cultural Conflict and Common Ground in Contemporary American Society*, ed. N. J. Smelser and J. C. Alexander (Princeton, NJ: Princeton University Press, 1999), 236.

32. Demerath, *Crossing the Gods*, 218.

IS MORALISTIC THERAPEUTIC DEISM THE NEW RELIGION OF AMERICAN YOUTH? IMPLICATIONS FOR THE CHALLENGE OF RELIGIOUS SOCIALIZATION AND REPRODUCTION
*Christian Smith*

1. Thomas Luckmann, *The Invisible Religion* (New York: Macmillan, 1967), 36.

2. Christian Smith with Melinda Lundquist Denton, *Soul Searching: The Religious and Spiritual Lives of American Teenagers* (New York: Oxford University Press, 2005).

3. Along these lines, see Terri Apter, *The Myth of Maturity: What Teenagers Need from Parents to Become Adults* (New York: Norton, 2001); Kay S. Hymowitz, *Ready or Not: What Happens When We Treat Children as Small Adults* (San Francisco: Encounter Books, 2000), and *Liberation's Children: Parents and Kids in a Postmodern Age* (Chicago: Ivan R. Dee, 2003); Robert Shaw, *The Epidemic: The Rot of American Culture, Absentee and Permissive Parenting, and the Resultant Plague of Joyless, Selfish Children* (New York: HarperCollins, 2003); David Elkind, *All Grown Up and No Place to Go* (Cambridge: Perseus, 1998). Also see Institute for American Values, *Hardwired to Connect: A New Scientific Case for Authoritative Communities—A Report to the Nation from the Commission on Children at Risk* (New York: Institute for American Values, 2003).

4. Smith with Denton, *Soul Searching*, 118–171.

5. Many of the ideas in this section were suggested in the postscript of Smith, *Soul Searching*, 265–271.

6. Charles Taylor, *Sources of the Self* (Cambridge: Harvard University Press, 1989) and "Self-Interpreting Animals," in *Human Agency and Language* (Cambridge: Cambridge University Press, 1985), 45–76.

7. See, for example, Dorothy Bass and Don Richter, eds., *Way to Live: Christian Practices for Teens* (Nashville, TN: Upper Room Books, 2002); and Dorothy Bass, ed., *Practicing Our Faith: A Way of Life for a Searching People* (San Francisco: Jossey-Bass, 1997).

8. In this I tend to agree with recent empirical observations—though not necessarily normative assessments—in Alan Wolfe's *The Transformation of American Religion: How We Actually Live our Faith* (New York: The Free Press, 2003).

9. For other relevant sociological works on this point, see Patrick McNamara, *Conscience First, Tradition Second: A Study of Young American Catholics* (Albany: State University of New York Press, 1992); William D'Antonio and others, *American Catholics* (Walnut Creek, CA: Alta Mira Press, 2001); Robert Wuthnow, *After Heaven: Spirituality in America Since the 1950s* (Berkeley and Los Angeles: University of California Press, 1998); Conrad Cherry, Betty DeBerg, and Amanda Porterfield, *Religion on Campus: What Religion Really Means to Today's Undergraduates* (Chapel Hill: University of North Carolina Press, 2001); Richard Flory and Donald Miller, eds., *GenX Religion* (New York: Routledge, 2000); James Davison Hunter, *Evangelicalism: The Coming Generation* (Chicago: University of Chicago Press, 1987); Dean Hoge, William Dinges, Mary Johnson, and Juan Gonzales, *Young Adult Catholics: Religion in the Culture of Choice,* (Notre Dame, IN: University of Notre Dame Press, 2001); Dean Hoge, Benton Johnson, and Donald Luidens, *Vanishing Boundaries: The Religion of Mainline Protestant Baby Boomers* (Louisville, KY: Westminster / John Knox, 1994); Wade Clark Roof, *Spiritual Marketplace: Baby Boomers and the Remaking of American Religion* (Princeton, NJ: Princeton University Press, 1999); Phillip Hammond, *Religion and Personal Autonomy* (Columbia: University of South Carolina Press, 1992).

10. Such as Thomas Nelson's *Revolve* Bible, first published in 2003, with covers such as the one that appears at the top of page 282.

11. See Christian Smith and others, *American Evangelicalism: Embattled and Thriving* (Chicago: University of Chicago Press, 1998), 89–199.

THE "INTERIOR" LIVES OF AMERICAN COLLEGE STUDENTS:
PRELIMINARY FINDINGS FROM A NATIONAL STUDY
*Jennifer A. Lindholm*

The findings presented here are part of collaborative work that was conducted by the author with Alexander W. Astin, Helen S. Astin, Alyssa N. Bryant, and Katalin Szélenyi. John A. Astin assisted with focus-group interviews.

1. See e.g., A. W. Chickering and L. Reisser, *Education and Identity*, 2nd ed. (San Francisco: Jossey-Bass, 1993); and P. G. Love, "Spirituality and Student Development: Theoretical Connections," in *The Implications of Student*

*Spirituality for Student Affairs Practice 95*, ed. M. A. Jablonski, 7–16 (San Francisco: Jossey-Bass, 2001).

2. See e.g., A. W. Astin, *What Matters in College? Four Critical Years Revisited* (San Francisco: Jossey-Bass, 1993); E. T. Pascarella and P. T. Terenzini, *How College Affects Students* (San Francisco: Jossey-Bass, 1991).

3. See e.g., C. Cherry, B. A. DeBerg, and A. Porterfield, *Religion on Campus* (Chapel Hill, NC: The University of North Carolina Press, 2001); J. J. Lee, A. Matzkin, and S. Arthur, *Understanding Students' Religious and Spiritual Pursuits: A Case Study and New York University* (Research Report, 2002).

4. K. L. Todd, "A Semantic Analysis of the Word Spirituality," 2004, http://web.nwe.ufl.edu/ ~jdouglas/spiritual.pdf.

5. See S. Ellingson, "The New Spirituality from a Social Science Perspective." In *Dialog: A Journal of Theology* 40, no. 4 (2001): 257–63; J. A. Lindholm and H. S. Astin, "Conceptions of Spirituality among Undergraduate Students: Defining Constructs and Experiences" (unpublished manuscript, 2004); P. L. Marler and C. K. Hardaway, "Being Religious or 'Being Spiritual' in America: A Zero-Sum Proposition?" *Journal for the Scientific Study of Religion* 41, no. 2 (2002): 289–300.

6. Fetzer Institute/National Institute on Aging Working Group, *Multidimensional Measurement of Religiousness/Spirituality For Use in Health Research* (Kalamazoo, MI: Fetzer Institute, 2003), 2.

7. A. W. Astin, "Is Spirituality a Legitimate Concern in Higher Education?" (opening keynote address, "Spirituality and Learning" conference, San Francisco, April 18, 2002).

8. See J. Dyson, M. Cobb, and D. Forman, "The Meaning of Spirituality: A Literature Review," *Journal of Advanced Nursing* 26 (1997): 1183–88; N. C. Goddard, "A Response to Dawson's Critical Analysis of 'Spirituality' as Integrative Energy," *Journal of Advanced Nursing* 31 (2000): 968–79; D. M. Hindman, "From Splintered Lives to Whole Persons: Facilitating Spiritual Development of College Students," *Religious Education* 97, no. 2 (2002): 165–83; A. S. King, "Spirituality: Transformation and Metamorphosis," *Religion* 26 (1996): 343–51; R. A. Tanyi, "Towards Clarification of the Meaning of Spirituality," *Journal of Advanced Nursing* 39, no. 5 (2002): 500–509.

9. P. G. Love and D. Talbot, "Defining Spiritual Development: A Missing Consideration for Student Affairs," *NAPSA Journal* 37, no. 1 (1999): 361–75; P. C. Hill and others, "Conceptualizing Religion and Spirituality: Points of Commonality, Points of Departure," *Journal for the Theory of Social Behaviour* 30 (2000): 51–77; B. J. Zinnbauer, K. I. Pargament, and A. B. Scott, "The Emerging Meanings of Religiousness and Spirituality: Problems and Prospects," *Journal of Personality* 67 (1999): 889–919.

10. E. J. Tisdell, "Spirituality in Adult and Higher Education" (Columbus, OH: ERIC Clearinghouse on Adult Career and Vocational Education, 2001).

11. D. Zohar and I. Marshall, *Spiritual Capital: Wealth We Can Live By* (San Francisco: Berrett-Koehler, 2004).

12. I. I. Mitroff and E. A. Denton, "A Study of Spirituality in the Workplace," *Sloan Management Review* (1999): 83–92.

13. G. H. Gallup, Jr., "Remarkable Surge of Interest in Spiritual Growth Noted as Next Century Approaches," *Emerging Trends* 12 (1998): 1.

14. A. W. Astin, "Why Spirituality Deserves a Central Place in Liberal Education," *Liberal Education* 90, no. 2 (2004): 34–41.

15. See, for example, G. M. Marsden, *The Soul of the American University: From Protestant Establishment to Established Nonbelief* (New York: Oxford University Press, 1994); and A. M. Cohen, *The Shaping of American Higher Education: Emergence and Growth of the Contemporary System* (San Francisco: Jossey-Bass, 1998).

16. A. W. Astin and others, "Spirituality in Higher Education: A National Study of College Students' Search for Meaning and Purpose, Summary of Selected Findings" (unpublished manuscript, 2004); M. DeSouza, "Contemporary Influences on the Spirituality of Young People: Implications for Education," *International Journal of Children's Spirituality* 8, no. 11 (2003): 269–79; M. Harris and G. Moran, *Reshaping Religious Education* (Louisville, KY: Westminster John Knox Press, 1998).

17. C. E. Ellison and J. S. Levin, "The Religion-Health Connection: Evidence, Theory, and Future Directions," *Health Education and Behavior* 25 (1998): 700–720; Hill and others, "Conceptualizing Religion and Spirituality."

18. See L. Duff, "Spiritual Development and Education: A Contemplative View," *International Journal of Children's Spirituality* 8, no. 11 (2003): 227–37; D. M. Lee, "Reinventing the University: From Institutions to Communities of Higher Education," *Journal of Adult Development* 6, no. 3 (1999): 175–83; J. Lewis, "Spiritual Education as the Cultivation of Qualities of the Heart and Mind: A Reply to Blake and Carr," *Oxford Review of Educa-*

*tion* 26, no. 2 (2000): 263–83; M. Tatarkowski, "Should Spirituality Be Taught in Post-Compulsory Education? Justifications for its Inclusion in Further Education Curriculum," *Pastoral Care* 15, no. 3 (1997): 23–29.

19. See e.g., J. Bradley and S. K. Kauanui, "Comparing Spirituality on Three Southern California College Campuses," *Journal of Organizational Change* 16, no. 4 (2003): 448–62; S. W. Cook and others, "College Students' Perceptions of Spiritual People and Religious People," *Journal of Psychology and Theology* 28, no. 2 (2000): 125–37.

20. The CIRP survey was created by Alexander W. Astin in 1966 and is now completed annually by over four hundred thousand students at more than seven hundred institutions nationwide. CIRP Freshman Survey findings are used widely to document an array of demographic, attitudinal, and social changes involving the nation's students entering college.

21. The first set of weights was designed to adjust for nonresponse bias. The second set of weights was designed to bring the respondent file counts up to the "population," which in this case was the total number of first-time, full-time freshmen from fall 2000 who were still enrolled in spring 2003 at the same institution. The final weight used for each respondent consisted of the product of the two weights. To keep the degrees of freedom at an appropriate level for purposes of statistical inference, these final weights were "normalized," such that their sum equaled the actual number of respondents (i.e., $N = 3,680$). The weight variable used in deflating the sample to 3,680 was derived by dividing the original weight by the ratio of the weighted sample to the unweighted sample.

22. See e.g., A. W. Astin and others, *The American Freshman: Thirty-Five-Year Trends* (Los Angeles: Higher Education Research Institute, UCLA, 2002).

23. See e.g., A. N. Bryant, J. Y. Choi, and M. Yasuno, "Understanding the Religious and Spiritual Dimensions of Students' Lives in the First Year of College," *Journal of College Student Development* 44 (2003): 723–45.

24. P. Wink and M. Dillon, "Spiritual Development Across the Adult Life Course: Findings from a Longitudinal Study," *Journal of Adult Development* 9, no. 1 (2002): 79–94.

25. K. Stokes, "Faith Development in the Adult Life Cycle," *Journal of Religious Gerontology* 7 (1990): 167–84.

26. P. T. Terenzini, E. T. Pascarella, and G. S. Blimling, "Students' Out-of-Class Experiences and Their Influence on Learning and Cognitive Development: A Literature Review," *Journal of College Student Development* 37, no. 2 (1996): 149–62.

27. See e.g., H. Bowen, *Investment in Learning: The Individual and Social Value of American Higher Education* (San Francisco: Jossey-Bass, 1977).

28. See e.g., Pascarella and Terenzini, *How College Affects Students.*

29. See e.g., Astin, *What Matters in College?*; P. T. Terenzini and E. T. Pascarella, "Living With Myths: Undergraduate Education in America," *Change* 26, no. 1 (1994): 28–32.

30. G. D. Kuh, "The Other Curriculum: Out-of-Class Experiences Associated with Student Learning and Personal Development," *The Journal of Higher Education* 66, no. 2 (1995): 123–55.

CURRENT EXPRESSIONS OF AMERICAN JEWISH IDENTITY: AN ANALYSIS OF
114 TEENAGERS
*Philip Schwadel*

1. For more information on the NSYR data, see Christian Smith and Melinda Denton, "Methodological Design and Procedures for the National Study of Youth and Religion (NSYR)" (Chapel Hill, NC: National Study of Youth and Religion, 2003), http://www.youthandreligion.org.

2. Every teen in the full sample was asked the same series of questions. While this was beneficial for the purposes of comparison across religious traditions, it may have also obscured the data among non-Christian respondents. For example, asking Jewish or Muslim teens a question using Christian-centric nomenclature (such as "religious faith") might elicit a different response than would a question using in-group language.

3. Note that 40 percent of Jewish teens reported attending religious services at least once a month. Yet for only 33 percent of those who attend Jewish services at least once a month, a synagogue is their primary or secondary place of worship.

4. Barry A. Kosmin, "Coming of Age in the Conservative Synagogue: The Bar/Bat-Mitzvah Class of 5755," in *Jews in the Center: Conservative Synagogues and their Members*, ed. Jack Wertheimer (New Brunswick, NJ: Rutgers University Press, 2000).

5. Rosh Hashanah, Yom Kippur, and the days between these two holidays are considered the High Holy Days or High Holidays. The ten days from the beginning of Rosh Hashanah to the end of Yom Kippur are also called the Days of Awe.

6. The extent of an individual's civic activity and voluntary service is frequently correlated with socioeconomic status. See Sidney Verba, Kay Lehman Schlozman, and Henry E. Brady, *Voice and Equality: Civic Voluntarism in American Politics* (Cambridge: Harvard University Press, 1995).

7. Of the teens surveyed by NSYR, 23 percent live in households with incomes under $30,000, while only 6 percent of the Jewish teen respondents live in households with incomes below $30,000.

•

A SPIRITUAL CROSSROADS OF EUROPE: THE TAIZÉ COMMUNITY'S
ADVENTURE WITH THE YOUNG
*Brother John of Taizé*

1. "Conformément à l'exemple du Christ nous devons nous impliquer nous-mêmes dans cette transmission [de la foi] et nous constituer nous-mêmes en don pour les autres. . . . La tradition chrétienne est autolivraison. Elle s'effectue par des témoins qui s'impliquent eux-mêmes, qui font geste avec toute leur vie." *La Théologie et l'Église, Cogitatio fidei 158* (Paris : Éditions du Cerf, 1990), 201; translated as *Theology and Church*, 1989.

2. Interview with Paul Ricoeur, *Letter from Taizé*, April–May 2001. Also available online at the Taizé Web site, http://www.taize.fr; and published in *Taizé, au vif de l'espérance* (Paris: Bayard Éditions, 2002), 205–209.

RELIGIOUS IDENTITY AND BELONGING AMIDST DIVERSITY AND
PLURALISM: CHALLENGES AND OPPORTUNITIES FOR CHURCH AND
THEOLOGY
*Peter C. Phan*

1. The slogan is now the title of a helpful book by Robert C. Fuller, *Spiritual, But Not Religious: Understanding Unchurched America* (Oxford: Oxford University Press, 2001).

2. The most comprehensive, one-volume study of religious experience is Ralph W. Hood Jr., ed., *Handbook of Religious Experience* (Birmingham, AL: Religious Education Press, 1995).

3. On contemporary religious diversity in the United States, see Diana L. Eck, *A New Religious America: How a "Christian Country" Has Become the World's Most Religiously Diverse Nation* (San Francisco: HarperSanFrancisco, 2001). An accessible book on American religious diversity is John H. Berthrong, *The Divine Deli: Religious Identity in the North American Cultural Mosaic* (Maryknoll, NY: Orbis Books, 1999).

4. For a brief discussion of these options, see Peter Byrne, *Prolegomena to Religious Pluralism: Reference and Realism in Religion* (New York: St. Martin's Press, 1995), 1–30.

5. Of Erikson's many writings on personal identity, see *Childhood and Society* (New York: Norton, 1950); *Identity, Youth, and Crisis* (New York: Norton, 1968); and *Dimensions of a New Identity* (New York: Norton, 1974).

6. See W. E. B. DuBois, *The Souls of Black Folk* (1903; repr., Milwood, NY: Kraus-Thomson Organization, 1973).

7. See Erik Erikson, *Young Man Luther: A Study in Psychoanalysis and History* (New York: Norton, 1958).

8. On the sociology of religious belonging, see Hervé Carrier, *The Sociology of Religious Belonging* (New York: Herder and Herder, 1965).

9. I am referring to the following studies discussed or presented at the conference "Faith, Fear and Indifference: Constructing Religious Identity in the Next Generation," at the University of Southern California, October 10–11, 2004, the basis for the present volume: "Spirituality in College Students: Preliminary Findings from a National Studies" (SCS) conducted by the Higher Education Research Institute, University of California, Los Angeles; "National Study of Youth and Religion" (NSYR), published in Christian Smith with Melinda Lundquist Denton, *Soul Searching: The Religious and Spiritual Lives of American Teenagers* (New York: Oxford University Press, 2005); "A Portrait of Detroit Mosques: Muslim Views on Policy, Politics and Religion" (PDM) by Ihsan Bagby, Institute for Social Policy and Understanding, Clinton Township, Michigan; and Christian Smith, "Is Moralistic Therapeutic Deism the New Religion of American Youth? Implications for the Challenge of Religious Socialization and Reproduction," the third chapter in this volume.

10. See Smith, "Is Moralistic Therapeutic Deism the New Religion of American Youth?"; and his book *Soul Searching*.

11. See his *De controversiis,* vol. 2, bk. 3; *De ecclesia militante,* ch. 2; "De definitione Ecclesiae" (Naples: Giuliano, 1857), 2:75.

12. See Joseph Neuner and Jacques Dupuis, eds., *The Christian Faith in the Doctrinal Documents of the Catholic Church* (New York: Alba House, 2001), 44.

13. Austin Flannery, ed., *Vatican Council II: Constitutions Decrees Declarations* (Northport, NY: Costello Publishing Co., 1996), 99.

14. In his *The Nature of Doctrine: Religion and Theology in a Postliberal Age* (Philadelphia: Westminster, 1984), 34, George Lindbeck rightly notes the important role of the "external word" for the origination of faith in his critique of what he calls the "experiential-expressive model," but he goes overboard in placing the priority on the external word, contradicting what he wrote elsewhere: "Turning now in more detail to the relation of religion and experience, it may be noted that this is not unilateral but dialectical. It is simplistic to say (as I earlier did) merely that religions produce experiences, for the causality is reciprocal. Patterns of experience alien to a given religion can profoundly influence it" (33).

15. Corresponding to the different conceptions of faith are the various models of revelation. In his *Models of Revelation* (Garden City, NY: Doubleday, 1983), 68–83, Avery Dulles presents five models of revelation: as doctrine, history, inner experience, dialectical presence, and new awareness. The conception of faith under criticism corresponds to the model of revelation as inner experience.

16. On this inculturated character of the Christian faith, see Peter C. Phan, "Catechesis and Catechism as Inculturation of the Christian Faith," *Salesianum* 65 (2003): 91–122.

17. Karl Rahner, *Foundations of Christian Faith: An Introduction to the Idea of Christianity*, trans. William Dych (New York: Crossroad, 1976), 344.

18. See Paul F. Knitter, *Introducing Theologies of Religions* (Maryknoll, NY: Orbis Books, 2002). For a classic exposition of the Roman Catholic standpoint on religious pluralism, see Jacques Dupuis, *Toward a Christian Theology of Religious Pluralism* (Maryknoll, NY: Orbis Books, 1997). For an Evangelical viewpoint, see Harold Netland, *Encountering Religious Pluralism: The Challenge to Christian Faith & Mission* (Downers Grove, IL: InterVarsity Press, 2001).

19. For a fuller discussion of this model, see Peter C. Phan, "Multiple Religious Belonging: Opportunities and Challenges for Theology and Church," *Theological Studies* 64 (2003): 495–519. This model has been called by Jacques Dupuis "inclusive pluralism" or "pluralistic inclusivism."

20. The possibility of salvation for non-Christian believers and non-believers, with requisite conditions, is explicitly affirmed by Vatican II in its dogmatic constitution on the church, *Lumen Gentium*, no. 16.

21. Vatican II's decree *Ad Gentes*, no. 9.

22. Dupuis, *Toward a Christian Theology of Religious Pluralism*, 387.

23. Jacques Dupuis, *Christianity and the Religions: From Confrontation to Dialogue* (Maryknoll, NY: Orbis Books, 2002), 257.

24. For extensive reflections on these three issues, see Peter C. Phan, "To Be Catholic or Not To Be: Is It Still the Question? Catholic Identity and Religious Education Today," *Horizons* 25, no. 2 (1998): 159–80; and "Multiple Religious Belonging: Opportunities and Challenges for Theology and Church," *Theological Studies* 64 (2003): 495–519.

25. I am inspired by Karl Rahner's "indirect method" as it is deployed in his *Foundations of Christian Faith*. See my "Cultural Pluralism and the Unity of the Sciences: Karl Rahner's Transcendental Theology as a Test Case," *Salesianum* 51 (1989): 785–809.

26. I am indebted to Cardinal John Henry Newman's theory of religious knowledge as expounded in his *An Essay in Aid of a Grammar of Assent* (1870; repr., Westminster, MD: Christian Classics, 1973).

27. Richard McBrien makes a distinction between *characteristic* and *distinctive*. What is *characteristic* may also be found in others, but what is *distinctive* is found in oneself alone. *Characteristic* of Roman Catholicism is the insistence on the triumph of grace over sin, tradition and continuity, community, sacramentality, and mediation. *Distinctive* of Roman Catholicism is its teaching on the Petrine office. Also *distinctive* is the particular *configuration* of the various characteristics mentioned above. See his *Catholicism* (Minneapolis: Winston, 1981), 1171–84. Needless to say, Christian identity is constituted by both *characteristic* and *distinctive* elements.

28. I am in broad agreement with George Lindbeck's view of religion as a cultural-linguistic system, though I think he unduly underestimates the cognitive and expressive dimensions of doctrines. See his *The Nature of Doctrine*.

29. Greeley speaks of four basic elements of the Catholic heritage: sacramental experience, the analogical imagination, the comic story, and organic community. See Andrew Greeley and Mary Greeley Durkin, *How To Save the Catholic Church* (New York: Viking Penguin, 1984), 33–102. With regard to the analogical imagination, see also Andrew Greeley, *The Catholic Myth: The Behavior and Beliefs of American Catholics* (New York: Simon & Schuster, 1990), especially chapter 3, "Do Catholics Imagine Differently?" Greeley takes the analogical imagination as the root characteristic of Catholics. I agree with Greeley that Catholics tend to imagine "analogously" but I do not think that this is specific to Catholics. The analogical imagination works as powerfully among the Orthodox and the Anglicans, for example, as among Catholics; by the same token, the "dialectical imagination" is no less in use among Catholics than among Protestants. My point is that Catholic identity is formed not by their differences from others as long as these remain superficial but by their deep structures, even though these may be shared extensively by others. This is not an idle point, since Catholics can thus strengthen and nourish their own identity in a truly ecumenical way. In this way, ecumenical dialogue is not seen as diluting Catholic identity but fortifying it.

30. Newman, *An Essay in Aid of a Grammar of Assent*, 492. On this notion of "illative sense" and its role in the formation of conscience, see Linda L. Stinson, *Process and Conscience: Toward a Theology of Human Emergence* (Lanham, MD: University Press of America, 1986).

31. See Diane Winston, "Campuses Are a Bellwether for Society's Religious Revival," *The Chronicle of Higher Education*, January 16, 1998, A60.

32. For a theological discussion of multiple religious belonging, see Catherine Cornille, ed., *Many Mansions? Multiple Religious Belonging and Christian Identity* (Maryknoll, NY: Orbis Books, 2002).

33. See Robert C. Fuller, *Spiritual, But Not Religious*, 5–7.

34. Raimundo Panikkar, *The Intrareligious Dialogue* (New York: Paulist Press, 1978), 2.

35. See Peter C. Phan, "Multiple Religious Belonging," 508–15.

36. Of course one should not dismiss every search for "unchurched" spirituality, especially among youth, as a self-indulgent, fuzzy-minded, feel-good,

neopagan exercise. It often signals a failure of the official church to respond effectively to the spiritual needs of the young and represents a sincere attempt to find meaning in one's life amidst rampant consumerism and materialism. Interestingly, publishers know that books with the word *spirituality* in the title sell! Pastorally, this search for spirituality is a golden "teaching moment" that the church must take advantage of. The literature on the "spiritual but not religious" movement has been growing. Beside the works by Robert Fuller, see also Robert Ellwood, *The Sixties Awakening* (New Brunswick, NJ: Rutgers University Press, 1994) and *The Fifties Spiritual Marketplace: American Religion in a Decade of Conflict* (New Brunswick, NJ: Rutgers University Press, 1997); Robert Wuthnow, *After Heaven: Spirituality in America Since the 1950s* (Berkeley and Los Angeles: University of California Press, 1998); and Wade Clark Roof, *Spiritual Marketplace: Baby Boomers and the Remaking of American Religion* (Princeton, NJ: Princeton University Press, 1999).

37. See Aloysius Pieris, *Fire & Water: Basic Issues in Asian Buddhism and Christianity* (Maryknoll, NY: Orbis Books, 1996), 154–61.

38. Swami Abhishikananda, *Ascent to the Depth of the Heart: The Spiritual Diary (1948–73) of Swami Abhishikananda (Dom Henri Le Saux)* (Delhi: ISPCK, 1998), 19.

IDENTITY AND COMMUNITY IN A NEW GENERATION: THE MUSLIM COMMUNITY IN THE EARLY SEVENTH CENTURY AND TODAY
*Ghada Osman*

My thanks go to Prof. Reuven Firestone for his comments on an earlier draft of this essay. Any shortcomings or errors are clearly mine alone.

1. Sulayman Nyang, *Islam in the United States of America* (Chicago: ABC International Group, 1999), 13–16.

2. John Esposito, "Muslims in America or American Muslims," in *Muslims on the Americanization Path?* ed. Yvonne Yazbeck Haddad and John L. Esposito (Oxford: Oxford University Press, 2000), 3.

3. Gary David and Kenneth K. Ayouby, "Being Arab and Becoming Americanized: Forms of Mediated Assimilation in Metropolitan Detroit," in *Muslim Minorities in the West: Visible and Invisible*, ed. Yvonne Yazbeck Haddad and Jane I. Smith (Oxford: AltaMira Press, 2002), 135.

4. Esposito, "Muslims in America," 4.

5. Yvonne Yazbeck Haddad, "The Dynamics of Islamic Identity in North America," in Haddad and Esposito, *Muslims on the Americanization Path?*, 20.

6. Esposito, "Muslims in America," 4.

7. Garbi Schmidt, "The Complexity of Belonging: Sunni Muslim Immigrants in Chicago," in Haddad and Smith, *Muslim Minorities*, 107.

8. Ibid., 108–113.

9. See Nyang, *Islam in the United States*, 96, for an example of this.

10. See Haddad, "Dynamics of Islamic Identity," 28–29 for more on this.

11. Karen Armstrong, *Muhammad: A Biography of the Prophet* (San Francisco: Harper, 1992), 8.

12. Yahya Emerick, *The Life and Work of Muhammad* (Indianapolis: Alpha Books, 2002), 93.

13. W. Montgomery Watt, *Muhammad at Mecca* (Oxford: The Clarendon Press, 1960), 104.

14. Subhash C. Inamdar, *Muhammad and the Rise of Islam: The Creation of Group Identity* (Madison, CT: Psychosocial Press, 2001), 8. See also R. Hogan, G. J. Curphy, and J. Hogan, "What We Know About Leadership: Effectiveness and Personality," *American Psychologist* (1994) 49: 493–504, for more on this.

15. Armstrong, *Muhammad*, 104. See also Muhammad ibn Sa'd (d. 845), *Al-Tabaqat al-Kubra* (Beirut: Beirut Publshing House, 1978), vol. 1, for more on this.

16. Watt, *Muhammad at Mecca*, 95.

17. Armstrong, *Muhammad*, 93.

18. Ibid., 146.

19. Emerick, *Life and Work of Muhammad*, 68.

20. Armstrong, *Muhammad*, 102.

21. Sulayman Nyang and Zahid Bukhari, "American Muslim Poll," 2001, http://www.projectmaps.com/PMReport.htm (accessed October 13, 2004).

22. Carol Anway, "American Women Choosing Islam," in Haddad and Esposito, *Muslims on the Americanization Path?* 146.

23. Nyang and Bukhari, "American Muslim Poll."

24. U. S. Department of State, "Muslim Life in America," 2002, http://usinfo.state.gov/products/pubs/muslimlife/ (accessed October 13, 2004).

25. Nyang and Bukhari, "American Muslim Poll."

26. Anway, "American Women Choosing Islam," 146–7.

27. Armstrong, *Muhammad*, 53.

28. As was noted by Prof. Reuven Firestone in his reading of an earlier draft of this piece, it is striking that as Jews and Judaism were finally becoming more integrated in the United States, Muslims and Islam seem to have begun picking up the old Jewish outsider status.

29. Council for American-Islamic Relations (CAIR), "Poll: 1-in-4 Americans Holds Anti-Muslim Views," 2004. http://www.cair-net.org (accessed October 13, 2004).

30. Inamdar, *Muhammad and the Rise of Islam*, 108.

31. Armstrong, *Muhammad*, 8.

32. Emerick, *Life and Work of Muhammad*, v.

33. Ibid., 66.

34. Anway, "American Women Choosing Islam," 146.

35. Emerick, *Life and Work of Muhammad*, 64.

36. Ibid., 78.

37. Ibid., 74.

38. Ibid., 73.

39. Andrea Elliott, "Study Finds City's Muslims Growing Closer Since 9/11," *New York Times*, October 4, 2002.

40. CAIR, "Poll."

41. Nyang, *Islam in the United States*, 116.

42. Schmidt, "Complexity of Belonging," 114–5.

43. Ibn Sa'd, *Tabaqat*, 1:430, 441; Ahmad b. Muhammad b. Hanbal (d. 855), *Musnad* (Beirut: 'Alam al-Kutub, 1998), 3:337; Abu al-Husayn b. Muslim b. al-Hajjaj (d. 875), *Sahih* (Beirut: Dar ibn Hazm), 1:187.

44. U.S. Department of State, "Muslim Life in America."

45. Elliott, "Study Finds City's Muslims Growing Closer."

46. Uri Rubin, *The Eye of the Beholder: The Life of Muhammad as Viewed by the Early Muslims* (Princeton, NJ: The Darwin Press, 1995), 128.

47. Kambiz GhaneaBassiri, *Competing Visions of Islam in the United States: A Study of Los Angeles* (Westport, CT: Greenwood Press, 1997), 23.

48. U.S. Department of State, "Muslim Life in America."

49. GhaneaBassiri, *Competing Visions of Islam*, 26.

50. Ibid., 44.

51. U.S. Department of State, "Muslim Life in America."

52. Elliott, "Study Finds City's Muslims Growing Closer."

SECOND-GENERATION MUSLIM IMMIGRANTS IN DETROIT MOSQUES: THE SECOND GENERATION'S SEARCH FOR THEIR PLACE AND IDENTITY IN THE AMERICAN MOSQUE
*Ihsan Bagby*

1. Ihsan Bagby, Paul M. Perl, and Bryan T. Froehle, *The American Mosque: A National Portrait* (Washington, DC: Council on American-Islamic Relations, 2001).

2. Ihsan Bagby, *A Portrait of Detroit Mosques: Muslim Views on Policy, Politics and Religion* (Detroit: Institute for Social Policy and Understanding, 2004).

3. This paper does not focus on second-generation Muslims who do not attend a mosque. It might be assumed that the assimilation story of the non-mosque-going second-generation Muslim will differ markedly, but that is not a given. No data exists to estimate what percentage of second-generation Muslims attend a mosque. However, anecdotal information from interviews indicates that the percentage of mosque attendance among the second generation varies greatly within ethnic groups and sections of town.

4. W. Lloyd Warner and Leo Srole, *The Social Systems of American Ethnic Groups* (New Haven, CT: Yale University Press, 1945); Herbert Gans, "Introduction," *Ethnic Identity and Assimilation: The Polish Community*, ed. N. Sandberg (New York: Praeger, 1973).

5. Herbert Gans, "Second Generation Decline: Scenarios for the Economic and Ethnic Futures of the Post-1965 American Immigrants," *Ethnic and Racial Studies* 15 (1992): 173–92.

6. Richard Alba and Victor Nee, "Rethinking Assimilation Theory for a New Era of Immigration," *International Migration Review* 31 (1997): 826–72; Herbert Gans, "Toward a Reconciliation of 'Assimilation' and 'Pluralism': The Interplay of Acculturation and Ethnic Retention," *International Migration Review* 31 (1997): 875–92.

7. Robert E. Park and Ernest W. Burgess, *Introduction to the Science of Sociology* (Chicago: University of Chicago Press, 1921).

8. Herbert Gans, "Symbolic Ethnicity: The Future of Ethnic Groups and Cultures in America," *Ethnic and Racial Studies* 2 (1979): 1–20.

9. Milton M. Gordon, *Assimilation in American Life: The Role of Race, Religion, and National Origins* (New York: Oxford University Press, 1964).

10. Gordon, *Assimilation in American Life*, 70.

11. Gordon, *Assimilation in American Life*, 79.

12. Gordon, *Assimilation in American Life*, 81.

13. Kelly H. Chong, "What It Means To Be a Christian: The Role of Religion in the Construction of Ethnic Identity and Boundary Among Second-Generation Korean Americans," *Sociology of Religion* 59, no. 3 (1998): 259–286; Carl L. Bankston III and Min Zhou, "The Ethnic Church, Ethnic Identification and the Social Adjustment of Vietnamese Adolescents," *Review of Religious Research* 38, no. 1 (1996): 18–37; Rebecca Y. Kim, "Second Generation Korean American Evangelicals: Ethnic, Multiethnic, or White Campus Ministries?" *Sociology of Religion* 65, no. 1 (2004): 19–34; Prema Kurien, "Becoming American by Becoming Hindu: Indian Americans Take Their Place at the Multicultural Table," in *Gatherings in Diaspora*, ed. R. Stephen Warner and Judith G. Wittner (Philadelphia: Temple University Press, 1998); Ho-Youn Kwon, Chung Kim Kwang, and R. Stephen Warner, *Korean Americans and Their Religions: Pilgrims and Missionaries from a Different Shore* (University Park: The Pennsylvania State University Press, 2001); Pyong Gap Min, ed., *The Second Generation: Ethnic Identity Among Asian Americans* (Walnut Creek, CA: AltaMira Press, 2002); Nazli Kibria, *Becoming Asian American: Second Generation Chinese and Korean American Identities* (Baltimore: The Johns Hopkins University Press, 2002); Raymond Brady Williams, *Religions of Immigrants from India and Pakistan: New Threads in the American Tapestry* (New York: Cambridge University Press, 1998).

14. Yvonne Yazbeck Haddad and Adair T. Lummis, *Islamic Values in the United States: A Comparative Study* (New York: Oxford University Press, 1987); Raymond Brady Williams, *Religions of Immigrants from India and Pakistan: New Threads in the American Tapestry* (New York: Cambridge University Press, 1988).

15. The eight mosques included two Arab mosques (one of recent immigrants and one of older immigrants), two South Asian mosques (both older immigrants), three African American mosques, and one ethnically mixed mosque (recent immigrants). A proper mosque distribution of ethnicity and age was, therefore, maintained. In each mosque, the number of mosque participant questionnaires collected equaled at least half of the attendance at Friday prayers.

16. Bagby, *A Portrait of Detroit Mosques*, 31.

17. See Chong, "What It Means To Be a Christian," 262.

THE LEISURE OF WORSHIP AND THE WORSHIP OF LEISURE
*Jack Miles*

1. In Christian Smith, ed., *The Secular Revolution; Power, Interests, and Conflict in the Secularization of American Public* (Berkeley and Los Angeles: University of California Press, 2003), the thesis is pursued that "the historical secularization of the institutions of American public was not a natural, inevitable, and abstract by-product of modernization; rather it was the outcome of a struggle between contending groups with conflicting interests seeking to control social knowledge and institutions" (vii). Against this agonistic vision, Martin Marty argues that only a new, more syncretic model can account for

the mixtures of secularism and religion that are encountered in "the world that we actually inhabit," which "is neither exclusively secular nor exclusively religious, but rather a complex combination of both the religious and the secular, with religious and secular phenomena occurring at the same time in individuals, in groups, and in societies around the world" (*Daedalus,* Summer 2003, 42). In the Muslim world, the likelihood is vanishingly small that pluralism can be achieved through anything other than some blend of Muslim religion and secularism with an Islamic face. Cf. Abdulahi An-Naim, *Human Rights in Cross-Cultural Perspective* (Philadelphia: University of Pennsylvania Press, 1995). And the Muslim world is no longer a place apart from the West.

2. James Traub, "The Stuff of City Life," *New York Times Magazine,* October 3, 2004, 23–28.

3. Christian Smith, "Is Moralistic Therapeutic Deism the New Religion of American Youth? Implications for the Challenge of Religious Socialization and Reproduction," the third chapter in this volume.

4. Nancy Ammerman, "Journeys of Faith: Meeting the Challenges in Twenty-First-Century America," the second chapter in this volume.

5. Peter C. Phan, "Religious Identity and Belonging Amidst Diversity and Pluralism: Challenges and Opportunities for Church and Theology," the ninth chapter in this volume.


Teach Your Children Well: Closing Observations on Constructing Religious Identity in the Next Generation
*Diane Winston*

1. Jay Michaelson, "Notes on Camp: How a Summer Choice for Kids Became a Linchpin of the Jewish Community," *The Forward,* June 11, 2004.

2. Amy L. Sales and Leonard Saxe, *How Goodly Are Thy Tents: Summer Camps as Jewish Socializing Experiences* (Waltham, MA: Brandeis University Press, 2003).

3. Christian Smith, "Is Moralistic Therapeutic Deism the New Religion of American Youth? Implications for the Challenge of Religious Socialization and Reproduction," the third chapter in this volume.

4. Smith, "Moralistic Therapeutic Deism."

5. Higher Education Research Institute, "Spirituality in College Students: Preliminary Findings from a National Study" (University of California, Los Angeles, 2004), 9.

6. Higher Education Research Institute, "Spirituality in College Students," 1.

7. Peter C. Phan, "Religious Identity and Belonging Amidst Diversity and Pluralism: Challenges and Opportunities for Church and Theology," the ninth chapter in this volume.

8. Susan M. Barbieri, "Daybreak Devotion," *Minneapolis Star Tribune,* May 22, 2004.

9. S. Mitra Kalita, "Supporting the Hunger for Faith," *Washington Post,* November 3, 2003.

10. Christina Preiss, "Teen Center to be Place to Play and Pray," *Minneapolis Star Tribune,* August 18, 2004.

11. Nancy Tatom Ammerman, *Pillars of Faith: American Congregations and Their Partners* (Berkeley and Los Angeles: University of California Press, 2005).

12. Nancy Ammerman, "Journeys of Faith: Meeting the Challenges in Twenty-First-Century America," the second chapter in this volume.

13. Phan, "Religious Identity and Belonging."

# Contributors

**Nancy Ammerman** is professor of sociology of religion at Boston University, with appointments in the School of Theology and the Department of Sociology. She is the author of *Pillars of Faith: American Congregations and Their Partners* (2005), *Studying Congregations: A New Handbook* (1998), and *Congregation and Community* (1997). In 1993, Ammerman served on the panel of experts convened by the U.S. Departments of Justice and Treasury to make recommendations in light of the government's confrontation with the Branch Davidians at Waco, Texas.

**Ihsan Bagby** is associate professor of Islamic studies at the University of Kentucky. He is the author of *The Mosque in America: A National Portrait* (2001), the first comprehensive study of mosques in the United States, and of *A Portrait of Detroit Mosques* ( 2004). He is working on a book on African American Muslims. Bagby serves on the advisory board of the Hartford Institute for Religion.

**Tobin Belzer** serves as research associate at the Center for Religion and Civic Culture at the University of Southern California and as senior research associate at the Berman Jewish Heritage Center for Research and Evaluation in Jewish Education. She is the author of *Jewish Identity at Work* (forthcoming) and is coeditor, with Julie Pelc, of *Joining the Sisterhood: Young Jewish Women Write Their Lives* (2003).

**Richard W. Flory** is associate professor of sociology at Biola University and a research associate at the Center for Religion and Civil Culture at the University of Southern California. He is editor of *GenX Religion,* (Routledge 2000) and associate editor of *The Encyclopedia of Fundamentalism* (Routledge, 2001). Flory has published articles on various aspects of religion and American culture.

**James L. Heft, S.M.,** is president of the Institute for Advanced Catholic Studies at the University of Southern California and serves as the Alton Brooks Professor of Religion at USC. The author of more than 130 articles and book chapters, he is editor of Charles Taylor's *A Catholic Modernity?* (1999) and of *Faith and the Intellectual Life* (1996), *Beyond Violence: Religious Sources for Social Transformation in Judaism, Christianity, and Islam* (2004), and *Believing Scholars: Ten Catholic Intellectuals* (Fordham, 2005). He is also the author of *John XXII (1316–34) and Papal Teaching Authority* (Mellen Press, 1986).

**Brother John**, a member of the Taizé community, is the author of seven books on Scripture and spirituality—*The Pilgrim God: A Biblical Journey* (1985); *The Way of the Lord: A New Testament Pilgrimage* (1990); *Praying the Our Father Today* (1992); *God of the Unexpected* (1995); *The Adventure of Holiness: Biblical Foundations and Present-Day Perspectives* (1999); *At the Wellspring: Jesus and the Samaritan Woman* (2001); and *Reading the Ten Commandments Anew: Towards a Land of Freedom* (2004). The Taizé community, located in the village of that name in France's Burgundy region, was founded in 1940. The community is monastic in inspiration and is made up of more than one hundred brothers, Catholic as well as from various Protestant backgrounds, who come from more than twenty-five different countries.

**Jennifer Lindholm** is project director for Spirituality in Higher Education: A National Study of College Students' Search for Meaning and Purpose, which is sponsored by the Higher Education Research Institute (HERI) at the University of California, Los Angeles, Graduate School of Education and Information Studies. Lindholm also directs HERI's Triennial National Faculty Survey and the Institute's newest program of research on spirituality in higher education. Her research is focused on the structural and cultural dimensions of academic work; the career development, work experiences, and professional behavior of college and university faculty; and issues related to institutional change within colleges and universities.

**Brie Loskota** is assistant director and research associate at the Center for Religion and Civic Culture at the University of Southern California. She is researching successful models of Jewish-Muslim dialogue. Loskota has served as project manager for research Lilly-funded projects on young adults in congregational life.

**J. Rolando Matalon** is a rabbi at Congregation B'nai Jeshurun in New York. He serves on the boards of the American Jewish World Service, Human Rights Watch/Middle East, Americans for Peace Now, U.S. Interreligious Committee for Peace in the Middle East, Givat Haviva, and Plaza Jewish Community Chapel.

**Jack Miles**, visiting scholar at Occidental College, serves as senior fellow with the Pacific Council on International Policy. He is the author of *God: A Biography* (1995), for which he was awarded a Pulitzer Prize in 1996, and of *Christ: A Crisis in the Life of God* (2001). A MacArthur Fellow (2003–7), Miles has taught at several universities and worked as an editor for the *Los Angeles Times* and for book publishers.

**Ghada Osman** is assistant professor of linguistics and Oriental languages at San Diego State University (SDSU) and a principal investigator for the Language Acquisition Resource Center at SDSU. She is the author of, among other articles, "Pre-Islamic Converts to Christianity," *Muslim World* (winter 2005), and "Representing the West in the Arabic Language," *Journal of Islamic Studies* (summer 2004). Osman's doctoral dissertation is "The Christians of Late Sixth and Early Seventh Century Mecca and Medina: An Investigation into the Arabic Sources" (Harvard, 2001).

**Peter C. Phan** holds the Ignacio Ellacuría Chair of Catholic Social Thought at Georgetown University and is on the faculty of the East Asian Pastoral Institute, Manila and Liverpool Hope University, England. He is the author of hundreds of articles and ten books, including *Christianity with an Asian Face: Asian American Theology in the Making* (2003) and *Grace and the Human Condition* (1988). Phan has served as president of the Catholic Theological Society of America.

**Amira Quraishi** serves as advisor to the Muslim Student Association at Johns Hopkins University. She cofounded Muslims Against Terrorism in New York City in September 2001. Quraishi is doctoral candidate in religious studies at the University of Pennsylvania, where she will write her dissertation on intersections between Islamic law and Sufism.

**Nadia Roumani**, research associate at the Center for Religion and Civic Culture at the University of Southern California, serves as senior associate with the Carnegie Council on Ethics and International Affairs in New York City, where she is a specialist in international development policy specialist, focusing on macroeconomic policies in developing and transition countries and on the role of civil society.

**Melchor Sánchez de Toca** is undersecretary of the Pontifical Council for Culture, which was established in 1982 and in 1993 assumed duties formerly assigned to the Secretariat for Dialogue with Atheists, on the grounds that culture is the privileged forum for dialogue with non-believers. A Catholic priest, Sánchez de Toca has long worked on issues involving the pastoral and cultural implications of science. In his current position he promotes dialogue between faith and science and is concerned with the study of unbelief and religious indifference.

**Philip Schwadel** is assistant professor of sociology at the University of Nebraska, Lincoln. As research associate for the American Religion Data Archive and as a postdoctoral researcher with the National Study of Youth and Religion (NSYR), he has worked extensively with data on American religion. He is coauthor, with Christian Smith, of the NSYR report *Portraits of Protestant Teens: A Report on Teenagers in Major U.S. Denominations* (2005).

**Christian Smith** is the William R. Kenan Jr. professor of sociology and director of the Center for the Study of Religion at the University of Notre Dame, after having taught for twelve years at the University of North Carolina at Chapel Hill. He is the author of *Soul Searching: the Religious and Spiritual Lives of American Teenagers* (2005), *Moral, Believing Animals: Human Personhood and Culture* ( 2003), *Christian America? What Evangelicals Really Want* (2000), and, with Michael Emerson, of *Divided by Faith: Evangelical Religion and the Problem of Race in America* (2000).

**Diane Winston** holds the Knight Chair in Media and Religion at the University of Southern California Annenberg School for Communication. She is author of *Red-Hot and Righteous: The Urban Religion of the Salvation Army* (1999) and coeditor, with John M. Giggie, of *Faith in the Market: Religion and the Rise of Urban Commercial Culture* (2002). Winston has been a reporter for several U.S. newspapers, including the *Baltimore Sun* and the *Dallas Morning News.*

# Index